Nahanni Journals

Edited and with an Introduction by
RICHARD C. DAVIS

Nahanni Journals

R.M. PATTERSON'S
1927–1929 JOURNALS

Published by
The University of Alberta Press
Ring House 2
Edmonton, Alberta, Canada   T6G 2E1

First edition, second printing, 2010.
Printed and bound in Canada by
    Marquis Book Printing Inc.,
    Montmagny, Quebec.
Copyediting by J. Lynn Fraser and
    Leslie Robertson.
Index by Adrian Mather.

Library and Archives Canada
Cataloguing in Publication

Patterson, R. M. (Raymond Murray),
    1898-1984 Nahanni journals :
R.M. Patterson's 1927-1929 journals /
R.M. Patterson ; Richard C. Davis, editor.

Includes bibliographical references.
ISBN 978-0-88864-477-0

    1. Patterson, R. M. (Raymond
Murray), 1898-1984—Travel—Northwest
Territories—South Nahanni River. 2.
Patterson, R. M. (Raymond Murray),—
1898-1984—Diaries.
3. South Nahanni River (N.W.T.)—
Description and travel. 4. Northwest
Territories—Description and travel.
I. Davis, Richard C., 1939- II. Title.

FC4195.S6P375 2007
917.19'3042   C2007-901537-9

The University of Alberta Press is
committed to protecting our natural
environment. As part of our efforts, this
book is printed on Enviro Paper: it contains
100% post-consumer recycled fibres and is
acid- and chlorine-free.

The University of Alberta Press gratefully
acknowledges the support received for
its publishing program from The Canada
Council for the Arts. The University of
Alberta Press also gratefully acknowledges
the financial support of the Government
of Canada through the Book Publishing
Industry Development Program (BPIDP)
and from the Alberta Foundation for the
Arts for its publishing activities.

The publisher gratefully acknowledges
Dr. Margaret Hess's generous donation
in establishing a revolving fund for the
University of Alberta Press that has helped
make possible the publication of this book.

Canada Council   Conseil des Arts
for the Arts   du Canada

Canadä

Alberta Foundation for the Arts

for Kjell Fohlström
(1944–2006)

...another life lived fully...

"Believe me, my young friend, there is nothing—absolutely nothing—
half so much worth doing as simply messing about in boats."

—KENNETH GRAHAME

Contents

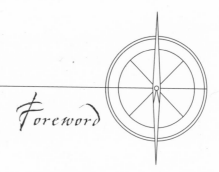

Foreword

IN THIS RAPIDLY URBANIZING CIVILIZATION, WE HAVE LOST OUR BALANCE. Our current environmental crisis stems from the fact that we act as if we are not a part of the world, but somehow outside of it. In the cities in which we all increasingly live, our food comes from supermarkets, our water from taps, and our electricity from power lines. As our weather grows more extreme, we watch from within our comfortable climate-controlled homes and shake our heads, and promise ourselves that we'll definitely make an effort to try to recycle a little bit more.

But at the same time, when you ask Canadians to describe their country, it is usually our great wilderness that springs to mind. The true north strong and free: remote, raging rivers, untouched forests, unexplored mountain ranges, and free spaces where wildlife roams undisturbed.

This disconnect is alarming. Our drive for resources with which to fill our cities and homes has accounted for large portions of Canada's wilderness. The great open spaces of our imagination are not as infinite as they once seemed, yet we continue to coast on an idea of a Canada that simply no longer exists. Instead of taking our wilds for granted, we need to begin to value them and to use them as a resource, not for our appetites, but for our souls.

The Nahanni River is one of those places that is too magnificent to put at risk for the sake of shareholders' balance sheets. A couple of weeks on the Nahanni can recharge your spirit for a year. That's why parks aren't just places to be protected "out there"; they are places we go to learn about what we need to do "right here."

R.M. Patterson's journals offer us moments in which to reflect upon the nature of the wilderness we are rapidly losing. Although Patterson's journey cannot be replicated in a world of satellite phones, GPS devices, and freeze-dried, vacuum-sealed camp food, the relationship he had with the land can. As we read Patterson's journals, we realize once more how much we require contact with an elemental life, with nature's bounty, in order to achieve contentment and wholeness within ourselves.

Nahanni Journals is a book that will offer Canadians an opportunity to re-establish contact with their history and allow visitors a glimpse into what makes our nation unique. From our First Nations to our voyageurs, from the coureurs des bois to Patterson himself, this country was shaped by people who were deeply connected to its land and rivers, and our greatest hope for the future lies in rediscovering those connections once again.

And if, like me, reading these journals gives you a mind to grab your paddle and go measure yourself against the land, by all means, do. I promise you, the land will not find you wanting.

JUSTIN TRUDEAU

Preface

R.M. PATTERSON'S ADVENTURES ON THE
SOUTH NAHANNI RIVER in the 1920s were the stuff of dreams. For
modern readers, tethered to desks or staring into computer monitors, Patterson's
ramblings by canoe or snowshoe represent the very essence of personal freedom,
independence, and self-reliance. His decision to embrace an elemental life in the
wilderness speaks volumes to those who would like to make similar choices, but
who—for whatever reasons—cannot. Indeed, much of our pleasure in learning
about Patterson's Nahanni travels grows out of a perhaps unconscious admiration
for a man who succeeds at breaking the fetters that we still allow to encumber
us. As we observe Patterson fulfill his dreams, we fulfill our own, albeit vicari-
ously, and so sustain ourselves for another day of dancing to a drum that we do
not beat.

The wilderness regions of Canada have changed substantially since Patterson
first left his footprints behind. The frontier between settlement and wild land has
pushed back dramatically in 80 years. Developments in aviation and communication have rendered all but meaningless such once-familiar romantic descriptors
as "in a remote valley" or "beyond an isolated mountain range." Replicating
Patterson's adventures in the Nahanni valley is no longer possible: the region
is now protected as a national park, where abundant use by ecotourists has
necessitated regulation, the very antithesis of the freedom, independence, and
self-reliance we admire in Patterson.

Is it, then, the simple fact of an altered social geography that keeps unfulfilled
urbanites from walking away from their daily chores, from leaving mortgages for
others to sort out? Is it only that the vast resource of the North has disappeared
and experiences such as Patterson's are no longer available to us? I suspect not.
Canada still offers an abundance of space in which the "rugged individualist" is

free to roam. Rather, we have found new ways to satisfy the human need for identity and autonomy. Many of us have evolved different ways of engaging with the land, ways that will accommodate thousands of others who have similar needs, and as a result, we are able to leave the land much as we found it. The land can and will nourish us, if only we manage our relationship with it. Nonetheless, managing that relationship in Nahanni country has to look considerably different in this century than it did in the early years of the last. And as *Nahanni Journals* demonstrates, our best ideas about how to manage that relationship can change dramatically in a much shorter span of years.

Certainly, when I first read *The Dangerous River*—Patterson's 1954 account of his Nahanni adventure—all my thoughts were with the man on the river. His experiences became mine, from the peaceful reveries evoked while lying on a sun-drenched boulder beside the rushing water to the icy chill as a moccasined foot broke through overflow ice in mid-winter. I admired—even envied—the adventurer for being where he was, instead of where I was, which, almost by definition, seemed prosaic and uneventful. Rarely if ever did I think beyond the imagined experience of being on the Nahanni. In this way, *The Dangerous River* enabled me to escape my own chafing routine, and that brief respite from the dull domesticity of reality was enough to carry me—for the moment, anyway. And in the longer term, the vision of a future "Nahanni adventure" of my own sustained me, even though my more rational self knew it to be an unlikely event.

But as I revisited *The Dangerous River* over the years, and as I read other books of travel and adventure—some about the Nahanni, some about worlds away— I began to reflect on *The Dangerous River* as a piece of writing, not merely as a vehicle for my own imaginary time-travel. I read Patterson's other accounts of an outdoor life. Much later, David Finch's *R.M. Patterson: A Life of Great Adventure* appeared in bookstores; it helped solidify my interest in Patterson as a writer, and not simply as a magician who could transport me to a more elemental world. Patterson's skill as a writer, of course, is exactly what had enabled him to perform the magical relocation I had initially felt, but my enthusiasm had been nonetheless for the world he created, not for the act of creating it. Most importantly, Finch's book led me to the 1927 and 1928–1929 journals that Patterson kept as he travelled on the Nahanni.

The primary goal of *Nahanni Journals* is to provide the reader with a clean, uncluttered text of this record R.M. Patterson kept when he was on the river in 1927 and 1928–1929. It is an engaging, personal account of a young man in the prime of his life and travelling in one of the most beautiful parts of the world. Because each entry was composed on a more or less daily basis, the collective journals possess an appealing immediacy and emotional honesty not found in *The Dangerous River*, which was written more than a quarter-century after the fact. If reading these journals offers a respite from the humdrum of workaday routine, or if the journals inspire the reader to accept the challenge of self-reliance, then making them available to the public will have been worthwhile.

These daily journal entries—written in small bound volumes by the light of smoky campfires, often while the weary traveller huddled under a net to ward off swarms of insects—provide both a fresh perspective on the Nahanni experience and another opportunity for temporary escape from the "comforts" of urban life. But they also reveal a man as in love with language as he is with the outdoors. The journals enable us to see Patterson simultaneously embrace the unarticulated life of a solitary wilderness traveller and the unquenchable desire to communicate to others all that he experiences.

Patterson was never a brilliant writer, but he was indeed one of competence, skill, and humour. Like the authors he read (Robert Surtees and early Dickens, but not James Joyce), he was more interested in entertaining than enlightening his audiences. Yet his command of language was sophisticated enough that it served him admirably as he employed it in subtly diverse ways. As these journals reveal—especially for those familiar with *The Dangerous River*—Patterson's language could capture the complete range of his daily emotions and his complicated relationship to the land he travelled.

Patterson's bold choice of how to live the life he was given is impressive. But that achievement is further enhanced by his writerly accomplishments, and *Nahanni Journals* seeks to frame these daily journals in a context that heightens the reader's ability to appreciate that verbal aspect of the record. The same man who could choose self-reliance and individual freedom over material security and creature comfort could, as well, evocatively transform his personal experience into words. Those are not personality traits often found in a single individual, something we should not lose track of in the excitement of canoeing the South Nahanni alongside Patterson.

For about 18 months between 1927 and 1929, R.M. Patterson travelled in the vicinity of the South Nahanni. There is little to dispute about that fact. But while the experience remains the same, two very different autobiographical accountings of it have evolved—the journals and *The Dangerous River*. The

Introduction and other editorial support found in *Nahanni Journals* try to tease out an understanding of the different relationships Patterson developed with his Nahanni experience, relationships he developed through writing. These various relationships—with environmental issues, with the author's personal life, with popular audiences—demonstrate that Patterson was not only an accomplished traveller but an accomplished travel-writer as well.

Acknowledgements

ALL BOOKS ARE THE PRODUCT OF MANY
MINDS WORKING TOGETHER, and *Nahanni Journals* is no exception. So
many individuals and institutions have contributed to making this book possible
that my acknowledgements here seem a wholly inadequate way of recognizing
them. While all contributions have been both welcomed and essential, some have
been outstanding. Whatever the level of assistance, these acknowledgements are
tendered with the most sincere appreciation and thanks.

The editorial aspect of this project began a few years ago as a senior under-
graduate course at the University of Calgary. After familiarizing themselves with
R.M. Patterson's *The Dangerous River*, and after receiving some instruction in
scholarly editing, the class developed a set of editorial practices, which they used
to transcribe Patterson's 1927 and 1928–1929 journals. Working from photo-
copies of the original manuscripts, each student checked the transcriptions of
other students, thereby producing a sound preliminary transcription. I then
took the students' work to Victoria, where I carefully checked it against the
manuscript journals. I trust the students learned from the experience; certainly
their considerable efforts helped produce a highly reliable edition of Patterson's
journals. Students also wrote essays that explored some of the differences between
the journals and Patterson's much-later book account of the same experience,
and these essays are posted at http://www.ucalgary.ca/~rdavis/rmpatterson/.

I have repeatedly enjoyed the pleasure of consulting with David Finch,
author of *R.M. Patterson: A Life of Great Adventure*. In fact, it was his biography
of Patterson that first made me aware that Patterson's journals were accessible.
Never in my experience as an author has anyone been as generous with his time
or resources as has David. He spoke about Patterson to my class, he offered me
unlimited access to the boxes of documents he accumulated in his research for

the biography, and he has repeatedly answered my various questions to the best of his ability. I cannot thank him enough for the help he has given, or the generosity with which it has been offered.

Preparing this book has also brought the unexpected pleasure of introducing me to Janet Blanchet, R.M. Patterson's daughter. In the early 1980s, I had the opportunity to meet Raymond and Marigold Patterson, and all the spirit of warmth, grace, and vigour embodied by that delightful couple has clearly been passed on to their daughter. Janet Blanchet has been unstinting in her assistance to this undertaking, especially in her efforts to make hundreds of photographs and letters available to me.

Many individuals have advanced this project in ways too numerous to mention, but several warrant special mention. Sophie Borcoman of Parks Canada has answered many pestering questions about Nahanni National Park Reserve. Verity Andrews of University of Reading generously provided me with copies of correspondence between Patterson and his New York publisher. The staff at the British Columbia Archives Division, especially Katy Hughes and Ann ten Cate, provided me access to Patterson's journals. Alison Woodley updated my understanding of environmental issues related to the Nahanni. Douglas P. Tate assisted with questions about natural history related to the Nahanni. The Interlibrary Loan staff at the University of Calgary has been patiently and abundantly helpful in carrying out the bibliographic aspects of this project. Professor Robert Cockburn first introduced me to *The Dangerous River* and to the possibility of bringing serious scholarship to bear on outdoor writing. Professor Emeritus M.T. Myres shared Patterson's inscription on the title page of an edition of *The Dangerous River*, and both Mrs. Pat Myres and Pat Clarke were most helpful in sending a copy that could be reproduced here. Dr. Robert Craig Brown, Dr. Cormack Gates, and Dr. W. Gillies Ross supported my efforts to secure leave time to complete this project. Marilyn Croot prepared the maps, and Janice Swanson, Mary Sullivan, and Stephanie Thwaites generously assisted me with securing permissions.

The Elisha Kent Kane Foundation assisted me with some essential early funding and, without that support, Patterson's journals would still be accessible only to those with the time and inclination to read them in the British Columbia Archives. The Isaak Walton Killam Foundation provided me with a brief period of time during which I could devote all my energies to this undertaking and, again, without that opportunity to focus, there would be no book. The Dr. Frederick

Cook Society helped cover some of the costs involved in preparing maps for *Nahanni Journals*. Finally, I wish to thank the Artic Institute of North America and the Faculty of Humanities at the University of Calgary for their support in the form of a small starter grant that first took me to Victoria.

Some of the ideas presented in the Introduction were initially developed for papers read at various conferences in the United States and Canada. My thanks go out to the conference organizers and to those participants who helped me better understand how to read Patterson's journals.

The University of Alberta Press would like to thank Dr. Margaret Hess for her generous donation in establishing a revolving fund to assist our publications program. *Nahanni Journals* is the third book to benefit from this fund.

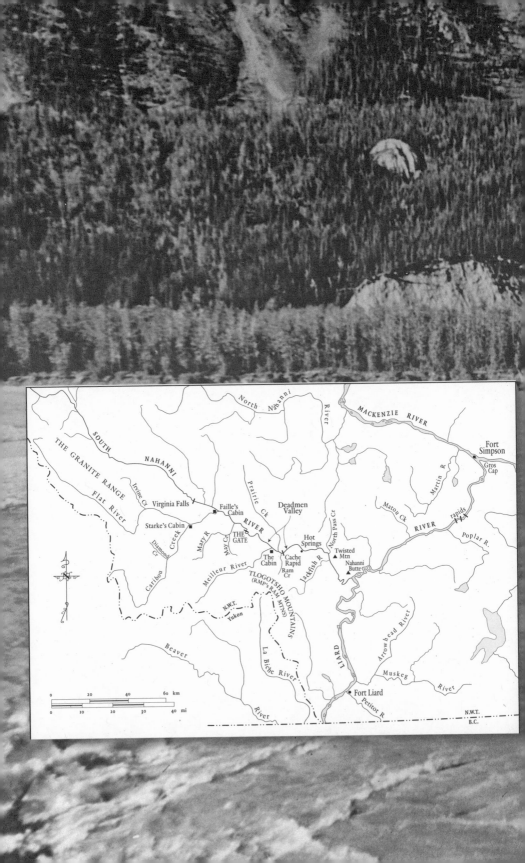

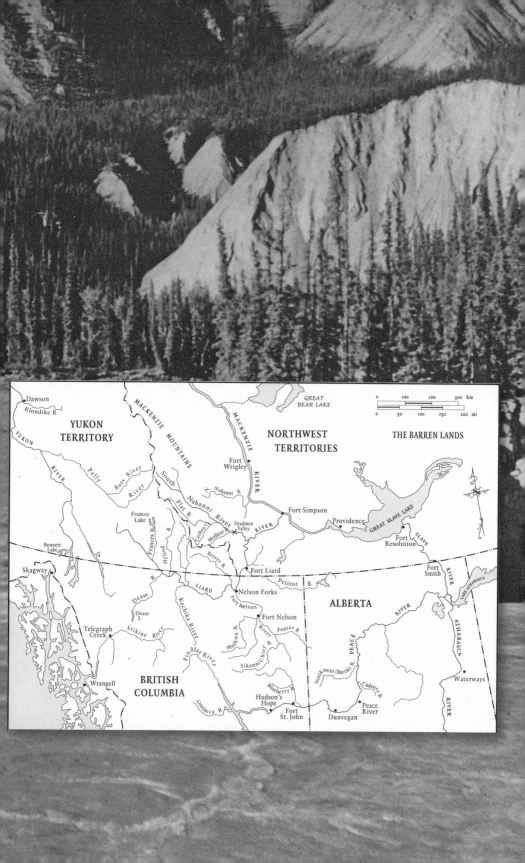

Prologue

IN THE SUMMER OF 1923, A TALL, SOMEWHAT GANGLY YOUNG MAN LOOKED UP FROM HIS CUBICLE in the Bank of England's London office and saw—not the dark wainscotting on the wall or the clock and appointment book on his desk—but the blue haze of faraway mountains. His position at the Bank of England was relatively new, having followed soon after he completed his degree at Oxford University; the image of a faraway horizon was more deep-seated, having haunted him since childhood. He had dreamed it from the window of the substantial family home in Darlington, County Durham, gazing westward over the rolling hills of the Yorkshire Dales. He had dreamed it as a schoolboy in Lancashire, transforming the Pennine Hills into towering, unnamed mountains in the remotest parts of Canada. And now he dreamed it again. But this time, the dream had an unfamiliar sense of finality about it. No longer content with the dream of a bolder and more elemental life, he would give his notice that afternoon. He would begin to live the dream.

His new life began on a dairy farm in southwestern British Columbia's Fraser Valley in 1924. But cow udders, hay rakes, and sanitizing solutions soon proved to hold little more appeal than had the London ledgers and account books. Seizing advantage of the Soldier's Settlement, a 26-year-old Raymond Patterson laid claim to 320 acres of scrub land in the Peace River district of northwestern Alberta. All he needed to do was clear the land and build a cabin on it. Homesteading was an enticing opportunity for the thousands of immigrants who came to Canada during the nineteenth and twentieth centuries, immigrants seeking to improve their status from a past life where landownership had been intimately linked with social privilege and inheritance. But Patterson came from no such disadvantaged family. His grandfather, with whom he lived, had made a fortune in the foundry business, and he had no problem with his grandson benefiting from his engineering skills and business acumen. What motivated the young Patterson to homestead, then, was a pure sense of adventure, not a necessary search for livelihood.

Still, even from his homestead in Peace River country, the haze of faraway mountains beckoned. Returning to England to enjoy Christmas holidays in 1925—the sort of holiday that is so much easier for those who homestead for recreation rather than for subsistence—Patterson read Michael Mason's *The Arctic Forests*. And if Patterson's autobiographical self-construction can be taken at face value, he was drawn to the blank space on a map of the Northwest Territories (NWT) that was printed on the end papers of Mason's book. With his apparently insatiable romantic imagination once more engaged in overdrive, Patterson decided that he must follow those speculative tracings on the map, must seek out parts of the Empire so unknown that they could not be properly set down on paper.

By the spring of 1927, he was on his way to the fabled and mysterious South Nahanni River, lying in the NWT near where the NWT, the Yukon, and British Columbia connect. Although not entirely unknown, it was only sketchily mapped. It certainly could provide nothing man-made in the way of supplies or security. Hence, it was an ideal site for geographical adventure *à la* those of Sir John Franklin, David Livingstone, and any number of sons of the Empire from a rapidly fading age. Indeed, the bush plane, which struck the final death knell of that age, actually made several appearances on the Nahanni while Patterson was there.

That summer, Patterson ascended the Nahanni to the point where it drops over a steep wall—Virginia Falls—some 127 miles upriver from its mouth. On this upward journey, he also scouted up the Flat River, one of the Nahanni's tributaries, where he prospected for gold, but without success. For the most part, he travelled alone, but he intermittently met up with Albert Faille, a trapper from Minnesota, who was also ascending the Nahanni that summer. Faille was an important mentor to Patterson, who had learned his limited canoeing skills by punting on the canal-like rivers meandering through Oxford University. Yet Patterson was clearly intent on travelling as much as possible under his own power. Many years later, he even claimed to have reached Virginia Falls on his own, although, as these journals reveal, he had to enlist Faille's assistance in order to get that far. It should not minimize Patterson's 1927 journey, however, to observe that his attainment of the Falls required the assistance of a companion. This was, after all, an unprecedented journey for a bank clerk.

+

*RMP at the Twisted Mountain. The photograph was taken by Faille
at the beginning of the adventurer's 1927 summer on the Nahanni.*

The summer of adventure was far from over. At the Falls, Patterson and Faille turned their bows downstream and descended the South Nahanni. Faille travelled as far as the mouth of the Flat River, where he built a cabin and prepared to spend the winter. Patterson journeyed to Nahanni Butte, where the South Nahanni drains into the Liard River. In less than three days, Patterson raced down the same river that had taken him as many weeks to ascend. Once upon the wide Liard, Patterson steered his canoe upriver, ascending the Liard as far as Nelson Forks, where he then ascended the Fort Nelson River to Fort Nelson. From there, the romantic former bank clerk struck out overland for Fort St. John in northern British Columbia. It was this overland trek at the summer's end that nearly cost Patterson his life.

The spectacular South Nahanni, Canadian Heritage River and World Heritage Site.

In the five months since he had left his homestead on Peace River, Patterson, according to his own count—proudly recorded on the final pages of the journal he kept—had travelled a total of 2,888 miles, 905 miles of which were in his canoe, and 775 of them while travelling solo. Much of the mileage, of course, had been logged in reaching the Nahanni and on his return to Edmonton, but he records that he poled, paddled, and tracked 310 of those solo miles on the Nahanni and its tributary, the Flat—no small feat, when one remembers that half of that mileage was upriver and that at the beginning of the summer, Patterson didn't know how to lift a canoe for portaging!

Those five months only whetted his appetite. He was not even back on his homestead before he was scheming to return to the Nahanni the following spring, accompanied this time by a fellow British expatriate living in Canada. The two adventure-seekers were equipped to spend the winter. By the final day of May 1928 Patterson and his companion, Gordon Matthews, were already on the Nahanni and had ascended partway up to a section known as the Splits, where the river broadens out and becomes a maze of islands, snyes, and a myriad of diverse channels extending up to two miles from riverbank to riverbank. By the time the two men had navigated a year's worth of supplies through the Splits, which necessitated moving portions of gear ahead, caching them where they would be

+

RMP's romantic cabin in the woods at 44° below.

safe from foragers, then turning back downstream for another load—a process repeated over and over again—too much time had elapsed. They would not be able to make it up the Nahanni as far as Flat River, where they had planned to overwinter and where they intended to prospect for gold. Because of the delay at the Splits, they decided to make their winter camp well below the Flat at a place known to Patterson as Deadmen's Valley, although properly "Deadmen Valley" on modern maps.

Most romantic young men, especially those reaching their majority in the age of Robert Baden-Powell and Ernest Thompson Seton, want to build their own house and live in it. Patterson had already done that in homesteading the Peace River half section. But never content merely to realize the dreams of "most romantic young men," the 30-year-old Patterson needed to do it again. So he and Matthews built a cabin across from where Prairie Creek enters the Nahanni on its north side, and beside a small snye that Patterson named Wheatsheaf Creek after a property in Dorset, U.K., that bore special meaning for his fiancée and him. The name still appears on modern maps, although often shortened to Sheaf Creek. In truth, having already satisfied some of that romantic urge to build his own house, Patterson left much of the building of the Wheatsheaf Creek cabin to Matthews. While his companion got the initial construction under way, Patterson—somehow still eager for the freedom of the trail and seeking the independence that only solo travel can provide—struck out for Flat River. He spent close to a month—from August 13 to September 8—travelling solo up the Nahanni, then up the Flat and one of its tributaries, ostensibly in search of gold, but he found nothing, and according to his journal, he didn't waste a great deal of time panning or seriously prospecting for it. Although he acknowledged what a generous and essentially good companion Gordon Matthews proved to be, R.M. Patterson preferred R.M. Patterson's company to any other. Solitude and adventure, as much as any yellow mineral, seem to have been what lured him onward.

The cabin Matthews built was small, 14ft. x 13ft. inside the log walls. It was certainly too small to shelter two six-footers at a time for very long. So even when both men were back in Deadmen's Valley, they spent a great deal of time laying traplines, hunting, and sleeping in snow camps well removed from the tiny cabin, in spite of sub zero temperatures and the darkness of a Subarctic winter. In mid-December, Matthews began a long solo snowshoe journey to Fort Simpson on the Liard for supplies, leaving Patterson alone in Deadmen's Valley. Six weeks later, having seen nothing of Matthews, who should have made it back to the cabin long ago, a nearly starving Patterson began the same long journey to Fort Simpson. The thermometer stood at -50° and the venture nearly cost Patterson his life. Finally meeting up with Matthews, who had been delayed at Fort Simpson, the two returned to Deadmen's Valley, where they remained for two extremely profitable months of trapping. In mid-May, they bid goodbye to their tiny cabin and left for life on the "outside."

+ + +

While R.M. Patterson's name is not a household word, many armchair travellers, ecotourists, northerners, and outdoors people—especially canoeists—who are familiar with the name know it because they have read *The Dangerous River*. Published in 1954, *The Dangerous River* is Patterson's book-length narrative account of his experiences on the Nahanni in the late 1920s. Presumably, many who pick up *Nahanni Journals* will do so because they know Patterson's *The Dangerous River*, which has not been out of print since it was simultaneously published in Britain and the United States more than 50 years ago. It has been translated into Spanish and Dutch. It has been read around the globe by ecotourists and adventurers alike, whose dream—often realized, often remaining only an alluring carrot dangling at the end of another urban and routine week—is to canoe down the South Nahanni River. A somewhat dispirited Parks Canada employee at Nahanni National Park Reserve once complained that people arriving in Fort Simpson in preparation to descend the South Nahanni in guided groups of rafters or canoeists had generally read *The Dangerous River*, but knew almost nothing about the aboriginal peoples who had inhabited the Nahanni watershed for centuries. To have penned such a widely read and long-lived book of adventure travel is remarkable; to have done so as a much-delayed afterthought by a man himself over a half-century old with no prior books to his credit suggests that Raymond Murray Patterson was not only an innovative man—he was an extraordinary one.

What is not so well known, even among Patterson and Nahanni enthusiasts, is that throughout nearly all his travels on the South Nahanni, Patterson kept a daily journal that has survived. The journal from the first summer on the river spans from June 7, 1927 to October 23, 1927, when Patterson returned to Edmonton. No account of this return journey, by the way, has been in print for the past 25 years because of anomalies in the publishing history of *The Dangerous River*, a matter addressed later in the Introduction. The journal from the next year starts on March 17, 1928 and runs through January 29, 1929, when a hungry Patterson set off for Fort Simpson in search of his overdue partner. The journals remained in the possession of Patterson for most of his life, and he consulted them on numerous occasions as he wrote up other accounts of his time on the river. Five years after Patterson's death on October 20, 1984, his widow, Mrs. Marigold Patterson—herself now deceased—entrusted the journals and many other documents of interest to the Royal British Columbia Museum, where they are currently housed within the British Columbia Archives.

Accessible to the public, these archived manuscripts provide the text for *Nahanni Journals*. The transcription that follows offers the general reader a clean and unencumbered edition of Patterson's lively journals. But the edition has been prepared in accordance with exacting editorial practices, and the Annotations section toward the end of the book provides more detailed information about the physical manuscript from which this clean transcription has been prepared.

Throughout, the entries are engagingly written responses to an experience virtually unattainable in this century. Their value, however, lies not only in the historical experience they reflect, but in the evocative creativity of the words themselves, for they reveal a very different man enjoying a very different experience from what appears in *The Dangerous River*.

Introduction

R.M.P.

THE FOLLOWING JOURNALS ARE AT LEAST AS
MUCH ABOUT THE MAN WHO WROTE THEM AS THE RIVER
THAT INSPIRED THEM, so let me begin by fleshing out something of
Raymond Patterson's biography, especially from his early years. Patterson was
fond of "creating" his youthful persona in many of his travel books, and as his
Nahanni River journals will illustrate, taking everything that Patterson wrote at
face value is not always reliable. David Finch's biography *R.M. Patterson: A Life
of Great Adventure* brings additional biographical information to the table, but it
necessarily relies heavily on Patterson's own autobiographical accounts. While
Finch's engagingly written biography is carefully researched and documented,
the author's main source of information is the archival record primarily assem-
bled by Patterson himself. *A Life of Great Adventure*, consequently, is the sort of
biography of which Patterson himself would have approved, circumstances that
can sometimes restrict a biographer's ability to plumb the depths of a complicated
and complex personality, which, indeed, is an apt description of R.M. Patterson.
Nonetheless, Finch's study is an important work that weaves together thousands
of details into a delightful narrative. Little of this introduction to Patterson's life
could have been written without it. More importantly, Finch's book drew my
attention to the very existence of Patterson's journals and reignited my interest
in him after a hiatus of more than two decades.

Raymond Murray Patterson was born to a Scottish father and English
mother in 1898 at Darlington, County Durham, in northern England. His
parents had married only two years prior to his birth, and Raymond was their
only offspring. Soon after the boy's third birthday, his parents' marriage fell apart.

A young RMP with his mother, Emily Taylor Coates.

Henry Patterson, Raymond's father, sailed to South Africa, where he worked as a newspaper correspondent. Only once, and briefly, was he reunited with his son, when the younger Patterson was in his early twenties. The failure of his parents' marriage and his father's departure to distant South Africa were formative events in the younger Patterson's life.

His mother, Emily Taylor Coates (later, after remarriage, Lady Scott), was the daughter of a highly successful engineer and businessman whose foundry supplied ironwork for the London Underground and steel for gas storage tanks around the world. After her husband left for South Africa, Patterson's mother and her young son moved into the Coates family home, and if the young Raymond lacked a father, he certainly did not lack for financial security or for loving attention from his mother. Mother and son forged a very close relationship. When—at the Coates family's expense—Patterson was sent away to be educated at Rossall school in Lancashire, beside the Irish Sea, he regularly wrote letters to his mother to keep her informed about his school life. But these letters were much more than letters home from a dutiful son; they were clearly a vehicle for the boy's need for self-expression. In fact, in 1951, when he turned 53, Patterson edited the letters he had written to his mother between 1911 and 1917 and self-published 75 copies of a book he entitled *Dear Mother*. That he would still have the letters 35 or 40 years later and that he would go to the trouble and expense of self-publishing them speaks volumes—both about his relationship with his mother and about the seriousness with which he took his writing.

Only a few months after leaving Rossall, early in 1918 Second Lieutenant Patterson found himself in the trenches of France, where, soon after, he was taken prisoner. He remained a prisoner of war until the Armistice nine months later. As an officer, Patterson took the initiative of setting up a prison library for himself and his fellow captives. After the war, Patterson attended St. John's College at Oxford, perhaps more the result of ample financial assistance from his mother's side of the family and the government's commitment to make education accessible to veterans, than of his own record of academic achievement. His rather mediocre studies at Oxford led to a second in political science and philosophy and, soon after, a position in the Bank of England in London. From this point forward, Patterson's life became at once more unusual and more interesting.

The catalyst for Patterson's travels was a visit from his father, whom he had not seen for 23 years. Evidently, the younger Patterson felt—or displayed—no abandonment issues; rather, he was enthralled by the sense of exotic adventure that his father represented. Out of respect for his mother, he did not follow his father back to South Africa, but soon after that unexpected visit Patterson resigned from the Bank of England and set sail for Canada.

First arriving in this country in 1924, Patterson worked on a dairy farm in the Fraser Valley before moving to northern Alberta, where he homesteaded 320 acres of free land under the Soldier Settlement. For some, clearing land and building a log house in Peace River country in the 1920s might have been a sufficient change from the dull, grey routine of a banking job in London, but it was only the beginning for R.M. Patterson. By the spring of 1927, he was on his way still farther north to the Nahanni River, lying in the Northwest Territories near where the NWT, the Yukon, and British Columbia abut. Of course, simply to get to the Nahanni in the 1920s required a fair amount of work, much of it in a canoe. This presented a somewhat special problem for Patterson, because, although he had considerable experience punting on the Cherwell and Isis rivers while at Oxford, he had virtually no experience paddling a canoe in fast water. But he had

+

RMP on the Slave River, Spring 1927, en route *to the Nahanni.*

a powerful romantic ambition for adventure; he was young and clever and reasonably fit; and he certainly wasn't the sort of person who suffered from debilitating periods of self-doubt.

The South Nahanni River was not a totally unknown entity in 1927—not at all the sort of veiled *terra incognita* that others had explored in the previous century. Gold-seekers on their way to the Yukon had struggled up the Nahanni. During the 18 months Patterson spent on the river, he found blaze marks on trees and several derelict structures, presumably left by previous white travellers, prospectors, and trappers. But the watershed was only sketchily mapped, and it provided nothing man-made in the way of supplies or security. In short, the South Nahanni was an ideal place for adventure.

The preface to the adventure began at the end of May 1927, in Edmonton, where Patterson and Dennis France boarded a train bound for Waterways, or what is known today as Fort McMurray, Alberta. According to Finch, France had just quit his job and was looking for a daring enterprise for the summer before returning home to England. He intended to travel with Patterson as far as Fort

Simpson and then take a steam-powered riverboat back. For his part, Patterson acknowledged that travel in pairs was both easier and safer, although such good sense did not prevail for long. At Waterways, the two novices loaded their canoe and set off down the Athabasca River, paddling for the first time in their lives. Blessed by considerable luck, they reached Lake Athabasca and survived the windy crossing to Fort Chipewyan, where they began their descent of the Slave River. Only a short way down the Slave, however, they were overtaken by the HBC launch *Canadusa*, which Patterson and French boarded as far as the portage at Fort Smith. From the portage they loaded their canoe and supplies on another scow that was being pushed downriver by a motor launch, and arrived on Great Slave Lake a little over a month after they had left Edmonton. Still aboard the scow, they crossed the lake and followed the Mackenzie River down as far as Fort Simpson, where the Liard River enters on the southwestern bank. There, Patterson traded his 18-foot canoe for a smaller 16-foot Chestnut Prospector, a cedar and canvas classic. This canoe model was manufactured by the Chestnut Canoe Company up until the 1980s when the iconic canoe manufacturer closed its doors for good. France, much to Patterson's satisfaction, turned back. Patterson then hitched a ride up the Liard on a scow, on which he travelled to a point about 50 miles downstream from the entrance of the South Nahanni River.

Here the real adventure began. Travelling alone for the most part, Patterson ascended the river as far as Virginia Falls, where the entire South Nahanni plunges over a drop in the rock that is more than twice the height of Niagara Falls. At the time of his visit, the cataract was not even named—Patterson only ever referred to the "Falls of the Nahanni," although only a few years ago there was a strong, but ultimately unsuccessful, movement to rename them Trudeau Falls. They were christened Virginia Falls by Fenley Hunter the summer after Patterson's initial visit. Hunter had seen them for the first time on his daughter's birthday, and through a presumptuous act of personal possession—all too common by those who see something for their first time and correspondingly assume everyone else up to that moment in time has been similarly benighted—named them after his daughter Virginia. The name stuck, even surviving the attempt to name them after the former prime minister of Canada, who had once flown in to them in 1970.

Unlike on the Saskatchewan, which a *canot du maître* manned by 16 pemmican-fed voyageurs could ascend by paddling, Patterson—travelling alone—had to pole or track his canoe almost the entire way. To pole a canoe requires the traveller to stand up and propel the craft forward by means of a long pole pushed against the river bottom; poling came easy to Patterson, thanks to his recreational punting on the ditches-cum-rivers of Oxford. Tracking was another matter. It involves walking along the shore and pulling the canoe forward, easy enough so long as the water is calm and the shore is level, but neither condition describes the Nahanni. Its waters are often turbulent, and as one pulls the bow of the canoe from the shore, the bow is understandably obliged to point shoreward, leaving the canoe broadside to the current and inevitably filling it with water. Add to this a shoreline composed of a tumble of irregularly-sized boulders, or a shoreline peppered with sweepers, i.e., fallen trees extending far out into the river, the soil from their exposed roots eroded away by the endless surge of the river. Irrespective of how secure the footing along the bank might be, considerable skill is required to stand on the shore and, by pulling a rope, coax a loaded canoe far out into the river so that it can pass beyond a sweeper. It was Albert Faille who taught Patterson how to manage his canoe in such situations. Perhaps an even worse scenario for tracking a canoe arises when there is no shoreline at all, but only steep cliff walls through which the river cuts.

But the following journals vividly describe Patterson's summer journey and his return the following year to trap and overwinter with Gordon Matthews, so there's little point in repeating the bare events here. Suffice it to say that no gold was found, but that, at Fort Simpson the next spring, Patterson and Matthews sold the marten they had trapped for nearly $2000, and that figure did not include what they received for pelts from weasels, foxes, mink, coyote, and at least one wolverine.[1]

Soon after he returned from the Nahanni in 1929, Patterson went back to England for the express purpose of marrying. On July 4, 1929, he exchanged vows with 26-year-old Marigold Portman, and thus began a match made in heaven. Only a woman with her own very special penchant for adventure and a willingness to forego routine creature comforts could have enjoyed the next half-century of Patterson's life. Marigold Patterson was indeed that woman.

The couple moved to Alberta, where they bought a sheep ranch west of Calgary. Patterson, of course, knew nothing about raising sheep, but he was as eager to learn the intricacies of sheep ranching as he had been to learn river travel. The crash of the stock market, however, made it nearly impossible for even the most seasoned sheep rancher to survive, and after only four years, Patterson sold out, "battered but not crippled."[2] These years, nevertheless, introduced him to George Pocaterra, an eccentric Italian-Canadian who shared Patterson's

+

RMP in tatters on his way back "outside," May 1929.

conflicting tastes for the cultural advantages of the city and the solitude and personal challenge of the wilderness. The two went on many horseback trips into the eastern slopes of the Rocky Mountains, and in 1933, Pocaterra sold his ranch—the Buffalo Head—to Patterson. Still standing today, the Buffalo Head is nestled in the beautiful Eden Valley on the north side of the Highwood River, west of Longview, Alberta. It became the Pattersons' home for the next 13 years, during which time they raised three children. Pocaterra had primarily raised horses on the ranch; Patterson converted it to a cow-calf operation, again in spite of the fact that he had no prior experience as a cattleman. The work was hard and the days were sometimes very long, but life on the Buffalo Head suited Patterson, situated as it was with its back up against the Kananaskis Range. Raising beef during the Depression always kept food on the table, and when the ledger-sheet occasionally grew troublesome, the Buffalo Head could turn a modest profit as a guest ranch. Such rejigging of the operation served Patterson well, as it enabled him to guide cultured visitors from the East or from Europe on horseback trips into the mountains he had come to love so dearly, thus allowing him to marry his love of culture and of wild nature. The nearly 17 years spent in southern Alberta immersed Patterson in the world of horses and in the Rocky Mountains, even if that immersion drew him away from his prior engagement with canoes and with the Canadian North.

Ever a restless man, however, Patterson sold the Buffalo Head in 1946, buying two properties in British Columbia in its stead. The first was an orchard at Shoal Harbour on the Saanich Peninsula of Vancouver Island. Marigold had often escaped part of the Alberta winters by visiting the island, and the two older Patterson children attended boarding school there. At about the same time, Patterson also purchased some ranching acres at Spillimacheen in the Columbia Valley of southeastern British Columbia, although it was never used for much more than hunting and riding activities before Patterson sold it and consolidated all his efforts in Shoal Harbour. Characteristically, when he and Marigold finally left the Buffalo Head, they did so on horseback in October of 1946, riding over the mountains to the new property in the Columbia Valley.

Clearly, 1946 was a busy year for the Pattersons, between selling one property, buying two, arranging for the removal of all their possessions, and riding over the mountains so late in the season that substantial snow cover was already accumulating. The next year, 1947, was busy in a different way. It began a new phase in Patterson's life. This man who so loved words that he retained his boyhood letters from boarding school to his mother, who spent hours in the northern bush either reading Dickens and Surtees or writing in his journal, and who organized a library in a prisoner-of-war camp now became a professional travel-writer. His first published article—"River of Deadmen's Valley"—appeared in *The Beaver* in June 1947. Even though it recounted experiences that had occurred nearly two decades previously, the article was an immediate success, in part, perhaps, because he could draw on the daily journal entries he had recorded 20 years previously. The "River of Deadmen's Valley" piece led to numerous other articles and stories in Canada (*The Beaver*), England (*Country Life*), and Scotland (*Blackwood's Magazine*). Like the man who fails because he drinks, and then drinks because he fails—but in a far more positive way!—Patterson fell into a cycle of writing about his outdoor travels and adventures, followed by a summer engaged in new adventures and travels so that he would have additional material about which to write. For example, rather than simply "retiring" to Shoal Harbour to write after selling off the Buffalo Head, Patterson made summer-long canoe trips into northern British Columbia in the late 1940s, canoeing the Stikine, Dease, and Liard rivers in 1948, and the Parsnip, Peace, and Finlay rivers in 1949. Later, those travels would provide the foundation of such books as *Trail to the Interior* (1966), *Finlay's River* (1968), and his ninety-eight page introduction to The Hudson's Bay Record Society's edition of Samuel Black's *A Journal of A Voyage From Rocky Mountain Portage in Peace River To the Sources of Finlays Branch And North West Ward In Summer 1824* (1955).

His practice of writing about adventures experienced long before started soon after Patterson left the Buffalo Head. Some time early in the 1950s, Patterson began writing the account of his 1927–1929 experiences that we know today as *The Dangerous River*. It was simultaneously published in both London and New York in 1954, having been completed in the autumn of the previous year. The catalyst for the book-length narrative came in June 1952, when the director of George Allen & Unwin Ltd.—having seen one of Patterson's magazine articles about the Nahanni in *Blackwood's*—wrote to ask if he had enough material to do an entire book. Patterson, of course, was flattered beyond belief. After all, George Allen & Unwin had just published Thor Heyerdahl's *The Kon-Tiki Expedition* (1950) and would publish J. R. R. Tolkien's *The Lord of the Rings* later in that same decade. Patterson must have set to work immediately, although he was also busy with other writing commitments. The director's expression of interest in Patterson's knack for storytelling was not the first of its kind, but it was the first by someone in a position to bring the work to fruition.

According to Patterson, friends and guests at the Buffalo Head had urged him years before to write down the stories of the Nahanni. He speaks of spending long summer evenings "equipped with a bottle of Chivas...," telling stories of the Nahanni country. Jim Bennett, a frequent guest at the ranch, had encouraged him to commit them to paper, but Patterson had doubted his ability to do so.[3] Now, fortified with a favourable public reaction to his magazine articles, the enquiry from a London publishing house came like a heaven-sent request to a man in love with the written word.

With no rapids to negotiate and no mountain passes to pry into on horseback, it is difficult to imagine just how Patterson might have passed his time in the post-Buffalo Head years. Clearly, he still passed many days exploring the world around him, but as he grew older, he spent more time reading and writing in his study. After the two summers of canoeing in northern British Columbia in 1948

+

Virginia Falls, photographed by RMP when he returned to the Nahanni in 1951.

and 1949, and after the various accounts of the Nahanni that were written and published in the late 1940s and early 1950s, Patterson put together a recollection of his days on the Eden Valley ranch in southwestern Alberta, published as *The Buffalo Head* in 1961. The first third of the book describes his early life, his home-steading in Peace River country, and his trip to the Nahanni; thus, this project is Patterson's first full-on attempt to reconstruct an autobiographical identity. Perhaps it is significant that Patterson wrote this lengthy autobiographical self-construction at the request of Helen King, one of the editors at William Sloane Associates, who told him that readers didn't just want to hear stories from the ranch, but wanted to know how he had ever come to be there in the first place. His personality was an essential component in the equation.

For a few years, he worked as a seasonal surveyor. In the early years of the 1950s, he was involved as a partner in the purchase of Big Coulee Ranch, but he sold his shares and returned to Shoal Harbour only two years later. At the same time he was involved in Big Coulee Ranch, Patterson revisited the South Nahanni, being invited to guide an American, Curtis Smith, up to the Falls of the Nahanni. Patterson was 52 years old at the time. The party of three took canoes from Fort Nelson to Nahanni Butte, via the Fort Nelson and Liard rivers. From the Butte, they made a deal with Fred Sibbeston to transport them as far as the Falls in a scow, and return them as far as the Flat River, where Patterson met up with his mentor from the 1920s, Albert Faille. By mid-September, Patterson was back home in Shoal Harbour and writing an eight-page article entitled "Nahanni Revisited" that appeared in the June 1952 issue of *The Beaver*. He made one more trip to the Nahanni in the summer of 1955, again with Curtis Smith, but all travel was by air, and the complete journey did not last a fortnight.

Late in 1959, St. John's College, Oxford, conferred the M.A. degree on Patterson. The timing of the honour was ideal, as Patterson and Marigold had decided to return to Britain. Patterson wanted to use the old country as a base from which to tour Europe, where he intended to research a book on Napoleon. They spent two years travelling on the continent, and finally returned to Victoria, where they bought property near the university in 1962. Almost immediately, Patterson began work on a new book project, a compilation of some of his previously published articles interwoven with added narrative sections to contextualize and connect the rejigged material. The result was *Far Pastures*, published in 1963 by Patterson's friend Gray Campbell, who in 1966 published the first Canadian edition of *The Dangerous River*. 1966 also saw the publication of *Trail to the Interior*. Two years later, in 1968, *Finlay's River* appeared. These latter two books were accounts of the canoe travel he had undertaken in northern British Columbia in the late 1940s. Now in his 70s, Patterson was able to relive those experiences through writing them down for everyone to enjoy.

Here was a man who had not written anything professionally until he was in his 50s. Yet by the time he died on October 20, 1984, he had written numerous travel articles, stories, and book reviews, researched and composed an introduction to a scholarly volume, and published five full-length books of outdoor travel. Clearly, Raymond Patterson was a complicated individual, a man full of contradictions. As this biographical sketch and the following journals reveal, he not only ducked out of a comfortable and promising career with the

Bank of England in London to milk cows, but he turned in his dinner jacket and before-dinner drinks so that he could homestead land in the Peace River district, land he could have purchased outright with little effect on the family balance sheet. And he relinquished the luxury and privilege that wealth could command so that he could sleep in an open snow camp at -40° or portage a canoe through a thrumming haze of mosquitoes. But the best part of all is that he passionately loved not only the experience he so willingly embraced—he loved putting it down on paper for others to experience.

THE JOURNALS

Patterson's journals of his 1927 and 1928–1929 South Nahanni adventures, which appear in print here for the first time, are essential cultural documents in numerous respects. The fact that they have remained unpublished until now surely arises for one reason and one reason only: because people wrongly assume that the journals are mere rough drafts of a later "master narrative." Such an assumption is never a safe one. In the case of Patterson's journals and *The Dangerous River*, nothing could be farther from the truth. As this Introduction shows, the journals differ significantly from the narrative account Patterson later produced. In some ways, they provide a superior account; in others, they are limited in ways that the narrative is not. But there is no mistaking the essential difference of the two accounts.

Perhaps the most powerful effect of the journals is that, when read together with the narrative, they demand a shift of consciousness from the reader. No longer is he or she able to ignore the fact that written renderings of physical experiences can never be more than written renderings. As much as the romantic traveller in all of us wants the printed page to catapult us into the very bows of Patterson's canoe, to provide us with an adventurous escape to the banks of the Nahanni—and surely that is why most armchair travellers read—these two parallel but distinctly different renderings of the identical historical and autobiographical experience propel the reader into the world of postmodernity. Whether the reader goes there kicking and screaming or with eager enthusiasm is an individual matter, but after encountering both the journals and the public narrative, no reader can ever again approach travel writing from the fundamentally naïve position that the account is somehow the experience. Most of us recognize that when books are made into films, the ultimate success or failure of the film has little to do with the book to which it is linked. The same recognition needs to be made about adventure or travel writing. Written renderings can only reflect an event or experience, and the success of the reflection—or in this instance, reflections—has only minimal dependence on the event itself.

The record of the first summer travelling on the Nahanni and overland via the Nelson and Sikanni Chief rivers to Fort St. John runs from June 7, 1927 to October 23, 1927. The 1927 entries are written in pencil in a small bound volume (13 x 23 cm) of lined pages. The original volume was completely blank except for the words "A. H. ESCH & CO. LTD., EDMONTON" printed at the bottom of the first leaf. This first journal actually takes the form of a lengthy letter to his mother, who resided in England. Since he knew he would have no opportunity to post the letter-journal from any point along the river, Patterson planned to keep the daily record and to mail it back to England when the opportunity arose, although he clearly understood that doing so might not be possible until he had come back from the Nahanni. Years later, Patterson even told his daughter Janet that, should the unimaginable happen—a chance encounter with a sow grizzly, a slip of the canoe pole at a critical moment—the journals might survive to inform his mother about the final months of his life. Hence, the 1927 journal served not only as a daily record of his experience, but as an intimate form of communication with his mother. Perhaps as a result of this latter function, the 1927 journals are a more compelling read than are those from the next year. While the main focus of the entries is travel on the river, Patterson "speaks" to his mother about personal matters and about common experiences they have shared. A section of one page has been carefully cut out of the journal, presumably because that section contained information Patterson—or possibly his family—did not wish to be read by anyone else. Enticing by its having been consciously removed, the missing segment actually heightens the personal nature of what remains, suggesting that some levels of intimacy cannot be sustained or extended beyond the moment and beyond the bond between a son and his mother.

The 1928–1929 journals, while less intimate, are nonetheless equally engaging. Like the 1927 journals, they are recorded in pencil on lined paper in a bound volume, although of somewhat larger dimensions (19 x 24 cm). Nothing indicates that they were intended for anyone's eyes but Patterson's, yet they are far from the terse notes a traveller might record in order to remind himself of the day's weather or the distance travelled. Instead, they are carefully constructed attempts to capture the full emotional spectrum of daily experience. The journals begin on March 17, 1928, with Patterson and Matthews at Fort St. John, British Columbia, *en route* to the Nahanni, and end with a quickly-jotted entry for January 29, 1929, just as a poorly provisioned Patterson is about to leave the cabin on Wheatsheaf Creek. He will head to Fort Simpson alone to learn what had happened to his companion, now missing for more than a month. But the journals include nothing about Patterson's solo winter journey back to Fort Simpson, about his return trek with Matthews to the cabin, about the productive two months of trapping along the Nahanni, or about the return journey to the "outside." The only surviving written account of that period is *The Dangerous River.*

For the most part, Patterson composed his journals at the end of each day, although in the length of the entries, in their frequency, and in their occasional irregularity, the journals reflect something of the very freedom of Patterson's journey. The most common time for composing his journal entries was at bedtime. During the long evenings of a northern summer, after a day of tracking or poling upriver, Patterson would lie under his mosquito net beside his campfire and write. Unquestionably, the summer-long thrum of mosquitoes demanded that one either be actively engaged in physical activity or—when resting—protected from them by netting or smoke, and when the camp chores were finished for the night, Patterson often chose to use this physically inactive time to indulge his love of words. Too active a mind to spend endless hours staring into the fire, Patterson either read his few books or wrote in his journals. Occasionally, the dated journal entries are marked "Morning" or "Noon," indicating that they were written up earlier in the day, rather than at bedtime. Entries marked in this way are usually followed by another entry describing what occurred later on that same day.

Although it seems to have been common practice in expedition journals kept by nineteenth-century naval men or colonial explorers to compose a number of journal entries at one sitting by working from rough field notes kept on a daily basis, Patterson's entries were most often written on the day and at the time ascribed to them. On rare occasions, he summarizes the events of a brief period when he had been unable to make daily entries, but he explains clearly that he is reconstructing the events of those days, not recording them on the day they transpired. Whereas official sponsors might reasonably expect the leaders of explorations they financed to keep a close record, Patterson was free of any such obligation. He made his journal entries solely because he wished to. If he had no time to write, he simply did not write, although because writing was so essential to him, he almost always found the time. Consequently, he had little reason to contrive the small fiction of pretending to write up journal entries on the same day as the date heading under which they appear. Patterson was not averse to fiction, but his penchant for meandering from strict fact is usually more evident in his public performances than in his journals.

As we have seen, writing up his journals served an extremely important function for this educated, highly literate man, who was, while not a stellar student at Oxford, most certainly a great lover of words. Capturing the day's experience in his journals put him in touch with words, even when he couldn't stomach reading—perhaps for a third or fourth time—the few books he had poled and tracked and portaged against the unceasing current of the Nahanni. Especially in 1927 when he travelled alone, writing in his journals occupied his mind as he lay—tired from the day's travel but not yet ready to sleep—imprisoned under his mosquito net by the roar of thousands of hungry insects during the long, nearly-unending summer days north of 60°.

One sees, both in the journals and in *The Dangerous River*, Patterson's intense engagement with words, an engagement that makes reading and writing essential activities. While it is easy to comprehend the immense pleasure a 50-year-old Patterson must have felt when he succeeded in writing for a wide commercial readership in mid-century, the journals contain a more fundamental embryo of his deep-seated fascination with words. They bear witness to a man so committed to the written word that he willingly packs, paddles, and portages heavy volumes up the river. They record a running account of what titles he wants to purchase next time he is in England or that he wants his mother to send to him. They show a playful use of language, both as inside jokes between Matthews and him, and as dialect humour, possibly arising from his frequent reading of *The Pickwick Papers* and *Jorrick's Jaunts and Jollities*. What else could explain, for example, such phrases as "I say nuffin" (September 11, 1927) and "Opes I shallnt be sick" (September 27, 1927) from this literate, Oxford-educated traveller? Why else would a man who hardly ever misspells a word in his journals repeatedly write "I thing" when he means "I think"? As well, the journals document allusions to readings from school and from childhood, allusions to sources as diverse as Kenneth Grahame's *The Wind in the Willows* and Ernest Thompson Seton's story "Krag, the Kootney Ram." It is, in fact, to the good fortune of every armchair traveller that Patterson had the skill to render his amazing adventures so vividly in writing. Unquestionably, Albert Faille was a better canoeist and a better bushman, but he was not able to share his experiences with others to the extent that Patterson was.

On the Nahanni, his journals were as important to Patterson as his canoe pole—actually, they were more important, because he could always go off into the woods to cut a new pole. He made entries in the journals routinely, whether as he lay in his sleeping bag before a fire or as he lunched on a sun-drenched rock surrounded by the roar of the Nahanni at midday. Those entries were always vivid word-pictures of the country he encountered or were thoughtful attempts to capture exactly the right tone that would convey—through words—his feelings. Like his reading, this act of writing in his journals provided him with a sense that he was communicating with someone, that while he frequently chose to travel alone, he did not wish to be without human company. On August 12, 1928, for example, Patterson spoke of writing letters to his fiancée and her mother as being "almost like talking to them." Undoubtedly, conceiving his 1927 journals as a letter to his mother put this more-or-less fatherless boy in close—if vicarious—touch with his mother, who played such a special role in his life. But even the less intimate 1928–29 journals reveal a diarist who sought the challenge of communicating subtle and complex ideas, not one who simply recorded daily temperatures and distances travelled.

Nonetheless, the journals also provided him with a detailed account of his adventure. Even in 1927, he recognized that he might wish to consult his record in future, so he requested that his mother keep the journals in a safe place for future access. It is not known when Patterson retrieved the first set of journals from his mother, but he certainly had them at his desk when he wrote *The Dangerous River* in the early 1950s and, presumably, when he composed the magazine articles in the late 1940s that led to the book contract. When Parks Canada conducted interviews with him in the 1970s, he again had access to them. They obviously were in Patterson's possession when he died in 1984, since they made up an important component of his widow's gift to the Royal British Columbia Museum.

In fact, in his Foreword to all editions of *The Dangerous River*, Patterson writes that "[a]ny quotations that are without a reference are from a detailed diary which was written up from day to day, at the time,"[4] although such quotations are often less than accurate copies of what appears in the journals. Numerous items in the Annotations section remark on the physical nature of the manuscript, describing marks that Patterson later made in the journals' margins as he constructed new accounts of the experience. Such commentary can help the reader understand Patterson's processes of composition. While such close textual detail will interest only a few, anyone who has read *The Dangerous River* will inevitably want to reflect on the relationship the journals bear to the book.

Even though the journals proved an essential tool in writing *The Dangerous River*, they are definitely not mere handmaidens to that narrative. The entries that make up the text of *Nahanni Journals* are invaluable for their own sake. This is a richly articulated, intensely personal record of a bold and rewarding period in a young man's life. It is a record that captures the very emotional fabric of one man's journey. The journals are fundamentally important renderings of what took place on the South Nahanni River in the late 1920s. Like most journals, they engage the reader with a greater sense of immediacy than many writers can reconstruct years later, and this is probably truer for amateur writers than professional authors, whose skills at verbal artifice have been honed. This greater immediacy of the journals better enables them to convey the ungoverned exuberance of the day or the darker articulations of disappointment or fear than does the more artificially composed narrative, written long after the fact. By way of comparison with *The Dangerous River*—published 25 years after the event—nothing speaks more clearly for the freshness of the journals than Patterson's own words: "[S]ometimes I get days behindhand...owing to hard travel.... It is a pity as if I could write when things happen I could tell you much more vividly about them" (September 1, 1927).

This increased immediacy has a powerful effect on the reader. Instead of being escorted along a well-established itinerary, the reader engages as a primary participant, travelling for the first time through uncharted territory, just as Patterson travels. For example, when Patterson passes the "Roche qui Trempe à L'eau" on the Nelson River for the first time on September 12, 1927, he observes an unnamed cliff, bored with holes and colourful with fern and moss and lichens, but he knows nothing about it beyond its interesting appearance. The journal reader necessarily experiences the brilliantly coloured rockface in the same way. By the time Patterson wrote *The Dangerous River*, however, he had learned the feature's name and its history among the old voyageurs, so he introduces it as if he were a well-informed guide shepherding a collection of tourists along the river. The effect can be amazingly different: the journal reader feels like a first-time adventurer, while the reader of the book responds like a paying tourist under the responsible charge of an experienced and well-informed guide.

This effect of experiencing *with* Patterson and not as a passive spectator is also created by such journal entries as the one on August 20, 1928. The initial part of the entry ends with "The crossing to the mouth of the Flat will be difficult." This is immediately followed by an updated entry for later the same day: "It was." Short of writing up his journal while in the very act of making this difficult river crossing, Patterson's response can't get more immediate. There is no elaborately constructed narrative describing how the crossing was difficult. There is not even an attempt to recreate the experience for the reader. There is simply the impression that the reader is present right alongside the traveller.

Journals, by their very nature, also have an attractive naïveté about them. Because the person writing the daily record lacks the hindsight of the narrative writer, the reader engages with him differently, just as the audiences of classical theatre engage differently with Oedipus when they watch him attempt to avoid a fate they know he cannot escape.

As well as a sense of immediacy and naïveté, these journals have a candid quality that is missing in the more elaborately orchestrated book. Patterson says things about Dennis France and the Fenwicks that he would not have said publicly. And for all his close friendship with Gordon Matthews, he certainly grumbles about what he considers to be Gordon's inadequacies. Such occasional disgruntlement with friends and acquaintances is the fabric of which human relationships are woven, and the opportunity these journals give to view Patterson from such a frank perspective have no counterpart in *The Dangerous River*. Similarly, the journals reveal a rather competitive young traveller, one not about to be bested by others he encounters along the trail. They reveal a man capable of laughing at himself, but a man who likes best to be the one to make the jokes at his own expense, and not to be the butt of jokes by others.

The unguarded, candid nature of the journals also makes Patterson vulnerable to some deserved social criticism. Like all tourists, Patterson brought his cultural baggage along with him to the Nahanni. The critical reader will sense Patterson's prejudices in *The Dangerous River*, but that baggage is even more obvious in the journals, largely because his language is more open. While it was not Patterson's nature to give offence needlessly, several remarks about First Nations people here in the journals certainly are offensive. The same is true of some racially-charged words he uses. Unfortunately, the attitudes that such language reflects were all too common among people of European ancestry in the early years of the twentieth century, a condition of Empire, no doubt. By the time *The Dangerous River* was written, the most overtly derogatory remarks about other cultures had disappeared, although whether Patterson himself made the changes because he was older and wiser, whether he made them to accommodate a broader audience, or whether they were made by an editor is unknown. The language that remains in the book—he speaks of "Indian cabins" there, where the journals speak of "shacks"—might well reflect the much greater engagement Patterson had experienced with the First Nations people who were his immediate neighbours during his residence at the Buffalo Head Ranch. Remember that he had only arrived from Britain less than three years before he headed for the Nahanni, and perhaps one of the things he learned in this country was that some of the baggage he had brought with him was not useful in the New World. On the other hand, the journals described his own winter residence at Deadmen's Valley as a "shack" on more than one occasion, so it would be wrongheaded to make too much of his word choice. At any rate, the candid nature of journal-keeping brings us a step closer to R.M. Patterson, a man not without his flaws, but a man to be respected nonetheless.

Some outdoor enthusiasts will revel in Patterson's seemingly insatiable taste for adventure. Others will delight in the way his words forge a visual link between the reader and the experience, the ultimate mark of a successful travel-writer. But whether they read *Nahanni Journals* primarily for the adventure that lies behind the account, or for the creative aspect of the account itself, everyone will embrace the humanity of this young man.

Because no edition of *The Dangerous River* including "The Trail South" chapter has been in print for the past quarter-century, most who have read Patterson's book know nothing about his near-fatal journey homeward from Nahanni Butte in September 1927. Even those who do, know it only through the telling of a man in his fifties, who sits snugly in his study many years later and spins a tale of adventure for his audience. The perspective of the journals is quite a different one. While Patterson comes from a socially privileged place and while he exudes a sometimes abrasive ego, he voluntarily puts himself in situations where the privilege of wealth won't lighten his load and where his self-confidence is driven nearly beyond its capacity. The homeward trip in the autumn of 1927 almost extends him beyond his resources, both physically and psychologically. And it is in these circumstances, circumstances that bring his human vulnerability to the fore, that his journal entries can be most evocative, as when he writes to his mother, realizing that he has cast himself into an ominous and seemingly inescapable situation. He puts on his bravest face, solicits a bit of maternal sympathy for his chafed knees and empty stomach, and bids his mother "Night night." The heroic figure of *The Dangerous River* will never again appear quite the same.

THE EVOLUTION OF *THE DANGEROUS RIVER*

In contrast to the journals' immediacy, the success of the narrative account derives from its highly constructed nature. That is not to suggest that *The Dangerous River* is anything other than delightful reading, but it tells of a decidedly different adventure. The quarter-century that elapsed between Patterson's departure from the Nahanni and *The Dangerous River*'s appearance on bookstore shelves gave rise to many changes in how the adventure was told. Some of those changes were consciously orchestrated in order to compensate for the immediacy that had been lost. Let's look briefly at some of the shaping factors that necessarily make the book a decidedly different creature from the journals.

Undoubtedly, Patterson had many opportunities to revise and polish orally his Nahanni stories during the years at the Buffalo Head Ranch. At the ranch, he had frequently regaled listeners with anecdotes about the glorious summer of 1927 and about his sojourn with Gordon Matthews. As the Buffalo Head increasingly took in guests from far away, Patterson's tales made him an engaging host during the long summer evenings. In fact, he explicitly records that on summer evenings, "around eleven p.m. when the zoo had all gone to bed, Jim Bennett & I used to foregather by a certain window in the Buffalo Head livingroom well equipped with a bottle of Chivas. Thus equipped we would go at it—& it wd. not be long before J.B. had me telling stories of the Nahanni country & all that went with that. Then he began badgering me. 'You must write these things down.' [N]ow you have it all…just how telling stories in the old B.H. living room, inspired by Jim Bennett's liberal doses of that great whiskey, somehow dragged out the D.R. by means of whiskey & sheer bullying."[5] Over the years, audiences' responses to his oral renderings must have considerably honed his storytelling skills. When an eager and possibly gullible audience begs to hear of the long ago and the far away, who would wish to disappoint them? One can only imagine the extent to which such oft-repeated yarn-spinning in the Alberta foothills contributed to some of the differences between the journals and *The Dangerous River*.

That, of course, is only Patterson's autobiographical accounting of the book's origins, and as we shall see, every word that flows from his pen should not be taken as gospel. At least one Nahanni enthusiast provides a less likely explanation of how Patterson's stories about the Nahanni came about. Norman Kagan claims that it was on Patterson's 1952 return to the South Nahanni as a guide for Curtis Smith that the budding travel writer "developed the materials for his book by telling tall tales to Curtis."[6] While it would be incautious to accept unquestioningly Patterson's explanation that Chivas, Jim Bennett, and long twilights at the Buffalo Head were the parents of *The Dangerous River*, Patterson had obviously written about the Nahanni for *The Beaver* as early as 1947. So while "telling tall tales to Curtis" in 1952 might have helped shape some small parts of *The Dangerous River*, the idea of writing about the Nahanni was in place—in fact, in print—five years before Patterson ever met Smith.

Before those tales of his Nahanni adventures became the text of *The Dangerous River*, Patterson served an informal apprenticeship in the magazine industry. As mentioned, his Nahanni experiences took various forms as magazine articles before they were transformed into the book. "River of Deadmen's Valley" was the first to appear, in the June 1947 issue of *The Beaver*,[7] and a year later, "Trails of the Canadian West," which appeared in London's *Country Life*, also drew, in part, on the Nahanni journey. But it was an article published in *Blackwood's Magazine*, "Interlude on the Sikanni Chief," in July 1952 that prompted the director of London publishing house George Allen & Unwin Ltd. to inquire of Patterson if he did not have "sufficient material of this sort for a complete book?"[8] That welcome inquiry was addressed to Patterson c/o *Blackwood's Magazine*. In the interval between the first piece in *The Beaver* in 1947 and *The Dangerous River* in 1954, Patterson placed other articles having to do with outdoor travel in northwestern Canada, but not necessarily specific to the Nahanni. "A Thousand Miles by Canoe," for example, which appeared in *Country Life* in July 1950, told of travel on British Columbia's Finlay River. Other articles were no doubt rejected, and some that were ultimately placed were first sent back for substantial revision. This process taught him about the demands of addressing a diverse audience of readers, something about which he'd learned little in composing personal letters to a specific friend or relative, in preparing essays for his tutor at Oxford, or in making journal entries to himself. To varying degrees, the guidance came from professional editors. At other times, he learned by simple trial and error: one article was accepted, another rejected.

This magazine apprenticeship had a decidedly commercial aspect. Magazine publishers then, as now, were in the business of making money, and not only did Patterson need to learn to write for the people willing to pay, but the opportunity to supplement his investment income—not performing at its best at the end of the 1940s as a result of the devaluation of the pound sterling and exchange controls—by becoming an author must have seemed attractive indeed.[9] For a man in love with the written word, this opportunity to make a living from his passion could not be passed up.

Patterson continued this learning process as he nudged *The Dangerous River* toward completion. According to Finch, correspondence between Patterson and the publishers of his book reveals a process of submission and feedback, partial rejection accompanied by guidance toward revision, suggestions for marketable titles, and so forth. Patterson received this hands-on instruction from two sources, since the book was published in the same year in London (by George Allen & Unwin) and in New York (by William Sloane Associates). Correspondence from the British publisher makes clear that they required Patterson to cut part of his manuscript, but left the decisions about where to cut to the author.[10] And Patterson certainly received suggestions for "cutting parts" of the book to meet the concerns of William Sloane Associates, who were committed to publishing a still shorter text than what the British publisher was willing to engage.[11] Finch remarks that Patterson played offers from these two publishers against each other, creating a sweeter deal for himself,[12] although the exact contractual relationship between these two firms on opposite sides of the Atlantic is murky, making it difficult to know exactly what role Patterson himself might have played. Extant correspondence between the two houses suggests that publication with Allen & Unwin of London was secured first, and then the British firm granted—at a negotiated price—rights to William Sloane Associates to publish an American edition.

Substantial and interesting—although incomplete—correspondence survives about the initial publication of Patterson's book on both sides of the Atlantic. Because such bibliographic detail will, understandably, appeal only to a limited audience, a comprehensive analysis of that correspondence has been placed in the Appendix, rather than here in the Introduction. In this introductory section, it is appropriate only to note that more than four months elapsed between the British and the American publications of the book, suggesting that Patterson had ample time to benefit from the advice of editors on both sides of the Atlantic.

These two publications in 1954 set the stage for many other editions of *The Dangerous River*. Since the publishing history is treated in detail in the Appendix, it is appropriate here to say only that the book was translated into Dutch and Spanish, and it has not been out of print in English for over a half-century.[13] The original British edition was reprinted in 1955 and then reprinted as a joint venture in Canada in 1957. A separate Panther Books edition was released in Britain in

1957. The first truly Canadian edition was published by Gray's Publishing in 1966, followed by at least five reprintings, all of them, like their 1966 original, having much in common with the 1954 British edition. Although the original William Sloane American edition was not reprinted after its appearance in 1954, texts closely aligned with it have resurfaced in both the United States and Canada: Stoddart of Toronto in 1989, Chelsea Green of Vermont in 1990, and Boston Mills of Erin, Ontario, in 1999. The Boston Mills edition is the only edition in print today.

Especially curious about the book's publishing history is the fact that the original British and American editions of 1954 differ in two key respects: the use of the definite article "the" in the title (*The Dangerous River* vs. *Dangerous River*) and the inclusion or omission of a major chapter, "The Trail South." While the matter of "the" in the title is an inconsequential curiosity only, the deletion of the 24-page "The Trail South" chapter constitutes a substantive change. In place of the missing chapter, which is Chapter 3 (situated between the "South Nahanni River" and "Deadmen's Valley" chapters) in the London edition of *The Dangerous River*, Patterson has written a transitional paragraph of about 150 words and positioned it at the beginning of the "Deadmen's Valley" chapter, which—in the shortened *Dangerous River* version—follows immediately after the "South Nahanni River" chapter.

But new editions or reprintings of this perennial favourite keep surfacing and perpetuating these two different versions of Patterson's book, which is what makes the issue more than a mere publishing hiccup from a half-century ago. For at least 25 years, *both* versions—the lengthier British model and the shortened American model—appeared on the market, yet none made any reference to the differing content or to the differing titles. Perhaps of even greater concern is the fact that for the past 25 years, no edition of Patterson's book that includes "The Trail South" chapter has been in print. For this reason alone, *Nahanni Journals* fills a major vacuum.

That "The Trail South" chapter was deleted by William Sloane Associates, rather than added by Allen & Unwin, becomes clear from correspondence between the two publishing houses. It shows that the London firm first contracted the book. The U.S. company then agreed to publish an American edition, but wanted a shorter book, one they produced—presumably in consultation with Patterson—by actually working from the galley proofs that Allen & Unwin had already prepared for their British edition. As I mentioned, all subsequent editions have simply mimicked one or the other of these two models. Those that drop the definite article from the title (as the original Sloane edition had) also drop "The Trail South" chapter as Sloane had done; those that use the full *The Dangerous River* title always include the chapter.

The sometimes-present, sometimes-missing chapter narrates Patterson's homeward journey from the Nahanni in the autumn of 1927. Starting at the Twisted Mountain, situated on the South Nahanni, six hours of downstream paddling from its mouth, Patterson followed a route home that took him up the Liard, the Nelson, and the Sikanni Chief rivers and on a nearly fatal journey overland to Fort St. John on the Peace River. The chapter closes as he arrives in Dunvegan, just up the Peace from the settlement of Peace River, Alberta, and close to his homestead.

While the entire chapter has gone missing in the Sloane Associates edition, nothing in the extant publishing correspondence explains the omission, other than Sloane Associates' desire for a shorter text. Perhaps cutting a chapter that did not specifically involve the Nahanni watershed was an easy way to bring about the reduction. Perhaps even Patterson himself suggested that particular strategy for reducing the word count. But the events that transpired along those other watersheds—events that made near-lethal demands on Patterson's physical and mental fortitude in spite of how hard he had just been travelling on the Nahanni—were powerful. And when powerful events get reconstructed through Patterson's use of language, eliminating them to save a few dollars in printing costs is an unfortunate solution.

Some of the later editions that have kept Patterson's book in print for over a half-century follow the original Allen & Unwin model, which includes "The Trail South" chapter. Others follow the American William Sloane Associates model and drop the chapter. What makes the American publisher's solution an especially unfortunate one is that, given the subsequent publishing history, the last time "The Trail South" chapter appeared in any edition was 1980, when Gray's Publishing reissued its original 1966 Canadian edition of *The Dangerous River*. While some version of the book happily remains in print today, all editions published after 1980 follow the model established by Sloane Associates in 1954. Those include the 1989 Stoddart, the 1990 Chelsea Green, and the 1999 Boston Mills editions. Consequently, except for those who read library or second-hand copies, modern readers are not even aware of, much less familiar with, this omitted chapter.

Previously, I observed that one unavoidable spin-off of reading Patterson's journals in conjunction with *The Dangerous River* account would be a certain loss of innocence in how one reads travel writing. No longer can one confuse the *recounting* of experience with the *experience* itself. A similarly inevitable postmodern realization rears its head in respect to the different versions of Patterson's book, too. One comes up against the fundamental question of "What text did Patterson write?" Or to consider this from another angle, did Patterson write two texts—one titled *The Dangerous River*, which includes a substantial chapter sandwiched between the "South Nahanni River" and "Deadmen's Valley" chapters, the other entitled *Dangerous River*, and abandoning the author at the Twisted Mountain at the end of August 1927? And if you have read Patterson's book, which one have you read?

The complications multiply when one thinks about questions of authorship. Did Patterson write one text and publish it as *The Dangerous River*, while a team of editors working for William Sloane Associates wrote *Dangerous River*? They, after all, required that cuts be made to the manuscript submitted to them through Allen & Unwin, which the London firm had already agreed to publish. A partial answer lies in the correspondence between the London and New York publishers. An unidentified staff member from Sloane Associates writes that he or she "had a most friendly letter" from Patterson saying that "he [i.e., Patterson] would be amenable to further cutting."[14] In fact, the Sloane Associates' letter requests that Allen & Unwin send them an extra set of galley proofs so that they can make suggested cuts and post them with clearly referenced page numbers to Patterson, who will also have a copy of the same galleys. But in almost every respect, the published text of the American edition is exactly the same as that of the English edition, except for the omission of "The Trail South" chapter. So if numerous elaborately placed cuts throughout the manuscript were ever suggested by the American publisher, it is clear that axing the entire chapter and leaving the rest as it stood was a far simpler way to make the necessary reductions.

Whether that realization was made by Patterson or by his American editors is, in many respects, irrelevant. What is relevant is that Patterson was complicit in the creative alterations, whether he suggested them or acquiesced to them. But because the final American text differs so substantively from the London edition, R.M. Patterson has clearly not been the *only* author of *Dangerous River*: Sloane Associates' editors, working under unknown commercial and financial constraints, have also authored this book. Whether one dismisses these different texts of Patterson's book as uninteresting bibliographic trivia or embraces them as ways of engaging with his re-creation of the Nahanni experience in words, the differences raise fundamental questions about texts and authorship.

While the journal entries are certainly no substitute for the 24 pages of narrative that were cut from the book, the 99 journal pages that recount Patterson's homeward journey will hold special interest, especially for those who have never read an edition of Patterson's book containing "The Trail South" chapter. The return from the Twisted Mountain to Edmonton required close to two months of travel, a significant portion of the time Patterson was away from his homestead during 1927. As well, some of the dangers he encountered during that stage of the journey evoked expressions of anxiety and self-doubt rarely heard from Patterson.

Yet in spite of the various forms *The Dangerous River* has taken, Patterson's narrative remains a classic of the genre. It has transported many an armchair traveller to a place he or she would rather be; it has inspired many others to live their lives—at least temporarily—with something of the same enthusiasm that Patterson showed. To have penned such a widely read book and one so long in print is itself an achievement. To have done so as a much-delayed afterthought by a man already more than 50 years old and with no prior books to his credit steers us toward the realization that R.M. Patterson was not only a complicated man—he was an extraordinary one.

TWO ROADS DIVERGED

Hindsight and artifice, as we have seen, can significantly alter the shaping of events in a story, just as can a publisher's desire to cut publication costs. Having looked at some influences that shaped *The Dangerous River* as a distinctly different text from the journals, it remains to consider the ways in which the two differ. For one thing, the journals tell a far less heroic story of conquest than does *The Dangerous River*; they recount, instead, the small daily pleasures of living a life in a natural environment free of artificial restrictions and assigned responsibilities. For another thing, the attention to colour is constant and detailed in the journals, a fascination that, while it is still evident in the narrative, is decidedly reduced. Another difference is that the journals reveal an unusually close relationship between a grown man and his mother, which—like the revelling in the colours of the Nahanni—is present but muted in the book. Similarly, the daily journals make frequent and elaborate mention of Patterson's prospecting for gold on the Nahanni and Flat rivers, which was the ostensible "purpose" behind this young man's adventure. But when the "returned hero" tells his story many years later, the references to that failed enterprise—the search for gold—have receded into an indistinct background blur.

Not all readers of *The Dangerous River* and *Nahanni Journals* are interested in Patterson's development as a writer or how the intervening years inevitably gave shape to a different rendering. Rather, they are lured to these accounts for the events they describe. Readers wishing to engage with travel writing in this way will appreciate the journals because they more accurately record Patterson's experiences on the Nahanni, or, as in the case of Patterson's return from the Twisted Mountain to Edmonton, because they provide a record of travels that many editions of the book do not. Let's look first at a few places where the journals document a different reality than what is reflected in the book, and then we can explore Patterson's reasons for creating such fictions and consider the various effects they've had. Perhaps the most concrete distortion of *The Dangerous River* is Patterson's claim that he ascended the river all the way to the Falls of the Nahanni on his own.

In Chapter 2, "South Nahanni River," he describes events that supposedly occurred somewhere between a camp he made on the Nahanni and the Falls.[15] That camp was so near the Falls that he could hear and feel them, but he could not see them. Eight pages of the book are devoted to his ascent beyond this final camp and his actual attainment of the Falls, although some of the pages concern stalking and shooting a magnificent Dall ram. Nevertheless, the final three pages of this section explicitly describe his struggle beyond the "insuperable obstacle" that had halted his upriver journey and had forced him to make camp where he could only hear and feel the Falls' thunder.[16] Patterson describes so well his victory over what had seemed an "insuperable obstacle" that it warrants quoting a few sentences from *The Dangerous River*: "I drove up in the eddy and hit the riffle at a fine angle and as hard and as close to the sandstone point as I dared. The canoe did its best for a second to stand on its tail—it was like riding a horse that is going to throw itself back over on to you. But the rock in the nose saved the day, and I found myself out on the smooth green water, down on my knees and digging into it like mad with the paddle. Something huge and white flashed into view as I cleared the sandstone point—it was the Falls! Well, to hell with the Falls! They could wait: this racing water was all that mattered now."[17]

The Falls of the Nahanni or Virginia Falls, as photographed when a joint effort with Faille enabled RMP to reach them.

This rousing description of the ascent continues for another 200 words or so, followed by three ample paragraphs that evoke the author's reverie as he drifts back and forth all afternoon in the "tremendously deep...pool at the foot of the Falls."[18] These pages represent some of the best adventure writing in a book of many fine passages. The journals, however, reveal those pages of fine writing to be just that—fine writing—because they are pure fiction! Of course, Patterson knew them to be pure fiction and consequently felt the need to explain to his audience why he hadn't taken any photographs of the Falls: he had forgotten to bring his camera from his last camp, the one just below that "insuperable obstacle." Interestingly, in place of the "pretty cocky" feeling he ascribes to himself in the book upon reaching the Falls, the journals reveal a severely disappointed young man who had to face the fact that his enthusiasm and perseverance could not meet every challenge he set for himself.

Another point at which the journals record (and hence reveal) a different reality has to do with Patterson's initial skills in a canoe. Many canoeing enthusiasts regard Patterson as a guru of sorts, and there is no question that he developed many enviable whitewater skills during his time on the Nahanni. Nor does the protagonist revealed in *The Dangerous River* make himself out to be an expert with pole and paddle; he even acknowledges that he had learned his poling skills on the flat waters of the Cherwell and Isis rivers at Oxford. But few readers would ever have expected what the journals reveal: that on August 13, 1927, already well on his way up the South Nahanni and at the first place where a full portage was necessary, Patterson had to ruminate on the technique that had been described to him of flipping a canoe over his head for portaging, because he had never before done so! A few lines from his journals speak volumes: "the struggle to get the canoe up onto my head was intense—the tracks on the sands of the bay look as if a circus had been to town. I had never done it before—there is a trick to lifting it that I had been told & had forgotten, so I had to find it out, with much cursing, for myself." There are many places in *The Dangerous River* where the reader derives pleasure from the author's self-effacing jokes at his own expense, but when he wrote his book decades after the event, Patterson couldn't bring himself to admit just how green he was.

One final example of a somewhat different history recorded in the journals must suffice; the reader will surely find others of interest. The responsible hunter that Patterson portrays himself to be in the Foreword to *The Dangerous River* proudly announces that "no wounded animal was ever allowed to get away. Everything we hit we killed, and nothing was shot uselessly with the exception of one mountain sheep that was swept away down the rapids. That, I claim, is a clean record."[19] Unquestionably, Patterson acted in a generally responsible manner while he was on the Nahanni, given the era and its attitudes. Since he and Matthews needed meat in order to feed themselves and their dogs, Patterson was not hunting merely "for sport," a fact that in itself shapes the notion of "responsible" hunting. And so it shouldn't be an act of condemnation to observe that his hunting record was not quite as impeccable as he claims. In fact, it was a total fabrication. The journals reveal numerous other occasions when an animal was wounded or killed, but could not be recovered—an inevitable situation, given the circumstances in which Patterson placed himself. On August 14, 1927, he killed a cow moose that floated away downriver, while its calf ran off, an event he remembered well, for when he lost the ram nearly a year later on July 22, 1928, he wrote in his journal that it was "[j]ust the luck I had with a moose last summer." On June 9, 1928, he and his companions fired wildly at another moose cow and calf, killing the calf, but only wounding the cow, which slipped off into the woods to die as food for scavengers. On July 6, 1928, he wounded another moose, but never found the carcass. On October 14, 1928, he wounded a bull moose that he couldn't find, although, through good luck, Matthews accidentally came across the carcass four days later. This unfortunate list of game that never made it to the larder does not include the various birds or fish whose lives were wasted. So there is no doubt that Patterson was consciously constructing his *The Dangerous River* persona according to his wishes, not according to experience or even to the journal record of that experience, which he always kept in front of him as he reconstructed his Nahanni years.

The journals also reveal that Patterson didn't quite have the full instincts of a sport hunter, even though his ego rarely took a back seat to a well-placed shot or a better "head" than what someone else had managed to shoot. For example, after mortally wounding the cow moose on August 14, 1927, thereby wasting the meat and leaving the calf motherless, Patterson came across a number of animals—a bear on August 21, a cow and a bull moose on August 22, a caribou on August 23—that he could have shot, but consciously decided instead to photograph them or to describe the creature's beauty in his journal. Not only was he a hunter with a somewhat sullied "clean record," but he seemed occasionally troubled by the very idea of killing itself.

The more significant issue is that the real R.M. Patterson was not quite the saintly hero he portrayed himself to be a quarter of a century later. Nor does the book mention what the journal documents on August 19, 1927: he had to leave his trophy ram's head for Faille to take out to Fort Simpson the next year because, Patterson records, "I didn't bother to get an NWT game license—about £15—& I am a resident of Alberta." This is human but not quite princely behaviour for a man who could afford to make the annual journey back to England the next winter. And the £15 fee to hunt within the law is a paltry sum in light of the $10,000 Patterson made that winter when his mining shares split three for one, tripling his investment.[20] These revelations that Patterson—like all of us—had a shadow side add to his humanity, and when we see him more as someone like ourselves and less as an heroic figure on a pedestal, the light-hearted manner in which he makes courageous choices about life becomes even more admirable. And taken collectively, these sites where historical event and autobiographical retelling obviously part company should serve to caution the reader against confusing the act of writing about travel with the physical travel itself.

I have addressed only a few examples of where the journals contradict the experience recorded in the 1954 book. Readers will find numerous other discrepancies.

But holding up the journals as evidence that events did not always transpire as reported in *The Dangerous River* requires care and sensitivity. Nevertheless, the simple fact is the events in the late 1920s on the South Nahanni were not flawlessly mirrored in the 1954 account. Patterson's book—like all travel writing and autobiography—is a form of fiction based on fact. The same could be said about the journals, in that Patterson has selected the events about which he chooses to write. And he has chosen to present those events in a particular manner. Both Albert Faille and Gordon Matthews would have told different stories, had they taken on the challenge of writing about their experience, but they did not. And Patterson's acceptance of the challenge to record his experiences in words is what brings us all to this common page.

Some Patterson enthusiasts who are already familiar with the 1927–1929 journals make little of the distortions in the book, merely accepting them as the inevitable poetic licence associated with telling an adventure. What good storyteller would, for example, let his protagonist fail almost within sight of his goal? That's a reasonable question, one with an interesting array of answers. By enabling the protagonist of *The Dangerous River* to attain his goal of the Falls, Patterson makes a hero of him. But he had a choice to make a different sort of protagonist of him—the sort who appears in the journals. I think the reader of *Nahanni Journals* will agree that the man who ascends the South Nahanni in 1927 in the journal record is no less interesting a man. He is, in fact, a bit more like you and me. And nothing draws the armchair traveller into the distant scene of action more than the sense that he or she *could* be there, were it not for a myriad of domestic or economic constraints.

Those amiable readers who happily accept the distortions of historical experience in *The Dangerous River* might be a bit more unsettled by a related matter. Across the title page of a 1957 Panther Books edition of his narrative, Patterson has inscribed a personal note: "To Hilda & Theo from Tony (in Canada 'George.'). All is exactly as it happened except that I shifted one bit of country (pp. 166–171) from Prairie Creek to the upper Flat River."[21] According to Professor Emeritus M.T. Myres, in whose hands the particular book remains, Hilda and Theo Chaundy had been friends with Patterson in Oxford. Years later, Hilda Chaundy gave the book to Myres. The inscription is perplexing on a number of counts. Considerable correspondence between Patterson and Edwin Fenwick, his close childhood friend and long-time resident of County Durham, shows the two frequently played the game of referring to each other as "George," apparently for no reason

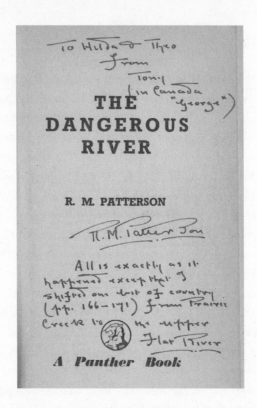

THE
DANGEROUS
RIVER

R. M. PATTERSON

A Panther Book

+

RMP—aka "Tony" and "George"—pledges the accuracy of his narrative to his friends.

---

other than juvenile playfulness. But why Patterson says in the inscription that he is known as "George" in Canada is confounding, although as Sloane Associates' editor Helen King grew increasingly familiar with Patterson over the years, she began her letters with the salutation "Dear George."[22] Less fathomable still is the name "Tony." Patterson's biographer David Finch has not heard of it, neither had Patterson's daughter Janet Blanchet nor wife Marigold any recollection of Patterson using the name "Tony," although both Janet Blanchet and Mariold Patterson were familiar with the nickname "George."[23] Interestingly, Finch also observes that Patterson used still another nickname on occasion—Bronzo![24] Given the historical era and the context of multiple identities, one cannot help but think of another Englishman-gone-bush in Canada, Archie Belaney, *aka* Grey Owl.

But of greater interest still is Patterson's personal insistence to friends that "[a]ll is exactly as it happened," even though the journals reveal the falsehood of that statement. Dr. Myres shared Patterson's title page inscription with me, and in our correspondence, Myres says that he is content with viewing any such "adjustments" as perfectly acceptable so long as the result is a "good travel book." I could not agree more. Certainly Patterson, whatever his methods, has written an excellent book of travel and adventure. But it is one thing to spin a yarn for an amorphous and ill-defined audience, and another to avow personally to friends the veracity of what was written. Perhaps Patterson's decision to affirm the truthfulness of his book is a manifestation of the Grey Owl phenomenon, where the individual feels forced to create a larger-than-life identity precisely because he knows his real identity to be a fabrication of sorts. Negotiating identity is difficult at the best of times; that R.M. Patterson *aka* George *aka* Tony *aka* Bronzo would unconsciously struggle with it—even overstep it—in this opportunity to validate his adventurous life in Canada to old friends from Oxford seems almost inevitable. Not content with a circumscribed life in England, the young Patterson had made bold choices and here, more than 30 years later, was his opportunity to prove the wisdom of those choices.

This probing into the factual nature of *The Dangerous River* is not, as I've said, intended to expose R.M. Patterson as an imposter or a charlatan. Nor is it designed to chip away at the gilding that many admirers—myself included—have laid on to his image. Yet to remain oblivious to the manipulative and creative possibilities of travel writing is unacceptable. Once this imaginative realm is genuinely acknowledged and embraced, are we not oversimplifying a complex phenomenon by simply accepting these jarring points of engagement between event and accounting as "adjustments"? Are we fully appreciating *The Dangerous River* when, without questioning them, we glibly accept the factual distortions as part of the frontier tradition of "yarning" and tall tales? To stop a serious inquiry into writing at that stage seems rather like coming to the mouth of the Nahanni, but not turning upstream to see what lies beyond the first obstacle.

In short, it is unnecessarily black-or-white thinking to say that *The Dangerous River* digresses from historical fact either because Patterson is a liar or because he is a storyteller. The spaces between these two options are too full of interest. For one thing, Patterson's hand was not entirely free when he wrote *The Dangerous River*. When the eager novice wrote his first published article, "River of Deadmen's Valley" in *The Beaver*, June 1947, he had already departed from simple factual truth. Not only had his 18 months spent on the Nahanni become a "three-year association with a...beautiful river,"[25] but he described drifting in his canoe in the pool below the Falls, and in his reverie nearly being drawn under the Falls themselves, but for a "frantic dig" with his paddle. This passage from the 1947 magazine article is closely paralleled in *The Dangerous River* some seven years later, although it is further developed there.[26] Since nothing of this sort appears in the journals, and since Patterson was accompanied by Faille and in Faille's big canoe when he actually did attain the Falls in late August, 1927, the author of *The Dangerous River* has obviously consulted closely with the "River of Deadmen's Valley" article as he wrote the book. In some respects, many years before publishing *The Dangerous River*, Patterson had already committed himself to reaching the Falls on his own. He would have had to given the lie to his own 1947 accounting if he were to tell the truth in 1954. Here is an excellent example of how prior written renderings of experience can shape subsequent accounts more than the original experience itself.

By the time Patterson wrote *The Buffalo Head* in 1961, he could tell how he, Faille, and Faille's big canoe had joined forces to reach the Falls.[27] No mention is made of Patterson's failed attempt to see them on his own, but that is reasonable, since *The Buffalo Head* largely concerns a much longer and later period of the author's life in southern Alberta and only summarizes his relatively brief time on the Nahanni.

In *The Dangerous River*, the troubled issue of attaining the Falls is of greater import. Here, the achievement of the Falls, like the matter of Patterson's expertise in a canoe and his "clean record" as a hunter, introduces a variety of deception in the book that can serve as a locus that encapsulates more systemic and ultimately more important variations. Consider, for example, how the solo attainment of the Falls recorded in *The Dangerous River* is almost a creative necessity in a story of man struggling against the wilderness. To have surrendered in his 1927 solo journey without reaching the Falls alone would have been to accept defeat. Many facets of the book reveal the protagonist as a conquering hero whose role is to defeat his adversary, in this case, the Nahanni River and the world of untamed nature it represents. Describing the upstream work as "a brute, head-on collision between me and the Nahanni,"[28] the heroic narrator lays the foundation in the first chapter, "The Legend," which introduces the reader to the many frightening and forbidding tales popularly associated with the river. It speaks of an aboriginal population "hostile to strangers" and of "white pioneers [who] have been done to death by them."[29] It records the ominous warnings that Patterson supposedly heard from locals when they learned he was about to enter the watershed, a country where—according to legend—"men vanish."[30] "The Nahanni, they said, was straight suicide,"[31] and if the river, which was "fast and bad,"[32] did not get you, the "wild Mountain Men—…Indians…who lorded it over the wild uplands,…made short work of any man…who ventured into their country." "No," so the dialogue goes, "we'd better all have another drink and be sensible and forget about the South Nahanni…."[33] Significantly, the journals mention nothing about the Nahanni's reputation; nor is there any mention of Patterson having been warned about the river as he approached it.

The narrative goes on to tell the popular legend of the two McLeod brothers who were supposedly murdered in 1906 for the gold they had found. According to the legend, their skeletons were later found tied to trees, but their heads were missing! Even though Patterson pokes and prods at the unlikely aspects of the rumour, going so far as to cite official RCMP reports that the brothers had probably died from starvation and exposure, the book takes great pains to revel in the ghastly and hyperbolic nature of hearsay evidence and a local penchant for the tall tale. The narrator chuckles at the absurdity of some of the names journalists have given to the place where the McLeods perished—"Headless Valley," "The Valley of Vanishing Men"—but he never misses an opportunity to draw the reader's attention to such epithets.[34]

That initial chapter of *The Dangerous River* lathers on stories of death at the hands of nature. Patterson tells of a man called Shebbach who died of starvation on the Flat River in 1949, of Jorgenson's death in 1910 or 1911, of the mysterious disappearance of Angus Hall in 1929, of the burned cabin and charred skeleton of trapper Phil Powers found in 1932. The chapter draws to a close with a paragraph mentioning three more men who mysteriously died or disappeared on the Nahanni—Holmberg in 1940, Eppler and Mulholland in 1936—and then ends with a quotation from Flynn Harris, an experienced northerner and an Indian Agent at Fort Simpson for 17 years: "The Nahanni is a nasty piece of water, and an arduous and dangerous waterway for the best of navigators."[35]

Set against such an introductory chapter, especially when one reflects on the book's title, anyone who enters the Nahanni voluntarily must indeed be a conquering hero. Who else could prevail against such a sinister environment? Mind you, Patterson has too much humour and modesty to cast himself in the same unabashedly intrepid role that Ranulph Fiennes constructs for himself in *The Headless Valley*, which recounts a militaristic assault on the Nahanni in 1971. An illustration facing page 32 in Fiennes's book shows the five expedition members attired very much like Navy SEALs or some other highly trained and equipped special forces unit. Avoiding the heroic self-styling courted by Fiennes (*The Headless Valley* includes a map marking out the exploratory paths of James Cook [1778], George Vancouver [1792–1794], Alexander Mackenzie [1793], Simon Fraser [1806],

David Thompson [1839], and Ranulph Fiennes [1971], which establishes a rather obvious context of British heroism), Patterson professes in his Foreword that "[w]e were never able to see ourselves in that heroic light."[36] Nonetheless, such a profession has more to do with Patterson's public modesty than it does with the spirit of the account he provides in *The Dangerous River*.

This sense of doing battle with the Nahanni pervades the book. Sometimes it is nothing more than a subtle nuance conveyed by imagery, such as when he writes that to watch Faille negotiate his canoe through whitewater is "like watching a fine swordsman seeking for an opening, feeling out his adversary."[37] At other times, the construction of a heroic protagonist is undercut by Patterson's frequent tone of self-mockery. But self-effacement has its limits, and *The Dangerous River* makes no mention of Patterson's first efforts to lift a canoe for portaging. Rather, as we've seen, the book disguises Patterson's novice status so well that it has become an instruction manual of sorts for recreational canoeists seeking tips on river travel. To admit inexperience hardly fosters the image of the conquering hero who can surmount all the myriad obstacles of this "arduous and dangerous waterway,"[38] and *that*, no doubt, is why such information has been expunged from the book. And one must bear in mind that Patterson worked closely with his journals as he composed *The Dangerous River*, frequently quoting or paraphrasing brief passages from them. The choice, then, of what to retain and what to omit was a very conscious one, not a mere accident of memory.

THE ETHOS OF THE JOURNALS: RATTY, MOLE, AND CHILDHOOD

The journals, however, record quite a different experience and, curiously and inexplicably, one more in keeping with the values of today's ecotourists who seek recreation and communion, rather than conquest, when they travel the Nahanni. Of the journey itself—not the written accounts of it—no one can deny that Patterson was drawn to the challenge the outdoor life offered. And, as we have seen, the story of meeting those challenges became an important element in *The Dangerous River*. But the journals reveal that this liberated bank clerk enjoyed a far more complex experience on the river, one filled with a child-like wonder, an immense capacity for self-indulgent play, and a deep spiritual apprehension of the natural world. At the same time, the Nahanni provided him with the tactile, physical challenges he sought.

In many ways, the journals—possibly because their intimacy puts them in touch with a different form of truth—better convey the full range of personal ecstasy that the traveller experiences. The joy of testing himself against challenges is ever-present, but that pleasure is only one of many surfaces on a multi-faceted jewel. His ecstasy on the Nahanni is the same ecstasy that lures people with green thumbs to gardens and attracts musical geniuses to strings or keyboards, the euphoria that makes atavistic individuals surrender themselves to the inevitable, involuntary impulse to immerse themselves in nature. It is not limited to the skills required to shepherd a canoe through rapids, not limited to the courage to press always onward and upward, although these attributes certainly provide one with the self-sufficiency to be able to travel ever more remotely into the realm of unspoiled nature.

To our great benefit, the full and complex range of ecstasy enjoyed by Patterson is delightfully passed on to those who read his journals. Joining Patterson on the Nahanni by means of his daily record not only offers vicarious danger from the safety of one's armchair; it creates the opportunity to participate in that same overwhelming sense of well-being and spiritual fullness that Patterson experiences through this deep and joyful submersion in the world of nature.

The spontaneity and immediacy of daily journals help convey this ecstasy, such as when Patterson's immense enthusiasm for yet another day prompts this Oxford-educated traveller to write "It grew slowly, like a flower, into the very perfectest day of all" (September 17, 1927). Or when—after a long string of such superlatives—he writes "This really is the most perfect day of all—better than all that have passed. I mean it this time" (October 19, 1927). What Patterson assumed were necessities in the book—a masculine and pragmatic purpose to the journey, a unified narrative—hold no sway in the journals, which are free to articulate his unrestrained exaltation of joy in nature.

Even though the journals describe the same historical journey as does *The Dangerous River*, the story they tell is not only an adventure of narrow escapes and struggle against the unknown, but the adventure of play, of shunning routine and social responsibility, of what Kenneth Grahame expressed as "simply messing about in boats."[39] They depict a joyous traveller communing with the universe as he basks in the glorious golden afternoon sun. On several occasions, Patterson remarks on how much happier he is on the Nahanni than he had been in London, and how much his general health has improved. For example, the young man who had been enraptured by such a string of "perfect" days on the Nahanni wrote on

+

Christopher Robin and Pooh gearing up for an "expotition."

Line illustrations from Winnie-the-Pooh by A.A. Milne, © E.H. Shepard,
reproduced by permission of Curtis Brown Group Ltd., London.

August 23, 1927 "I was perfectly happy—few people know what that means—
some never are." It is perhaps the joy of innocent youth—or even of someone
whose family circumstances had buffered him from many of the hardships others
must experience—but it is decidedly joyful.

The verbal portrait Patterson constructs of himself depicts a child at play,
not a hero engaged in struggle. He wrote in his July 26, 1927, entry "A young
day—& me in khaki with a red handkerchief round my neck, sleeves rolled up,
bare footed, open necked & hatless in the golden sunshine." It is almost rakish,
daring to be barefooted, *defying* convention to be open-necked and hatless, *boldly*
wearing a red handkerchief. One is reminded in this self-portrait of a naïve youth,
so immensely satisfied with himself and his costume that he could not even
conceive of the knowing amusement (or worse yet, sneering disapproval) with
which serious-minded and humourless adults might dismiss his inconsequential,
self-absorbed play. Again, the group portrait of Ranulph Fiennes's paramilitary
assault team provides a study in contrast of self-conception. Instead, Patterson's
self-portrait is reminiscent of *Winnie-the-Pooh*, especially when Christopher
Robin pulls on his Big Boots in preparation for an "expotition" to the North
Pole.[40] Suffice it to say that Patterson first set off on his playful adventure up the
Nahanni in 1927, the year after those similarly youthful and playful adventurers
headed off into The Hundred Acre Wood in Milne's book.

This nuance of *Winnie-the-Pooh* becomes more palpable when one considers
a very explicit reference to childhood reading in Patterson's journals. On the
evening of the last day of July 1927, the young traveller has camped just above
the Splits and is about to enter the Lower Canyon. His journal describes the "full

+

The Rat and the Mole are led to Portly in "The Piper at the Gates of Dawn"
chapter of The Wind in the Willows.

Line illustrations from The Wind in the Willows *by Kenneth Grahame,*
© *E.H. Shepard, reproduced by permission of Curtis Brown Group Ltd., London.*

beauty" of his surroundings: "a mass of wild raspberries, strawberries, black currants & red currants" on which he gorged, fresh marks of beaver, a moose drinking on the far shore. Patterson wrote that he "thought of the Rat & the Mole & the morning they saw Pan," an unmistakable reference to that other English classic of early twentieth-century children's literature, Kenneth Grahame's *The Wind in the Willows* (1908). Significantly, Ratty and Mole hear the pipes of Pan in an unusually mystical chapter in Grahame's book, one of immense spiritual weight in which a benevolent Nature deity protects a lost young otter and guides him back to his mother. Such images of the natural world as a nurturing mentor and a secure playground where the developing ego can explore its boundaries without fear of censure or danger stand in sharp contrast to the nature-as-adversary images that surface throughout *The Dangerous River*.

Patterson's reference to "the Rat & the Mole" has another effect as well. Not only does it link this Nahanni traveller's spiritual affinity for the wilderness with the benevolent deity of Grahame's book, but because the reference appears in the 1927 journals, which were addressed to Patterson's mother, the image of a warm and nurturing relationship between mother and son also springs to mind. Such a relationship, of course, has no role in the masculine, adult world of conquest that runs throughout the 1954 book. Sagas of heroic quest rarely mention the pleasures of youth, and they have even less to do with the comforts of bedtime, with which children's books are so often associated. It is not hard to imagine, then, why the later book retains no echo of the journal entry for Sunday, September 25: "A Chinook day—wet as the devil but warm—snow all slush. I am sitting by my fire in the woods having just had my apology for a supper, made my bed over the snow & cleaned my teeth. I travelled well—$9\frac{1}{2}$ hours on foot—& two more days like this will put me in Nelson—hungry but all right—if only I can find the way. Bits of todays trail were hard to find but tomorrow afternoon will be the worst. Both knees raw with wet cords rubbing on them but otherwise excellently fit—& tolerably sopping. Night night." Composing his entry just before he crawls into his sleeping bag after a long day, he grumbles a bit to his mother about being sopping wet and about having sore knees, dutifully records that he "cleaned [his] teeth," and after assuring his mother that he is "hungry but all right," he ends the entry with the words "Night night." The traveller is at low ebb, and his somewhat whimpering tone suggests he was eager for a bit of sympathy from a loving mother as she figuratively tucks her little boy in for the night.

Because their daily entries are not as consciously composed as are the pages of *The Dangerous River*, the journals are able to reveal a more complex and interesting map of the traveller's personality. They express the full emotional spectrum of Patterson's experience on the Nahanni in 1927, and they capture the exalted spirit of a life spent—to borrow Grahame's phrase again—"simply messing about in boats" the following year. Instead of the conventional and familiar hero, a twentieth-century Huckleberry Finn peoples their pages, a novice who struggles to swing the canoe over his head the first time for portaging, a hunter whose skill is not always as great as he would like, a man sadly disappointed with failing to meet his goals, and a youth totally immersed in irresponsible and socially unproductive play.

R.M.P., THE NAHANNI, AND THE ENVIRONMENT

That Patterson has written two substantially different accounts of his experience on the Nahanni will be obvious to any reader. What will be less obvious are the diverse ways readers will engage with the journals now that they are avail-

+

A twentieth-century Huck Finn seeks adventure on a more northern river.

able. Some South Nahanni aficionados or local historians might use these variant accounts as tools to understand—as much as possible—exactly what occurred on the river between 1927 and 1929. Armchair adventurers might seize the opportunity the journals provide to revisit the "old" Nahanni before it became a mecca for ecotourism. Others will treat them as cultural documents, exploring how the quarter-century that separates them from *The Dangerous River* reflects changed attitudes toward the North, the natural world, and the Canadian identity. Still another set of readers will want to understand the limiting conditions and the freedoms that distinguish personal diaries and public narratives. These and a myriad other pathways offer culturally and personally rewarding ways of thinking about what Patterson wrote.

Yet the most pressing issue facing the South Nahanni is an environmental one. To consider Patterson's 1927–1929 travels without reflecting on how his writing fits into this larger environmental picture would be wrongheaded indeed. The link between Patterson and the preservation of the Nahanni is complicated, however, and not easily ferreted out. Perhaps what links Patterson's writing with the notions of conservation will be more easily understood through reading these journals, rather than *The Dangerous River*. Nevertheless, it would be foolish to assert that two slim manuscript journals sequestered in a government archive could have had any direct influence on the protection of the region. This is a complex matter, one as complex as Patterson himself and the accounts he wrote. Nothing connected with the Nahanni, it seems, is simple and straightforward.

A brief summary of how environmental protection of the Nahanni has moved ahead can help us appreciate Patterson's influence. The Nahanni National Park Reserve was created in 1971 to protect the river from being dammed for hydroelectric production or exploited for mineral resources. Seven years later in 1978, the Park Reserve became the world's first site granted World Heritage status by the United Nations Educational, Scientific and Cultural Organization (UNESCO). And in 1987, the South Nahanni was designated a Canadian Heritage River. All these official and prestigious recognitions have been made with the same goal in mind: to preserve the natural wonders of the South Nahanni River. But as everyone knows all too well, designating a region as being worthy of preservation is not the same as preserving it. Recognition by national and international agencies, nevertheless, has been an essential first step in maintaining this jewel in the crown of Canada's northern wilderness.

How have Patterson's adventures on the river in the late 1920s been responsible for bringing about these protective measures? Not at all, most likely. Patterson's role in this regard came many years later when he began *writing* about those adventures. In spite of Patterson's claim that he and Faille "broke the spell" of mystery and foreboding that hung over the Nahanni—a claim he made 25 years after the event—patterns of travel in the region were little changed by his presence between 1927 and 1929. Inquisitive and independent white travellers had moved through the valley for decades before him. Jack Stanier and Joe Bird ascended the Nahanni beyond the Falls in 1898. Other prospectors in search of a route to the Klondike gold fields had ascended the South Nahanni, and when the lure of the Klondike began to wane, the Nahanni enjoyed minor gold rushes of its own. Never a productive one, the first Nahanni rush of 1922 lured a number of prospectors onto the Nahanni five years before Patterson arrived.[41] (In 1929, a larger rush was widely publicized in the *Edmonton Journal*, which carried two "gold rush on the Nahanni" items on the front page of the March 16, 1929 issue, although that rush was most likely stoked by Patterson's return to the Nahanni in 1928, rather than antecedent to it.) Patterson himself observed abandoned cabins along the river, portage trails around obstacles, blazes on trees, even a boot print in the sand. Perhaps, as Faille claimed, he and Patterson were the first men up the river "in seven years,"—that is, since the rush of '22—but their presence on the river was in no way an act of discovery that led to a major change in how the resource was used. Of course, even to debate who might have been the first white man on the Nahanni totally ignores that the region was first inhabited by the Nah'aa—the mysterious indigenous people referred to as Nahanies by early traders—long before men of European ancestry arrived. Even during the 18 months Patterson spent on the river, he met up with a surprising number of other travellers, including a group who had flown in aboard a small airplane. So Patterson's 1927–1929 travels themselves were clearly not what brought about the Nahanni's designation as a Park Reserve four decades later.

While the physical act of travel was not responsible for bringing about such protective measures, the act of *writing* about it did play a role in the environmental future of the region. But before exploring the relationship between Patterson's travel writing and the river's preservation, it will be useful to view the region's designation as a reserve from a more overtly political perspective.

The most visible public gesture toward environmental protection came from a far more political river traveller—the late Pierre Elliott Trudeau, a former prime minister of Canada. While serving as prime minister in August 1970, Trudeau was flown to Virginia Falls, where he was taken aboard a motorboat and carried downriver to Nahanni Butte. Hardly the exciting journey of Patterson 40 years previously, Trudeau's brief foray on the water nonetheless had an immediate effect. Soon after he returned to Ottawa, he directed his then-minister of Indian and Northern Affairs Jean Chrétien to look after the preservation of the South Nahanni. Although protecting the natural canyons from damming for hydroelectric production is usually understood to have been the sort of development Trudeau sought to avoid, a letter he wrote to David Finch says that his "enthusiasm for the idea developed" when he came off the river at Nahanni Butte and "heard that prospecting for oil had already begun in the area."[42] Notwithstanding Trudeau's words, hydroelectric and non-hydrocarbon mineral development were more threatening concerns. Regardless of what motivated Trudeau's protective instincts, however, his political sway was unambiguous. Finch writes that both Trudeau and Patterson "were instrumental in helping create the Nahanni National Park Reserve in 1971."[43] That an August journey down the river in 1970 could lead to the establishment of a National Park Reserve the very next year

+

The South Nahanni cuts through four deep canyons below Virginia Falls.

borders on a political miracle. Patterson could claim no such effect from his visits to the Nahanni!

But political machinery had been turning before Trudeau's drift down the Nahanni. The National and Historic Parks Branch had already requested the Canadian Wildlife Service to conduct a survey of the Nahanni region, a survey to be accompanied by recommendations for park boundaries. The National and Provincial Parks Association of Canada organized meetings in Toronto and Vancouver to promote the preservation of the Nahanni. George Scotter, one of the authors of the Canadian Wildlife Service survey (itself a 186-page document), gave over 20 presentations about the Nahanni, one of them with more than 3,000 people in attendance. Hundreds of letters of public support followed. The Department of Indian and Northern Affairs encouraged similar discussions, media interviews, and public talks. In fact, Indian and Northern Affairs had likely orchestrated Trudeau's trip to the Nahanni in the first place, so Chrétien probably took his instructions "to look after the preservation of the South Nahanni" as a political victory of sorts, rather than as a top-down direction from the prime minister.

So if, as Finch says, Trudeau was "instrumental" in the creation of the Nahanni National Park Reserve, he was as much an instrument of the public will and of his ambitious cabinet minister as he was the primary agent.

What Finch has in mind when he speaks of Patterson's "instrumental" role is also problematic. It is, of course, easy for an enthusiastic biographer to claim more for his subject than is warranted. Similarly, it is easy for an enthusiastic editor to imagine Trudeau being attracted to the Nahanni as a result of his having read *The Dangerous River*. It seems entirely reasonable to speculate that Trudeau—a well-read man, a proud Canadian, and a collector of canoes—would know Patterson's book. In fact, in a letter the late prime minister wrote to Finch, he acknowledged that he "had done some reading about the Nahanni in the years before [he] visited the river."[44] But Finch's work goes on to make clear that Trudeau's past reading did not include *The Dangerous River*, observing that in the autumn of 1970, Trudeau was "looking forward to reading Mr. Patterson's book, *The Dangerous River*." He would be reading from a copy that the author had personally inscribed to him.[45] So it was not a pathway leading through *The Dangerous River* that linked both Patterson and Trudeau as "instrumental" figures in the creation of the park. In fact, Trudeau had not even read the book.

Since Trudeau was not specific when he said he had "done some reading," one can only wonder just what he had read. Most of the Nahanni books available today were published in the decade *after* Trudeau's visit and *after* the creation of the park. George Scotter speculates that "done some reading" probably included the Canadian Wildlife Service survey commissioned by the National and Historic Parks Branch, and possibly a manuscript draft of an article on the Nahanni that was later published in *Nature Canada*. Neil Hartling says the former prime minister was influenced by environmentalist Gavin Henderson, who was the Executive Director of The National and Provincial Parks Association of Canada at the time, an influence lending further texture to Trudeau's possible reading.[46]

As well, Trudeau's long friendship with whitewater guru Bill Mason—who described canoeing the Nahanni as "the greatest canoe trip in the world"— would also have steered him toward some specialized reading.[47] Given Trudeau's personal interest in canoes and canoeing in the Canadian wilderness (many years later Trudeau would write the Foreword to Mason's *Path of the Paddle*), what he had in mind when he said he had done some reading "in the years before [he] visited the river" might well have been reading that was shaped by his friendship with Mason. It also might well have included Patterson's magazines articles about the Nahanni, especially those appearing in *The Beaver* magazine. To put

+
Mason Rock thrusting up amidst Virginia Falls.

---

this in other words, while Trudeau had clearly not read *The Dangerous River* prior to visiting the Nahanni in 1970, he had most likely done substantial background reading that ideally positioned him to respond when the Canadian Wildlife Service survey was submitted.

Patterson had begun writing for *The Beaver* in the summer of 1947, and his articles there and abroad led to increasing interest in the region. The image of the South Nahanni spread both within Canada and throughout the United Kingdom, and Patterson's articles in London's *Country Life* and Edinburgh's *Blackwood's* had considerable influence, especially as Patterson's winning prose was accompanied by photographs from his private collection. Inevitably, as the river became better known, the desire grew both to see it and to see its unspoiled beauty preserved. So even though a direct link cannot be established between Patterson's writing and Trudeau's political act, Patterson's efforts to evoke the Nahanni in words certainly influenced the immense public advocacy that, in turn, contributed to Trudeau's conservationist feat.

Trudeau and thousands of others also learned about the Nahanni through other textual and visual sources. In 1947, the young Pierre Berton, a cub reporter for the *Vancouver Sun*, flew to the Nahanni valley to investigate rumours that had been circulating on radio and in newspapers of a mysterious tropical valley where men had disappeared and their headless skeletons had been found. Just prior to Berton's visit, for example, the *Edmonton Journal* ran an article on its front page entitled "Where Is Headless Valley? Veterans of North Asking."[48] Upon Berton's return, he quickly debunked all the rumoured oddities of the valley: its tropically warm ecosystem, its wailing winds, its cliff dwellings and mongel caves, its headhunters—even its purported dinosaurs! Berton only allowed that gold could be found there, although not necessarily in significant quantities.[49] But the sensationalism and its debunking certainly contributed to popular knowledge of the Nahanni. Berton's radio dispatches from northern Canada were syndicated worldwide, and at one point, readers of more than one hundred newspapers followed the journalist as he fed the appetites of a populace grown weary of war news. Not only did this coverage make the Nahanni an all-but-household world for a year or so, it set the stage for Patterson's tale of heroic adventure along a threatening and dangerous river that appeared seven years later.

Nor is it mere coincidence that Patterson's first published article—"River of Deadmen's Valley"—appeared in *The Beaver* only three months after Berton's explosion of the Nahanni myths. And as we have seen, that story of Patterson's journey into such a threatening environment is what led to the birth of *The Dangerous River*.

The heroic-struggle theme was also taken up by the National Film Board's 1961 black-and-white classic *Nahanni*, which depicts a persistent but unsuccessful Albert Faille—now well advanced in years—struggling up the river to ascend beyond Virginia Falls. Surely Trudeau would have been familiar with NFB's cinematic piece, especially since his friend Bill Mason had worked extensively with the organization. And the excellent work generated by the NFB has become a vanguard by which international audiences have been made aware of Canada and Canadian issues, even far outside the country's geographical boundaries.

In the decade *after* the Nahanni National Park Reserve was created, the ways by which people and prime ministers came to know about the Nahanni blossomed unimaginably. The best known sources were Ranulph Fiennes's *The Headless*

Valley (1973), Dick Turner's *Nahanni* (1975), the *Nahanni National Park Historical Resources Inventory* conducted by W.D. Addison & Associates in 1975–1976 and published by Parks Canada, Joanne Ronan Moore's *Nahanni Trailhead* (1980), and Douglas Chadwick's 25-page "Nahanni: Canada's Wilderness Park" in *National Geographic* in 1981. Such ample publicity led steadily to greater use of the park. Visitor statistics supplied by Parks Canada record that there were more than 800 overnight users in 1995, with normal years registering between 650 and 700 overnight users. These numbers take on special significance when one considers that no road services the park. Consequently, all traffic to the Falls must arrive by air, unless, of course, the visitor follows the same route as Patterson! Yet very few people would pay the high cost of air travel to spend only one night in the park. So when Parks Canada statistics record a single overnight user, they mark a river traveller who spends, on average, ten days to two weeks "overnighting" along the Nahanni as he or she descends it.

Several other factors compound this vast increase in traffic since the Nahanni achieved park status. First, since visitors come to the park largely to experience the river, users are not spread evenly throughout the more than 4,750 square kilometers the park encompasses. Rather, virtually all park use concentrates along a thin corridor meandering through the centre of the park. Second, because the river cuts through such deep canyons, available campsites along the river are extremely limited, which forces almost all river travellers to stop at these same few campsites. Third, since nearly all river travel occurs in July or August when the river is usually most navigable and the weather finest, the annual use statistics could more accurately be said to show use during a brief two-month period.

The immense popularity of the Nahanni today is obvious, both at home and abroad. While we have seen a variety of sources all contributing to this public awareness, R.M. Patterson's *The Dangerous River* remains one of the most consistent inspirations to Nahanni travellers. Recall the Parks Canada employee I mentioned in the Prologue, who remarked that almost everyone stopping at the Fort Simpson visitor centre *en route* to canoeing or rafting down the river had read—or was at least familiar with—*The Dangerous River*. And this recreational use of the river increases the number of advocates who wish to see the Nahanni further protected, making Patterson's book a continuing factor in the preservation of the Nahanni region. If Finch was understandably enthusiastic in claiming that Patterson was "instrumental" in creating the park itself —his role was certainly important, although perhaps not "instrumental"—the ubiquity of *The Dangerous River* among those who travel the river today shows that Patterson is indeed "instrumental" in maintaining and promoting the preservation of the river.

One might assume that because the Nahanni is now protected by its National Park status, its environmental future is secure. Nothing could be farther from the truth. If the region is to remain a pristine wilderness, efforts to preserve it must be renewed. In the late 1990s, the Canadian Nature Federation ranked Nahanni National Park Reserve as the 8th most endangered park in Canada; in 2002, they changed the ranking to the 2nd most endangered, 2nd only to Prince Edward Island National Park, whose beaches and sand dunes are being washed back into the sea by the natural forces that created them. For the Nahanni, man is the primary force putting this natural wonder at risk.

The cause for serious concern arises from the fact that while the boundaries of the Nahanni National Park Reserve prohibit dams or mining activity within a narrow corridor along part of the Nahanni proper, what takes place on most of the Nahanni's tributaries is not subject to park regulation. Hence, whatever sort of resource development is deemed profitable from one year to the next can be carried on, and any effluents or by-products from mining, road construction, or the like that get into the nearby streams will flow directly downhill and into the South Nahanni itself. Imagine, for example, the efficacy of legislation that would prohibit industrial activities that produce toxic effluent on the lower Mississippi River, but permit such activity on the Ohio and Missouri rivers. The problem with the park legislation of 1971 is that it sought to protect the river, but did not protect the many waters that flow into it. In fact, the Canadian Wildlife Service's initial recommendation for park boundaries—which the National and Historic Parks Branch requested the Canadian Wildlife Service to make when the pre-park survey was commissioned—included the entire South Nahanni watershed, not simply the river and its immediately adjacent environs. Unfortunately, the government chose to protect only a serpentine strip alongside the river, about 1/7th of the entire Nahanni watershed. Not many years passed before the International Union for Conservation of Nature and Natural Resources (IUCN), which makes recommendations to the United Nations on World Heritage, responded with a recommendation that the entire watershed be included in the World Heritage Site, much as the Canadian Wildlife Service had originally conceived the park.

Even in the late 1960s when the Canadian Wildlife Service conducted its survey, its recommendations had been shaped by commercial resource development interests already in place. Today, the inadequate park boundaries are a matter of serious concern. For example, the Cantung Mine, a tungsten mine owned by North American Tungsten Corporation, has operated on and off for nearly 45 years along the headwaters of Flat River, abandoning and re-opening operations as world metal prices fluctuate. The facility temporarily shut down for 15 years between 1985 and 2000, leaving the mine and its industrial chemicals on site. After re-opening, the company spilled 20,000 litres of diesel fuel in 2002, and in the summer of 2006, the company was served with a notice from the federal government to shut down operations because of seepage from tailings ponds—an order that was later rescinded after discussions with the company. Consequently, the pressing environmental concerns with this mine are to insure that no further damage is done in the mine's remaining few years of viability, and that the company posts an adequate security bond to guarantee the cleanup is done by the company, not by the taxpayers of Canada. According to the Canadian Parks and Wilderness Society, the security bond currently posted by the company is far less than the projected cost of environmental cleanup.

A similar situation arises with a proposed mine owned by the Canadian Zinc Corporation on Prairie Creek, which flows into the South Nahanni near Deadmen Valley. The mine has the potential to feed highly toxic substances—40 tonnes of cyanide and millions of litres of diesel fuel are stored on site—into Prairie Creek and then into the South Nahanni. The ores themselves contain high levels of mercury. And in order to operate the mine, the company needs to build a road that would cross a sensitive landscape of globally significant limestone caves and canyons known as the Nahanni karstlands. The mine was first built as part of a scheme by the Texas-based Hunt Brothers to corner the world silver market in the early 1980s. When the U.S. Federal Reserve intervened, the price of silver plummeted, and the original proponent of the project went bankrupt. Twenty years later, a new junior mining company has taken over the site—now planned as a zinc project—and, as metal prices rise, interest in the investment community rise as well. Yet irrespective of zinc prices, the project is plagued with uncertainty, and the local Dehcho First Nations have challenged elements of the undertaking in court.

In fact, local support for conserving the region, rather than exploiting its resources, is strong among First Nations people. In 2000, the Dehcho—echoing the Canadian Wildlife Service and the IUCN in the 1970s—requested that the national park be expanded to protect the entire watershed of the South Nahanni River. As they have been for the past seven years, the Dehcho are currently negotiating a land and self-governance agreement with the Government of Canada for a vast area that includes the South Nahanni northward to the traditional territory of the Sahtu Dene and the Metis. As do the Dehcho, the Sahtu Dene and Metis wish to see the entire watershed brought within the park reserve.

Obviously, the issues are much more complex than the two immediate threats to the South Nahanni River—the operations of North American Tungsten Corporation and Canadian Zinc Corporation—would suggest. Other mining exploration projects are also at the preliminary stages, and some First Nations communities support resource development that will bring employment and wealth to their people.

What is clear, nonetheless, is that without further legislated protection of the entire Nahanni watershed, the South Nahanni River will inevitably be vulnerable to future environmental hazards. Indeed, relevant governments, environmentalists, aboriginal groups, small businesses, and resource developers are keenly aware of these complex issues and are working to find solutions. Still, one cannot help but wish Trudeau's government had taken the Canadian Wildlife Service's initial recommendations for park boundaries and designated the entire South Nahanni watershed as a park reserve in 1971.

In spite of the political will of the National and Historic Parks Branch, the Canadian Wildlife Service, The Department of Indian and Northern Affairs, Jean Chrétien, and Pierre Trudeau, what actually brought about the creation of Nahanni National Park Reserve was that people wanted the region protected. And they told their government that. No doubt, considerable leadership was necessary to encourage ordinary citizens to speak out and to write letters to their elected officials, but that did happen. Today, those same people who use the Nahanni for recreational purposes—whether in canoes, rafts, or armchairs—can have the same effect on expanding the park's boundaries.

Ironically, many of those same recreational users who can save the Nahanni from resource development are, increasingly, themselves a stress on the ecosystem. As we have seen, heavy use by large numbers of annual visitors is exacerbated by a short recreational season and limited camping spaces. These factors lead to demands on the environment that are sometimes more characteristic of an urban park than a remote wilderness.

But the irony goes deeper, because many of those who come to the waters of the Nahanni have been inspired to do so by R. M. Patterson's *The Dangerous River*. Like him, they seek opportunities for solitude, for communion with nature, for independence, and for adventure. Yet in order to accommodate the heavy use of the river, while avoiding as much as possible the environmental degradation that accompanies such heavy traffic, Parks Canada has had to place many restrictions on what visitors can and cannot do in the park. More than a quarter-century ago, Joanne Moore discovered that if she and her partner wished to build a log cabin and live on the Nahanni as had Patterson, they needed to do it outside park boundaries. Today, regulations are myriad. Rafters and canoeists must register with Parks Canada before accessing the river, they can only start their descent at prearranged times, camping or even stopping for a picnic is prohibited at certain spots along the river, camping at Virginia Falls is limited to two days only, metal fire pans must be used when building any fire, and they are encouraged (although not yet required) to carry out personal waste, as well as garbage. Nevertheless, while some individualists grumble at the regulations, most users accept the need to minimize human impact—whether industrial or personal—on the natural environment.

The elements that link Patterson's writing to the preservation of the South Nahanni are, as we have seen, both subtle and complex. While it is not possible to say definitively that *The Dangerous River* led to the creation of Nahanni National Park Reserve, it was surely Patterson's writing about the Nahanni and not his travel on it that had any influence at all. Since the park was created in 1971, numerous books and films have been published and produced about the river, but none has made the public more aware of it than Patterson's; hundreds of ecotourists arrive on the Nahanni every year inspired by *The Dangerous River*. While recent books and documentaries are far more explicit in their themes of conservation than was Patterson's, none has had any greater effect on the preservation of the Nahanni wilderness. Nor has any one of them sufficiently stirred the public to demand that the park boundaries be expanded to include the entire Nahanni watershed. But rivers cannot live isolated from the ecosystem of which they are an integral part.

Whatever other ways readers find to engage with these journals, the ideal response would be that the publication of *Nahanni Journals* inspires passion for preserving this wilderness jewel. Travellers can no longer live on the river in the manner Patterson did in the 1920s, but as long as the watershed remains in a natural state, modern travellers can find their own meaningful connections to a way of life that has been here since the dawn of man. To exchange that for a horde of dollars in a shareholder's bank account or a government's treasury just makes no sense.

EPILOGUE

Modern travellers on the Nahanni are generally a well-heeled demographic of educated, environment-sensitive tourists. They can, after all, afford to fly into the park and be shepherded downriver by experienced guides. For the most part, their sensibility is more comfortable with digital cameras than .303 Lee-Enfield rifles. Although *The Dangerous River* has lured many of these ecotourists to the Nahanni, Patterson's journals from the 1920s better capture the ethos of child-like play and spiritual rejuvenation befitting today's traveller.

For the most part, they show us a man "simply messing about in boats," a child secure at play in the nurturing natural world. The seemingly unstoppable protagonist of *The Dangerous River*—expert marksman and canoeist—steps aside for the vulnerable young man. He can be brash. He can be competitive. He can grumble about his companion's shortcomings. And when he meets obstacles that he is incapable of surmounting, whether a turbulent stretch of river below the Falls or a maze of trackless forest and an empty stomach, he can resort to that most child-like of behaviours—he can confide in his mother and be nourished by the knowledge that she loves him. These emotions of simple joy in the moment, of reverence for forces infinitely greater than ourselves, and of uncertainty that we can meet the challenges that lie ahead viscerally yoke the modern traveller to Patterson's journals.

The Dangerous River was written by a young British adventurer who grew up reading the heroic stories of big game hunters, intrepid sportsmen whose walls displayed the trophies of their sport. It comes as no surprise that the book reflects those values, in spite of Patterson's protestations that he and Matthews "were never able to see ourselves in that heroic light."[50] But much has changed since 1954, and Nahanni travellers feel more desire to photograph than to kill the wild creatures they encounter. What is interesting about the journals is that, while they were written by that same young adventurer so pleased with his ram's head, they often reveal Patterson's own unsettled thoughts about hunting. More than once, he writes in his journal that he has taken a photograph of a bear or moose, instead of trying to kill it. Such regret is most poignantly expressed on August 14, 1927, when he saw a cow moose and her calf, killed the cow, only to watch her carcass float irretrievably and uselessly downstream in the Nahanni's current. His sorrow—"I wish now I had taken their photograph instead—it would have made a beautiful picture"—speaks volumes. Not only does it reveal a capacity for empathy with wild creatures (what would become of the now-motherless calf?) more in keeping with the values of modern ecotourists, but if Patterson were to have the opportunity to tell his 1927–1929 Nahanni adventure yet another time and in the twenty-first century, the resulting narrative would undoubtedly look a lot more like *Nahanni Journals* than *The Dangerous River*.

The heroic adventurer's disposition lurking in *The Dangerous River*'s pages has passed far downstream and out of sight. Instead, today's travellers seek the values that are the very ethos of *Nahanni Journals*. We can only hope the publication of these journals encourages both the personal and spiritual values they embrace, and that society's complex relationship with the Nahanni National Park Reserve—indeed, all the natural world—will be approached with rich understanding and deep respect.

UPDATE ON CURRENT DEVELOPMENTS

In 2007, as this book was going through press, two events of great relevance to *Nahanni Journals* occurred. First, the Government of Canada announced its intention to expand the boundaries of the Nahanni National Park Reserve, an intention it followed up on in 2009 by increasing the size of the park reserve by over six times. Second, after a life of more than half a century, *The Dangerous River* went briefly out of print, but in 2009, TouchWood Editions once more took up the publication of the full text of Patterson's famous book.

Editorial Practices

THIS EDITION OF PATTERSON'S JOURNALS HAS TWO GOALS. The first and foremost is to produce a clean, easily-read text that nevertheless conveys something of the unpolished nature of a daily journal. The second is to generate a text that accurately conveys the physical nature of the handwritten manuscript, including its various alterations, marginal notes, and idiosyncrasies of format. To realize both objectives in a single text has been challenging.

In addressing the first goal, I have edited the journals in a way that creates an unobstructed but reliable text. For the most part, Patterson's handwriting is legible, his prose is composed with a keen awareness of the subtle possibilities of language, and his sense of writing as a tool for communicating with others is highly advanced. Consequently, achieving this primary goal has required little more than preparing a faithful transcription of Patterson's words. Even so, scores of decisions had to be made about how best to represent handwriting and all its accompanying idiosyncrasies in print. In order for the reader of this printed text to understand what Patterson wrote in longhand, then, the guiding principles behind these decisions need to be spelled out.

First, little or nothing has been silently corrected. If Patterson made an error in spelling, chose to divide a word commonly written as one (such as "every where" or "south east"), omitted an apostrophe, or accidentally left out a word that he obviously intended, the error appears in what follows. If I have added anything for clarity, it has been placed either in square brackets or, in the case of expanded abbreviations, in italics. If a word is reasonably certain, but can't be transcribed with full confidence, a question mark is placed after the word and everything is put inside square brackets, thus [doubtful?]. If, on rare occasion, anything has been silently removed, such as a word inadvertently repeated by Patterson, the removal has been unobtrusively observed in the Annotations section. But Patterson's journals are generally quite clear and his spelling and grammar more than competent, so an editor need do little to insure clarity.

This transcription has been checked meticulously by numerous sets of eyes, and while no editor is infallible, I have enough confidence in the accuracy of this transcription to dispense with [*sic*] as a way of indicating that an error exists in the manuscript, and is not a creation of the editor. Readers do not want a text littered with [*sic*] after every potential error in spelling, grammar, or punctuation, so a great deal of effort has gone into insuring that what is printed here is what Patterson wrote. In exceptional circumstances, however, [*sic*] is used after a confusing error, with the suggested correction appearing within the brackets. Thus, when Patterson writes "I thing," as he does on occasion, the transcription mirrors Patterson's usage, but adds [*sic*: I think] for clarity. Only because this unusual construction appears to be intentional on Patterson's part, and because its effect might well be confusing to readers, is it treated with such an obtrusive intervention. Any other sort of editorial addition made in the interest of clarity has been placed in square brackets, except for expanded abbreviations, which have been placed in italics. If words are underscored or double-underscored in the journal, they are reproduced that way here unless they are date headings. An ampersand replaces the shorthand symbol Patterson uses for "and."

The matter of date headings brings us to a few silent changes that have been made in the interest of standardization. All date headings appear here in bold type above each entry, although the headings in the journals are often underlined and just as frequently appear in the margin beside the entry as above it. Patterson's use of abbreviated months or of cardinal or ordinal dates has not been standardized, but reflects what is in the journals, although all abbreviations have been expanded in italic and raised letters in dates have been lowered. Times, such as "A.M." or "pm," have been standardized to read "a.m." or "p.m." in every instance, and colons have been used in all times of day, whereas Patterson often separated the hour from the minutes with a raised period. Thus, "5·30 PM" becomes "5:30 p.m." While Patterson frequently used dashes of varying lengths to punctuate his sentences, all dashes here have been standardized. As well, commas and periods before or after a closing quotation mark have been placed within the quotation mark in this transcription. Finally, Patterson's paragraphing has been respected, but a more standard practice of dropping down to a new line and indenting the first line of the new paragraph is always followed, whereas Patterson—in the interest of conserving paper in the 1928–1929 journals—often indicated a paragraph break by merely leaving a blank space of about 3 cm, then continuing on the same line.

In order to meet the second editorial objective—that is, to convey the physical nature of the manuscript—a special Annotations section has been prepared. This section contains detailed information about what the manuscript looks like, such as where Patterson has added words or struck them out, what marks and notes appear in the margin, and so forth. Where it is obvious that such alterations or marginal additions were made at the time of composition, the words appear in the transcription as though they were a core part of the journal entry, but their irregular placement is acknowledged in the Annotations section. Where Patterson made textual changes at a later time, or where there is uncertainty about when changes were made, brief descriptions of such passages are made in the Annotations section, and the transcription itself reflects what Patterson sought to write at the actual time of composition. In rare places where Patterson inadvertently wrote one word or name when he clearly meant another, the error is faithfully recorded, but, depending on the seriousness of the error, either a correction is offered within square brackets in the text or the error is recognized in the Annotations section.

To achieve the primary goal of creating a clean, easily read text, the typical arrangement linking endnotes to the main text by superscripted numbers has been avoided. Because the Annotations include a great deal of curiosity-driven information relevant to Patterson's journals, as well as the annotations that describe the physical manuscript, the text of the journal would necessarily become an uninviting maze of superscripted numbers. To avoid such scholarly barbed wire, individual annotations in the Annotations section are linked to the main journal text by page and line number, not by a superscripted tag. While such an arrangement enables a clean text, it necessarily requires the reader to check the Annotations section periodically to see if it includes information relevant to his or her interests, since no superscripted tag gives notice. Nonetheless, the current method permits the inclusion of a great deal of information of potential interest to specialists from many different fields, without encumbering the primary text.

This method allows *Nahanni Journals* to serve two audiences, one that simply wishes to read this well-told daily rendering of Patterson's adventures on the South Nahanni River in the 1920s, and another that has more exacting demands for understanding the written account. Editorial baggage can be useful, but it should never interfere with a reader's initial perception, and so it is placed "behind the scenes," available to those interested in cultural introspection, postmodern theory, or analyses of composition, but only accessible to those who look.

As mentioned, the annotations also provide supplemental information about people, places, and titles mentioned in the journals. These annotations reflect the fact that *Nahanni Journals* is essentially a book about Patterson's *writing* about his experiences on the Nahanni, and not about the time Patterson spent on the river or about the river itself. To that end, the annotations attempt to satisfy the reader's curiosity about Patterson's reading interests and about his British origins, rather than about people and places on the Nahanni. The excellent books listed in the Bibliography will better serve these other interests.

Notes to Introduction

1. R.M. Patterson, *The Dangerous River* (Sidney, B.C.: Gray's Publishing, 1966), 184, 195. All subsequent page references to *The Dangerous River* are to this 1966 edition. While it would have been desirable to use a more readily available edition, no edition published after Gray's has included the complete text. The numerous and more recent reprints of Gray's edition, however, all use the same pagination as the 1966 first Canadian edition.
2. David Finch, *R.M. Patterson: A Life of Great Adventure* (Calgary: Rocky Mountain Books, 2000), 155.
3. Ibid., 239.
4. Patterson, *The Dangerous River*, 9.
5. Letter from Patterson to Gray Campbell, May 21, 1978, quoted in Finch, *Life of Great Adventure*, 235–36.
6. http://members.fortunecity.com/albert_faille/calgary.htm/, accessed February 20, 2007.
7. Finch, *Life of Great Adventure*, 230.
8. Ibid., 239.
9. Ibid., 229.
10. Furth to Patterson, May 22, 1953. Correspondence between R.M. Patterson and various publishers, 1947–1979. British Columbia Archives and Records Service, Victoria, B.C. MSS 2762, box 6, file 5.
11. King to Furth, April 1, 1954. Correspondence between George Allen & Unwin Ltd. and William Sloane Associates. MS 3282, University of Reading Library, Reading, U.K. Records of George Allen & Unwin Ltd., AUC 655/10. This is a folder containing 24 items related to the publication of *The Dangerous River*.
12. Finch, *Life of Great Adventure*, 240.
13. Ibid., 241.

14. Sloane Associates to Furth, January 14, 1954. MS 3282, University of Reading Library, Reading, U.K. Records of George Allen & Unwin Ltd., AUC 655/10.

15. Patterson, *The Dangerous River*, 68–75.

16. Ibid., 68.

17. Ibid., 73–74.

18. Ibid., 75.

19. Ibid., 10.

20. Finch, *Life of Great Adventure*, 151.

21. Patterson's pagination here refers to the 1957 Panther Books edition, which describes his adventure in a box canyon he calls "the Caribou's Hole" on page 170. The corresponding pages in Gray's 1966 edition are 145–49.

22. See letters dated June 9, 1955; May 3, 1960; June 27, 1960. British Columbia Archives and Records Service, Victoria, B.C. MSS 2762, box 6, file 5.

23. E-mail communication with David Finch and Janet Blanchet, April 15, 2003.

24. Finch, *Life of Great Adventure*, 48.

25. Patterson, "River of Deadman's Valley," *The Beaver*, June 1947, 8.

26. Patterson, *The Dangerous River*, 74–75.

27. R.M. Patterson, *The Buffalo Head* (New York: William Sloane Associates, 1961), 78.

28. Patterson, *The Dangerous River*, 48.

29. Ibid., 18.

30. Ibid., 20.

31. Ibid., 21.

32. Ibid., 20.

33. Ibid., 21.

34. Ibid., 25.

35. Ibid., 34.

36. Ibid., 9.

37. Ibid., 35.

38. Ibid., 28.

39. Kenneth Grahame, *The Wind in the Willows* (New York: Charles Scribner's Sons, 1908), 7.

40. A.A. Milne, *Winnie-the-Pooh* (1926; Toronto: McClelland & Stewart, 1994), 112.

41. Patrick Keough and Rosemarie Keough, *The Nahanni Portfolio* (Don Mills: Stoddart Publishing, 1988), 49–51.

42. Pierre Elliot Trudeau to Finch, March 19, 1996, quoted in Finch, *Life of Great Adventure*, 245.

43. Finch, *Life of Great Adventure*, 245.

44. Trudeau to Finch, March 19, 1996, quoted in Finch, *Life of Great Adventure*, 244.

45. Trudeau to Mrs. G.C.F. Dalziel, November 16, 1970, quoted in Finch, *Life of Great Adventure*, 244.

46. *Northern Currents* (Spring 2002): 1; http://www.nahanni.com/newsletter, accessed February 20, 2007.

47. Ibid.

48. *Edmonton Journal*, January 18, 1947.

49. *The Vancouver Sun*, February 17, 1947.

50. Patterson, *The Dangerous River*, 9.

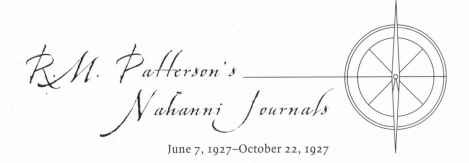

R.M. Patterson's
Nahanni Journals

June 7, 1927–October 22, 1927

[On the final day of May 1927, Patterson and companion Dennis France boarded a train at Edmonton, bound for the end of the railroad at Waterways, modern Fort McMurray, Alberta. Although they had arranged to travel onward from Waterways on one of mining engineer W.K. Cousins' scows as far as Fort Simpson, Cousins didn't appear as planned. So the two adventuresome novices, as Patterson later described, "carefully overloaded the canoe and shoved out into the river." The entry for June 7 was written on the Athabasca River between Waterways and Lake Athabasca, and the entry for June 10 had them on the big lake, waiting for an opportunity to cross to Fort Chipewyan.]

June 7

Camp on a little green water river a few hundred yards up from the Athabasca. Woke up at 5:30 a.m. Breakfast at six. Took the canoe down to the big river & had a look at the weather. Blowy & rainy & the river rough. So we baked bannock & re-sorted grub & kit more handily & dried wet things ready for an early lunch & a start at noon if weather permits, with a view to travelling until dark (11:00 p.m.) & camping on the coast of Lake Athabasca—from there to make a dash across to Fort Chipewyan (whence your fisher came) in the first calm water. A lovely morning now. Bluebells & cranberry blossom. Song birds, fish & wildfowl & no mosquitoes. What a relief.

Friday June 10

I am writing this sitting alone on the rock edge of a little island separated from Fort Chipewyan by one mile of rough, wind whipped water—Lake Athabasca. We landed here yesterday after a tough fight in the rough water & are still storm bound—from the point of view of a canoe—& unable to leave. I got up at 4:30

this morning to look at the water, but the wind was still churning it, so I went back to bed without waking Dennis & we slept on till eight. Good meals, bathing, washing clothes, writing letters & baking a store of bannock have filled the day, & all is done now. We can only read & rest till the lake calms & we can pull out on the ten miles of water that still separate us from the Rivière des Rochers.

This is one of Gods days that only seem to come in northern Alberta—the sun like a flame in a clear blue sky, not a trace of haze & all around the tumbling water & the lake gulls.

The south shore of the lake is fenland—flat & marshy & the home of wild-fowl. We can hardly see it now—it appears & disappears in curious mirages. The north shore & its islands form the edge of the Canadian shield—the Laurentian rocks—the oldest in the world. They are beautifully treed with spruce, white poplar & tamarack & on the shores of its bay are the buildings of Chipewyan gleaming white in the sunshine, the old fort standing four square on a rocky point. Around us are other islands—the smoke of a camp fire rising from one. The north shore stretches away & disappears in the distance, while to the east is only the water & the blue horizon. In this weather with its clear greens & blues & the sunshine glittering on the water, it seems the loveliest spot in the world. And the cool wind sends the mosquitoes to seek hiding—one can sleep without a bar.

Where I am sitting there are great wild gooseberries & strawberries in blossom, & wild thyme & honeysuckle. All manner of little flowering rock plants, mosses & small trees in the cracks of the veined & coloured rocks.

Below the waves are breaking & with me I have Jorrocks Jaunts & Jollities. Could money buy more than this?

Table of distances

Simpson to Nahanni. 109 miles.

Nahanni to Fort Liard. 79 miles.

Fort Liard to Nelson River 51 miles.

Nelson River to Beaver River 25 miles.

Beaver River to Hell Gate. 42 miles.

Nelson River to Fort Nelson 100 miles.

Fort Nelson to Sikanni Landing 100 miles.

+

Nahanni Butte, where the South Nahanni flows into the Liard.

[The crossing was nearly disastrous and included three days of being trapped on Mouse Island. From Fort Chipewyan, they paddled down the Slave River until being overtaken by the HBC launch Canadusa, which they boarded, complete with their canoe. Aboard the Canadusa, they carried on down the Slave and over the portage between Fitzgerald, Alberta, and Fort Smith, capital of the Northwest Territories at the time. Cousins showed up at Fort Smith, so Patterson and France jumped ship and hired on as temporary crew on Cousins' scow in exchange for passage. Once again, they were bound for Fort Simpson.

Spending a few days in Fort Simpson, where Patterson and France parted company on rather unhappy terms, Patterson traded his 18-foot canoe for a 16-foot Chestnut Prospector, a far more manageable vessel for a solitary paddler. Still aboard Cousins' scow, he then started up the Liard River to a point just upriver of the Liard Rapids, where he disembarked and began his journals in earnest on July 22, 1927.]

Friday July 22nd 1927

Spent the day wind bound at the west end of the Long Reach of the Liard, opposite the long island. Got up at 5:40 a.m. & had breakfast. Camp was in a lovely position, among spruce trees on the south shore & with a view over the Liard to the first range of the Rockies—the Mackenzie Mountains probably—with a great round mountain that should be Nahanni Butte at the south end. Broke up camp & as there was a good gravel beach, I repacked the canoe, balancing it better. Put out & immediately a head wind got up so strong that it was [a] waste of energy to fight it, so I put in to a little bay & made an atrocious bannock, shaved, ate wild fruit—raspberries & red currants—& had an early lunch. Soon after the wind dropped & I tried again but after a mile it rose to a gale & I had to land on a shallow lee shore. Nothing to do but to sleep & laze about—fortunately the wind makes the mosquitoes lie low. It is ten to eight now & I have had supper—the wind is falling & I am waiting to see if it will be calm enough for me to go ahead for another hour or two before I camp for the night. It is only 30 miles now to the mouth of the Nahanni & I had hoped to be there by tomorrow midday. Now it will not be till Sunday—damn wind on these big rivers, anyhow.

Saturday July 23rd   3:45 p.m.
The wind blew last night until sunset, when it was too late to make a start worth while. So I went very early to bed & was up at a quarter to three—some time about sunrise. I have never seen so many mosquitoes—I simply rolled up my bedding & mosquito net, oiled my face & hands, took some dried apples, a drink of water & some cold beans, put on my face net & fled. A lovely calm morning—the mountains looking very beautiful in their pale colouring. I went on until eight when I stopped & made breakfast. The wind rose again promptly but after I had fed & washed I decided to go on anyhow, so I started again—poling mainly—past some islands, over many little riffles on a shallow, gravelly bottom. Very fortunate that I learned to punt on the Cherwell & the Isis. Was caught suddenly by the wind about one & put on a lee shore—soft mud. Floundered madly & bare footed & lugged the canoe by hand into the shelter of a little point. Had lunch on the shingle & afterwards found the wind worse—a gale. So I cooked a pot of rice & raisins & had a bathe & change of clothes & am still waiting—what a life. Nahanni cant be much over 20 miles away—once in the smaller river I shall be safe from wind.

The day is like a June day—all glitters & sunlight & blue shadows. The mountains are deep blue, showing range after range now against the blue sky. White clouds bowling across, throwing dark blue shadows on the mountain slopes—the foothills in shades of blue according to their distance, & the unending green of the forest.

A young day—& me in khaki with a red handkerchief round my neck, sleeves rolled up, bare footed, open necked & hatless in the golden sunshine.

The wind is easing so I shall load up ready to go on if I can.

Tuesday July 27th

In Poole Field's shack at the mouth of the South Nahanni. A willow island in front—behind, the Indian village on a spruce flat with Nahanni Butte showing its precipitous eastern face above us—its head still in the rain clouds. Ten a.m. & the weather clearing to fair & windy.

Poled a good distance on Saturday evening along a stony beach & then crossed the end of a snye to a cut bank with fallen trees lying in the water. Current very swift—sun hot & the breeze fell & mosquitoes came out. The M.T. Liard River passed on the far side of some sand banks pushing her scows upstream—I landed at last on a sand & willow island, clean played out. Had supper & went to bed.

Up on Sunday about six. Sun shining brightly & no breeze—never in all my life seen anything like the mosquitoes. On a conservative estimate there must have been an easy 2000 outside my sleeping net alone. Took a hasty drink of water & a little cold rice & fled into the canoe & paddled on till about nine. Had breakfast under a cut bank on a sandy ledge—sand in everything, also mosquitoes & smoke—not much wood—upset tea pail on fire & burnt my fingers—dropped tea pail in river & had to fish for it, being bitten the while. Left thankfully.

Fairly good going up to a sharp point with a sweeping current. Crossed the Liard & came up the left bank in a blaze of heat, very tired & hungry & no place to land. Came at last to a sand bar about 3:00 p.m. & lunched—sand threw up the heat at me. A breeze got up about four so I washed & combed my hair & felt once more young & hearty. Heard Faille's kicker far behind as I started. He caught me up about five miles from Nahanni & towed me in.

Yesterday we were held up by pouring rain. I had my bed outside under my tarpaulin as I dont like sleeping inside, & we had our meals in this empty cabin—full of Hudson's Bay stuff for the new post above the splits. Baked, shaved, washed etc. & lazed about. Today I hope we shall get away. Not a soul in the village as all the Indians are down to Simpson for their treaty money.

Started at 12:00 p.m. Faille towed me as far as he could & left me where the swift water of the Splits began. Went a little way & camped on a shingle bar. Cold night—no mosquitoes.

Wednesday July 28th

Up at four. Lovely day—sun & breeze—no mosquitoes. Very hard going in the Splits—up to my knees in fast water, hauling the canoe, very often. Caught up Faille at midday but lost him in the afternoon when I had one devil of a time coming round two fast bends. Camp on a sand bar facing the twisted mountain. Cool night—no mosquitoes.

Thursday July 29th

Up early—various odd jobs to do so didnt start till eight. Slight smoke haze & north west wind—some clouds & very heavy dew. In trouble all day & didnt make much distance partly owing to strong head wind. Found a bad rapid at the shoulder of the twisted mountain & had to go round to another channel. Howling wind blew at lunch time & it looked like rain so I slept an hour on the sand. Passed Faille's empty canoes just before lunch—he was gone with his dogs, perhaps after a moose, as there are lots of tracks. Started at 2:30 & tracked canoe up a piece of fast water. Stopped to sharpen my pole which was worn down with much hard punting in the riffle when something caught my eye in the river, black & going hard down with the current. Thought it was a burnt stump at first—then a cow moose. Actually it was a black bear not seventy yards off. Never saw one swim before. It climbed out onto a shingle island—shook itself like a sheep dog, loped across, swam another branch of the river & disappeared in the bush. I had my rifle loaded in the canoe but a bear is not much use to me on a trip like this—couldnt pack the skin with me & could only make a few meals off it while it was still fresh. Also it looked so natural—wish I had had my camera out.

At least eight splits of the Nahanni here—the highest in the middle where I am. What with side chutes, fast water, timber & the head wind, I was forced to give up & camp early. Hope to make a very early start if it doesnt rain. Have the tarp up tonight in case of rain—bed made & mosquito net fixed. Not many fortunately—the worst is over thank God—they were awful on the Liard. August sees the beginning of the cool nights—or the end of July, as now. Also they cant breed in the fast water of the Splits.

Sleep from now on with a heavy automatic under the pillow—bears & wolverine & wolves are plentiful here—there are no men, not even Indians. Heard a wolf yesterday. Two eagles swooped at me at lunch today but I got a knife in one hand & a blazing torch in the other & they sheered off. Saw my first beaver on Sunday.

Mountains all round now—To the west the Yukon border.

Baked the best bannock that ever was seen tonight—it went well with honey & cheese.

+

"It looks like hell" — First or Lower Canyon.

Got wet up to the waist hauling the canoe across a side chute just before I camped. Changed & dried my things. Bed now. Twenty to ten—twilight comes much earlier than it did a few weeks ago.

Friday July 30th
Made good going in the morning until it clouded over & a cold wind got up which made it very difficult. Got into some big, stony, open bends & was pretty wet & very cold & hungry but had to go on until I could have the shelter of trees for lunch. Lunched late & went on for two more hours in the evening. Made a good camp, almost through the Splits & had supper in a shower of rain.

Saturday July 31st   Midday
Up at 5:30—glorious day of hot sun & breeze. Shaved this morning. Came through the last of the Splits & got beastly wet hauling the canoe across the head of a

rapid. Late lunch as I couldnt find a good place with firewood & a good landing when the proper time came. Am sitting on a sand & shingle slope by a whirlpool, below a rock, between the woods & the water. The mountains are all round & in front the river disappears into them by a huge cleft—the lower canyon of the Nahanni. It looks like hell—I wonder if I can get through it alone—I dont even know how long it is. Came by a cliff this morning with iron & salts & sulphur in it—found a little sulphur spring & had a drink & thought of Bath. I often think of Oxford & Lynmouth & the gardens of Hampton Court. Took two photos today—my canoe & trackline in the river & one of the canyon from the painted cliff. The forest here is very beautiful—untouched by fire or by man. Dried my clothes on the hot stones & took a sun bath as I had lunch. Now I must tackle the most difficult bit I have seen yet, as I must find a way round the whirlpool & cross to the other bank without going into the rapids below.

Evening   Camp on a sand bar in the cañon.

I crossed easily & saw the gateway of the cañon against the sun. I climbed a rocky point & saw the full beauty of it. Further up on my side was a green stream of warm sulphur water—there I had to cross again to a point where [there] were some old buildings, almost in the shadow of the cliffs—Indians probably. I landed & found, as usual on any cleared place, a mass of wild raspberries, strawberries, black currants & red currants & ate very hearty of fresh fruit. There was a newly cut tree that a beaver had cut & some of the bark that he had eaten. A moose came out on the far bank & drank, & I thought of the Rat & the Mole & the morning they saw Pan. There was a slight blue haze in the hot sunshine & with that great gateway in front it seemed that "a river came out of Eden."

I hadnt gone far into the cañon before I struck the worst rapid of all so far. I fought the canoe up it up to my waist in white water & am now changed & having supper by the fire with the huge cliffs all around—all colours of rock, now turning blue in the twilight & the yell of waters every where.

Sunday August 1

A cool morning & a blazing heat later—I could smell my old khaki shirt scorching at lunch time but it didnt matter as I was wading in the water at rapid after rapid & so kept cool—this would be an awful job in cold weather. The walls of the canyon are amazing—huge precipices all shapes & colours with the edge of the forest showing far above—trees on little ledges & trees along the flats at the points of the river. The river green & fast & all hard work—I very nearly lost the whole outfit, tracking it round a bad rock this afternoon. I can see the gold gleaming in the black sand all along the waters edge—fine yellow gold that glitters as the waves wash it—too fine to pan. I lunched on an old gold claim—I happened to notice the claim stake—a hewed tree. I think the name was Winter but couldnt be certain. The cliffs are getting more & more weird—no scene in a theatre or drawing by Rackham could equal this. Camped late & very tired.

Monday August 2
Bank holiday I suppose. Thank the Lord I'm here. Up at six—rather stiff & hands sore through much wetting. Washed them carefully & fixed up some lard & Eusol for them. Went back through the forest to the cliff foot & dug a panful of dirt & washed it—gold all the way—no more no less. Didnt start till ten—lunched at one in a very beautiful place—a bay of black sand under a moss grown cliff with the cotton woods behind. Over the river, spruce point & the walls rising in spruce covered turrets to the final sheer precipice. 500 *feet* anyhow. Walls up & down stream as the river winds like a snake & upstream against the sun a single rock in mid stream with a tree stranded against it. Yellow butterflies—also black, white & red ones—& the sound of water that I have so often longed for on the prairie. Could do without it now—should like a nice sluggish even running river—like the Cam or kindred ditch—that a fellow could make some headway against. However, every thing worth having seems to be well guarded.

Things went far too well for a while after lunch. I shot out from behind the rock & up a longish reach of the calmest water I have struck in the canyon. Round a bend, however, I heard the roar of water again. I crept up in the eddy & then struck slantwise across the boiling water & worked my way up the far side—a cliff which overhung in many places so that I had to bend my head to pass beneath. Hanging down in bunches were wonderful clusters of quartz crystals. Climbed a rock & took a survey of the water from above & thought I could manage to cross. Which I did but the water was so fast that I was carried into the very rapid that I had worked to avoid, so I had to swing & shoot down it & line up again from the eddy. I came at 4:30 to a point where there was the worst fall of all so I tied the canoe & climbed on over the rocks to see what I could do to pass through it. Went ahead a long way but could see nothing for one man alone but to go up as far as possible in the eddy & then unload & portage—over big rocks. So I went back & camped & beached the canoe to dry out the load. Think this is the end of the canyon as I could see a wider country ahead & blue ranges of mountains in the distance beyond the rapids, standing out sharp against the sun. Walls of the canyon here must be 800 foot precipices—almost sheer.

Tuesday August 3rd
Havent sneezed since leaving Edmonton—this has just occurred to me. I suppose a sudden return to the atmosphere of London would probably prove fatal.

Loaded the canoe & cached some heavy stuff up in the bush on a spring pole where I hope no bear will bother it. Was just going to tackle the portage when I heard Faille's engine & saw his two canoes in the distance, so I waited. He also went ahead to look things over & finally we worked our canoes up together & had lunch at the head of the rapid.

Immediately after lunch we tackled a strong riffle. His engine stalled & I beached my canoe & went out to help him & we worked his canoes to the head. Then I went back & brought up my little one & went on my way, passing Faille. I came, through the upper gateway of the canyon, to a lovely reach of calm water glittering in a burning sunlight. The walls went back & gave place to a wide valley with the forested mountains all round & streams of water clear as glass pouring in from clefts in the rock. The bush here is wonderful—generations of trees must have grown & died without fire. This must be the Eden—I may be the furthest man up this river—so far as is known there is no white man or Indian ahead of me. Saw a thunderstorm coming up—the heat was intense. I made a rush for a spot sheltered by trees & just got a big fire lit, my tarp up & myself & things flung under it & the stuff in the canoe tarped up when down she came[—]came with a flash & a bang—whole water. Sand blew off the bars, smoke from a fire in the Yukon, lightnigh [*sic*: lightning], thunder, river, rain, a gale, & the sun shone pale yellow over a mountain through it all—it looked just like hell. I sat under the tarp & fair cowered—torn between a desire not to get my rifle—loaded—wet & a wish to have it outside far away. Presently I took heart & wriggled out of my river things & into dry clothes—then I thought I would see how the chocolate was—untouched from Edmonton. Nothing wrong with it in the least. From that I went on to other things & by the time the rain was over, had made a very tolerable cold supper. Mosquitoes suddenly became active so I put up the net & went to bed at ten.

Wednesday August 4
Woke at four—before sunrise—a lovely morning. Lay thinking about getting up when I heard a grunting noise & turned my head to see a cow moose & her little

calf swimming the river some way up. They landed on a shingle island & the cow turned & nosed the calf—a pretty sight. Then I remembered that Faille & I could do with fresh meat so I chucked the mosquito net aside & reached for my rifle & took one long chance shot—600 yards—my old rifle which I always hated, not the one I bought in London. I saw the shingle fly just between them & they were off & into the river on the far side of the island. Was glad in a way, though I think the calf was big enough to fend for itself. It isnt everywhere where you get moose shooting from your pillow.

Then I got up & immediately the sun & wind rose too. I shaved & washed & had breakfast—later Faille caught me up & put in to the bay—he couldnt go on for wind, even with his engine. So we cooked, & washed & mended our clothes & lunched & still it blows. Faille has gone off after a moose & I have just finished going over the bottom of my canoe with canoe paint—it badly needed it as it got well scarred in the Splits & the canyon—I wonder what the next trouble will be. Shant be able to start till tomorrow now as the canoe has to dry, so later on I shall fish & bake bannock.

A beautiful day of sunshine & white clouds—but a God forsaken wind streaking round the bend. However, it will dry the canoe & the laundry.

War declared on Germany 13 years ago today.

Thursday August 5th
Overslept—lovely calm morning. Was loaded up & away at nine—Faille already gone as he was already loaded. Worked through four or five miles of splits & lunch at two on shingle facing the sun—in my shirt & hat—my other things drying on the hot stones. Out of the open valley & into the mountains again— there seems to be the gateway to a second cañon at the end of this reach, where the river turns south suddenly between two mountains—one forested & one of rock. Behind me is the forest—spruce here & smelling in the afternoon heat of gum & needles—a gorgeous smell. A great patch of tall blue flowers—a kind of lupin—& many black & golden butterflies. No mosquitoes—they are ending now, & only come a little in the evening & early morning & at times of rain.

On into the canyon—not so narrow & shut in as the last, mountains higher & water not so bad. Blew up for rain late in the evening & for the first time since early June I didnt put up my mosquito net. Laid the tarp over my sleeping bag & at times during the night a little misty rain fell on my face.

+

An unusual geological feature aptly called the Library Rock by RMP.

Friday Aug*ust* 6

Up at 5:30 & baked two bannocks before breakfast. Morning very fresh & beautiful when the sun broke through the clouds—I took a photo of camp. Made good time in the morning & by lunch was out of the canyon into a lovely valley, ringed by high mountains, yellow daisies & big purple daisies, also wild onions, by the stream where I lunched. Many bees & butterflies. No sign of Faille—or his dog tracks along the bank—surely we cant have passed the mouth of the Flat River, where he is going, already. Saw an enormous eagle this morning.

Later noticed Failles dog tracks. Made pretty good distance & camped in a canyon opposite a cliff at least 1000 *feet* high.

Saturday Aug*ust* 7

Up very early but owing to one thing after another cropping up didnt get away till ten to eight. Noticed canoe was punctured—caught on a sharp rock in an eddy—so pitched it temporarily. Went for five hours before lunch & made good time except in one place. Canyon pretty open—took photo of the library rock. Very hot at midday & a slight blue smoke haze. Lunched en deshabille—most of my clothes drying.

Everything went wrong, somehow, in the afternoon. I managed to make about four miles, I thing [sic: think], but it was a long stretch of uphill pulling—mostly on the track line—some poling—hardly any paddling. Didnt notice much of the scenery as what with watching ones feet on the slippery rocks & in the water, & the behaviour of the canoe on the end of the line one has more than enough to do. The canoe wouldnt track properly & swung all over the place, I slipped on the rocks, when I poled the pole slipped & I nearly went in several times, & when I paddled the paddle kept on striking the stones. As a matter of fact I think I had gone on too long without lunch & tired myself, as I was pretty played out when I made camp at 6:30.

Also I saw a black bear when I was in the middle of a long rapid—dropped the pole, grabbed the rifle & fired & missed of course as the canoe was bouncing downstream like a cork & almost split on a rock before I could get it under control again. A silly waste of ammunition but I had visions of a steak, & liver & bacon for breakfast.

Pulled myself together with chocolate & wandered wearily up the bank to cut logs for a baking fire. I ran into a hillside of raspberries & red currants & didnt return for an hour. I have never seen anything like it—the raspberries were thicker, bigger & more delicately flavoured than those of any garden. This redeemed the day from complete disaster.

I pitched & patched the canoe after supper, & slept again without a net—mosquitoes almost over here in the mountains—I thought they would be. The first frost should soon come now.

Sunday August 8th

Ten a.m. Up at five & ate cold porridge & milk & more raspberries. Then I baked, had breakfast, shaved, washed my hair, sharpened knives & axe. Didnt know it was Sunday—it was all most appropriate. As a matter of fact I have to wait for the pitch on the canoe to dry before I can start. So I shall probably have an early lunch here & travel about six hours on into the evening. In the meantime I shall take another stroll into the raspberry patch. 'Opes I shall'nt be ill, as Mr Jorrocks says.

Faille's canoe passing through The Gate, with Pulpit Rock towering behind.

Camp on a spruce point in the high mountains—a tremendous cliff opposite with gullies down which come occasional rock slides. Dont know how far I am up the Nahanni as the country is unmapped, except from information. Cant be far now from the Flat River where Faille is going to trap. He is the first white man to stay in here for seven years, & he & I are the first to come in alone for that period of time. I must tell you the story of the last ones sometime.

This delay is annoying but I believe one goes all the better for an occasional long rest in camp.

I hope you dont still say that I am neurotic, or that I ever sneer at you. This occurred to me yesterday when I was wading up a long rapid, pulling the canoe after me—if I had listened to Dr Stott I should have spent this summer in England instead of badgering a canoe up this stream of evil repute.

Had lunch & went on at once. After a long tough track & pull up a very steep rapid I came to a most wonderful place, where the Nahanni cuts clean through a mountain. The water beneath is calm & like glass—on the left a sheer precipice, & on the right the same but broken by a huge mass of rock that stands out like a pulpit. The rocks are tawny & red with iron, the water is green, above & beyond is the forest & over all hung a pale blue smoke haze. The whole thing was like a great gateway through which I glided silently midget like. I have seen many beautiful places in my life but never anything of this kind. I took two photos & will take another on my way down if I have enough left. Followed a long battle in rough water in the high mountains—a rock strewn country of red screes—trees only where the rock slides cannot come. Saw Failles foot prints on a sand bar. Also flecks of soft, red, river gold.

Only travelled six hours today but am ready for bed which is made & the net up. This poling, hard paddling, tracking & wading knee deep in swift water over rough, sharp, & slippery rocks is very tiring. I find it more so now that the river is almost continuously fast, with few calm stretches.

Monday August 9th

Went on for about a mile up a long stretch of swift water & then came to an impossible place—cliffs on both sides, a rock in the middle & a strong rapid. I saw Failles camp on the far side & went across, to find him lying under his mosquito net, discouraged & reading the life of Father Lacombe. He cheered up & we had a meal & then started to pack all our gear about quarter of a mile over the cliff & through the bush—to a little sand beach at the head of the rapid. I cut a trail down to the beach—it may be used in later years in some great gold rush up here. Faille cleared out an old trail through the bush. Finally all was portaged except the canoes. Faille saw a chance to get up the far side & track past the cliff. He bounced away over the waves &, after a struggle, made it & waved to me to come. I felt doubtful but took a holt on myself & put to sea. For about 90 seconds there seemed to be water in all directions racing past me & then I landed at the foot of the cliff & tracked up through the swirls & crossed to the new camp. Bathed, baked, washed my clothes & cleaned & bandaged a rock gash on my leg that I had neglected. A thunderstorm rolled up but did not break.

Tuesday August 10th

Faille made Norwegian Logging Cake for breakfast. I had bacon, honey & fruit & a pan of fresh raspberries, cranberries & hips & haws all stewed together—&

the last can of cream, so we did well. We set off together but his engine soon took him out of sight.

I found gold in larger quantities than ever before on a beach of black sand. The mountains seem to be a shade lower & I think we may be nearing the open valley & the Flat River. Sunshine pouring down as usual—one doesnt mind getting wet under these conditions. Lunch on the rocks by a little spruce covered island at the foot of a rapid.

Later 9:45 p.m.   Everything is done now & my bed & mosquito bar are made up on the deep moss under the trees.

It was a glorious afternoon—the whole lovely valley seemed to lie soaking in the warm sunshine & there was everywhere the scent of the spruce & the hum of bees. The canyon came to an end after a mile of particularly hard tracking—partly round a low cliff of sharp stratified rock with whirlpools at its base, on which rocks I tore off the patch I put on a few days ago.

After the canyon came a valley between rocky & wooded foothills with the mountains further back. Streams of water clear as glass run into the river from every side valley & draw, & signs of game are on all the sand bars.

The smoke haze has cleared away & the full colour of the mountain west has been showing—there is nothing more beautiful. In the south east the mountains of the canyon have been in yellow rock & deep blue shadows against a blue sky, & to the north west the mountains of tomorrow's trail have been blue against a sunset of gold & purple. Opposite is a yellow cliff with the green forest above it & the green river below. Behind, the tall spruce.

I am very fortunate to see these things. In years to come this will be a great play ground—now it is God's garden & only the animals & Faille & I are on the river—unless high up there are Indian parties from the North Nahanni or the upper Liard or men in from Mayo in the Yukon.

I expect a roaring cold as soon as I get in to Edmonton next winter—this life suits me & I can stand it & thrive when others would curl up & moan but a city seems to flatten me out.

The river is quieter here—there is less wallowing in rushing water & fighting with the canoe, but no doubt there is plenty ahead of me before I leave the canoe at the Sikanni Landing, 500 miles away.

Wednesday Aug*ust* 11   Lunch Time

Cold & clear at night & before sunrise but no frost. A day of clear sunshine & white clouds—like a May or June day—& a south west breeze. No trace of haze or smoke, & intensely clear & hot—a beautiful heat when one has to be in the water. Cloud shadows on mountain & forest a deep blue.

Started on the river at 7:30—it takes a goodish time to get breakfast, break up camp & load up, with all the odd jobs that there are to do—still dressing my ankle, which takes time. Travelled well & without too much trouble & must have come about 5 miles any how. Lunch on a shingle bar in a valley of the foothills—sitting like an urchin in ragged khaki shirt & light khaki trousers—head, arms, feet bare—& roasting on the hot stones. Passed one of Failles canoes drawn up on a sand bar, so his petrol must have given out. Saw a curious bird floating on the water—large, whitish head, red brown body & dark brown or black tipped wings & tail. In the eddy where my canoe is there is more of the light river gold in the ripples than I have yet seen—if only I could find where the coarse gold is.

Later   All I can say is—what an unspeakable afternoon. I went on up two long rapids & round two bends. Then the mountains opened out & in the distance over a broad valley I saw a hill that reminded me of the one Reeth is built on. It seemed to divide two river valleys & I thought that the one on the left must be the Flat River—a stream about 100 miles long. The sun was brilliant & glittering on the water, making mirages, & I couldnt be certain but thought I could see water of a deeper & cleaner green coming from the left hand valley. The Nahanni, however, had seized its little hour of liberty to split again into about five shallow & rushing branches—most difficult going & most tiring—& I had to leave the Flat River problem unsolved—having all I could do to wrangle the canoe on up the Nahanni without going across [the] quarter of a mile of mill race to see what the dark green water was.

Now, however, all signs of Faille have vanished, so it must have been the Flat. It is a pity that I couldnt be sure as I am going on as far as the falls & I had intended to leave some of my stuff with Faille. So now I am ahead again & going on alone—I have just fired a shot to let F*aille* know that I have gone on—otherwise he might wonder what had happened. I passed a good camping place amongst the spruce about six but didnt stop as I thought it looked bad for mosquitoes. Now I have got a bad camp & mosquitoes to boot—it must be going to rain, although it looks clear. I had to stop here as I had travelled for 10 hours—mostly wading—&

was dog tired, stiff & sore. The northern lights are flickering—the first time I have seen them as I have been going to bed at '10' but now it is getting dark at that hour. The fall is coming—the fruits are all ripe or ripening & a glow of red & brown is appearing in the undergrowth—not yet in the trees.

Thursday August 12

The glorious twelfth—& another day of strife for me. Only last year I was shooting prairie chicken on Battle River—far to the south. I can see Mr Fenwick at this moment & a lot of dull men standing awkwardly in the library in dinner jackets—I hate dinner jackets—give me my tails & a red rose & Marigold to come with me to the Berkeley & wassail, for an evenings joy. Too dark to write—I must put up my net & to bed.

Friday August 13th

Yesterday morning I was roused at four by the patter of raindrops on my net. I had been tired out the night before & had intended to sleep on till six, but it looked like rain for the whole day so finally I got up, ate some chocolate & rice & went off & cleared a camping place back in the bush—I had slept on the open sand bar by my canoe. Then the rain stopped & I went & lay down again in my clothes—but couldnt get off to sleep again. It started to drizzle so I rose gloomily once more & decided to have breakfast before it should pour—which I did & by the time I had finished the sun was blazing out of a blue sky—so much sleep lost for nothing.

I started & waded up a long rapid, tracking the canoe. At the top was a swift current & I had to struggle along under a cut bank—at times cutting away fallen trees with an axe from the canoe. Then the splits ended & another canyon began—rather pretty with low cliffs, but with very sharp rocks & bad rapids. I circumnavigated a fearful boil by a masterpiece of strategy & came at the top to an old camping place—whose I cant tell, but from the axe cuts it had been disused for years. Perhaps some of the mysteries of seven years ago had a part in it. Practically there have been no white men here since then. I felt awfully tired & it looked so beautiful—I camped there & took the afternoon to bathe & shave & bake & to care for my various scars. A rest once in four days or so, I think, helps one to travel faster. By the way, the bandages Carpenter rescued from my wastepaper basket & washed are invaluable—so are her socks, & I regret to say that I tore a hole in the big green pair on a spike

+
A motorized thirty-foot river boat pushing upstream through Hell's Gate Rapid.

in the bush on that last portage. Slept like a log until six this morning when I found the sun shining out of an amazingly blue sky—the smoke haze has completely gone.

August 13

I started early today & went up in the canyon between rock walls. I came about ten to a bay, beyond which the walls went on again with a swift current between them. At the far end I could hear the roar & see the boiling, white water of a bad rapid, so I beached the canoe & went ahead through the bush to a little point from which I could look down on the rapid. The worst so far—a most curious place—here is a little map which will show you what I was up against.

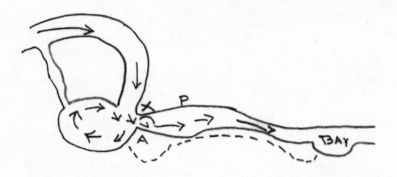

I was on the point A. The water boiled in waves six feet high past X & split on A & made two whirlpools—a sucking underneath A & a fast current between the cliffs to my little bay, six hundred yards away. I didnt know whether to try it or not[;] there were a few yards only between X & A in which one could cross that rush of water. So I went back to the bay & took out my axe & rifle, packsack, some food & clothes & laid them on the beach in case I lost the whole outfit but managed to reach shore myself. I left this notebook with them, took a bit of choco-late & set sail. I worked my way up the far side as far as P & beyond that I could not get, paddle as hard as I might. So after 5 tries I turned & shot back into the bay.

I took my axe & cleared a trail through the woods & down to the whirlpool bay where I am camped now & writing by the firelight. Over that trail I portaged every damned thing I have—the struggle to get the canoe up onto my head was intense—the tracks on the sands of the bay look as if a circus had been to town. I had never done it before—there is a trick to lifting it that I had been told & had forgotten, so I had to find it out, with much cursing, for myself.

I am glad I couldnt get beyond P—I now see that my little canoe could never have crossed those waves that are so close to me here—but I'm glad I had the nerve to tackle it. Its no disgrace to have portaged. Here & there I found an old axe cut in the bush, so the old timers must have done it too—one of the trails of '98 ran up the Nahanni but few ever saw the Klondike River—the Indians & the Nahanni settled them.

The night is cold, clear & beautiful after a hot day—no mosquito net tonight. The woods were a relief after so much water—the smell of balsam[,] moss & tamarack & the sunlit peace.

+

RMP portaging, some time after necessity taught him how to lift his canoe.

Saturday August 14   10:00 p.m.

A glorious day—never have I seen such a spell of wonderful weather as on this river—the warm afternoon sunshine seems to go clean through you & the scents of the woods can never be forgotten in years to come.

A day of joyous venture also. I crossed the whirlpool & worked upstream against strong water & at midday came to a little fall that the canoe wouldnt climb. So I lunched on the rock & then unloaded & portaged half my stuff about 100 yards—got into the water & lugged the canoe up by the nose—reloaded & started again.

I soon came to a canyon of red & yellow rocks & loose stones, sharp as knives, which played hell with the canoe & the soles on my old running shoes. Down the canyon was a mass of white water—I was almost disheartened but the Nahanni is a fine river for building character—it develops in one an appalling obstinacy. Up I went yard by yard—you must get me to tell you about it—its too long to write. Three times I crossed & once was swept out into the waves—shipping water & swearing hard as the white tops curled over the canoe. The last time I ate two bars of chocolate & smoked a cigarette before starting—like the last breakfast of the condemned. However, fortunately I seem to be getting rather handy with a canoe & we are still alive.

I must be 130 miles up the Nahanni now—I can hear the thunder of the falls which few living white men have seen—very few. One trapper had a photo of them but lost it and all his outfit in a rapid as he ran down the river to the Liard. I promised McDougall one for his office at Fort Smith if I should ever see them—& get there I mean to if I have to track every inch of the way.

Thank God Dennis isnt here—a useless encumbrance & he would have been scared thoroughly by this time. He told me afterwards that the only reason he paddled so hard in that storm on the lake was that he was afraid he was going to be drowned. No guts—that family—I'm afraid. Thank heavens I can travel alone.

I shot a cow moose this evening. I was baling out the canoe just after crossing the last swells to my camping place when I heard a grunting in the water, & I saw in front of me a cow moose & her calf swimming to shore. They landed a little way down & as the calf seemed well able to take care of himself I shot the cow. She fell & in her struggles rolled over the bank & died in the water. Before I could get to her she was swept away by the current & I saw my rump steak vanishing down the rapids—a meal for the wolves & a wicked waste of meat & game. I wish now I had taken their photograph instead—it would have made a beautiful picture.

The night is going to be cold & clear—a mosquito bar is becoming unnecessary except on muggy, rainy evenings.

Sunday August 15
Was roused early in the morning by the calf bleating for its mother. I thought a little young venison would go well & it was only 20 yards away watching me as I slept under the trees. I reached for my pistol but was so sleepy that I couldnt lay my hands on it & the calf trotted away. I went to sleep again & heard him at intervals—was finally roused at five by the patter of hooves on the shingle by the canoe & saw the calf swim away in the morning mists across the Nahanni just before sunrise.

Sunday always is a tough day for me. I started well on a golden morning but soon hit a little yellow canyon—spent the morning working through it & emerged at 12 bruised & battered, wet to the waist & fed up. I saw another immediately ahead & promptly put in to this little bay for lunch & to hang up my wet things to dry & twiddle my toes in the hot sand.

I am nearly to the second creek marked on the east bank of the Nahanni, on your map, above the Flat River. If I can get to it & as far beyond as is not too difficult, I shall camp & go the rest of the way on foot if possible as the river is too fast here for it to pay to go by canoe. I had to risk myself & my worldly goods once this morning in the rough water & twice I saw my home & bed & board swing madly on the end of the track line in a riffle. The falls are supposed to be at latitude 62° & it would be a pity to loose [sic] all for the sake of a five mile scramble. Also dangerous in this lonely country.

Later   I had a tough afternoon. I crossed the river & made my way up a long swift reach, tracking the canoe. The sharp stones cut my shoes to ribbons & the waves from the rapids kept lifting the canoe & dashing it on the rocks. Very hard to keep ones footing—my feet & socks are [jagged?] to pieces & in as bad a state as my shoes. I came to a point where it seemed I could go no further—I took its photo as my furthest north. Then by hard paddling I managed to look round it & saw a pebble shore & wooded banks in place of the cliffs & rocks—if only I could get across. I was so cheered that I slipped back into the eddy & laughed like an idiot. Then I tackled the crossing. The canoe leapt & pitched worse than on Lake Athabasca & twice white water came clean over the side. I got down on my knees & fairly dug into the water & just got her over—30 yards further down & I should have been under a cliff, heading for a bad rapid.

I tracked round the point & was sickened by the sight of another cañon with its red & yellow walls & curious battlements & pinnacles—the water wilder than ever. However, I pushed on & at last was stuck at a point where two fast riffles met with a bad rapid below them. To gain the far side I had to pass between them & either I had to go up into the riffles, which I didnt think my canoe could stand, or else go lower & chance being swept under a cliff. A place of sharp stones & miserable spruce—not a level spot to walk or lie—but I decided to beach the canoe & go on on foot.

I got the canoe fast between the stones & set out at five o'clock of a hot afternoon to climb out of the cañon to see what the country ahead towards the falls was like. I went up a rock slide in between the pinnacles of the canon, raising the warm dust, eating raspberries & hips and haws, & fearful of starting an avalanche of rock at any moment. Then I found above me a great hill covered with birch, jack pine & silver spruce & floored with cranberries. I went up that till the forest gave way to a little grassy down & I saw on top of it a birch log cut with a saw. I was amazed that any man should ever have been up there, much less have cut wood. And then suddenly I saw that it was the head & horns of a Rocky Mountain ram—the big horn sheep. Honestly, my heart almost stopped with pure joy—&

I pulled my pistol, but he was too far away. So I swung round the hill a little &
went up like a cat & came on him of a sudden perhaps fifty yards away. There was
no rot or waste of time—see any standard work on deer stalking. I just let drive
straight between his eyes. He stood still for at least a second & I was so afraid I
had missed him that I fired twice quickly at his body this time—& saw each bullet
strike. He gave a plunge & disappeared over the far side of the hill & I sobbed
& sweated after him to find that he had rolled under a tree & was dead. How he
didnt fall at my first shot I dont know—the bullet hit about one inch from where
I had aimed & was a shade nearer the right eye than the left—it must have gone
into his brain.

I was dog tired when I landed & must have climbed 700 feet, but my tired-
ness was gone. It was a lovely Sunday evening. The Nahanni was far below,
looking almost peaceful, & the sound of it was only a murmur through the
warm smell of the pines. To the south east were the mountains through which
I had come from the Liard—to the north east great stone capped mountains,
pearl grey in the smoke haze. Blue against the evening, across the canyon,
were groups of the Rockies, separating the Nahanni from the Beaver River
in the Yukon—& from behind them the smoke of a fire drifted over into the
Territories. And over all I could hear the boom of the falls—& what was more,
I had my sheep. Do you remember Ernest Seton Thompson's story "Krag, the
Kootenay Ram." I had it when I was little & I said then that I would get one,
as Shorty got his—some day. But I never dreamed of shooting it with a 9 milli-
metre Luger pistol—that is a truly western touch. Rich men come from all over
the world with the most expensive rifles—batteries of them—to hunt these
sheep, & I get one in a Sunday evening climb. The horns are big, I think, &
wonderfully symmetrical, but bear the scars of many battles—I meant to get
a head, but intended to take a day or two & hunt for it, not thinking I should
walk onto one. If only I can get it home to the flat. As I looked at the view I saw
three more rams with great curling horns looking at me from a little down not
400 yards away—& two more far across the valley. What a paradise for game—
these animals had probably never seen a man. I wonder what they thought of
their first—dusty, unshaved, an old red handkerchief of John's round his neck
& an old khaki shirt, ripped to tatters.

When I had my tonsils out that book I had in the home said that the possession of the head of a bighorn sheep placed a man in the first rank among hunters—I
very much wonder.

So back I slid[,] rolled and clattered to camp, raising dust, stones & hell, & up again I toiled with my camera, axe, hone, & a wet sack—& by eight the beautiful head was safe from insects in a pool in the river—a sack of meat was dangling in the trees, the steaks were sizzling & I was feeling that this Sunday had redeemed itself a little.

I looked very carefully at the river & came to the conclusion that at the present stage of water it would be foolish for me to cross & go on—not being a matter of life & death. So I decided to camp for one day to look after the ram's head, bake, cook, rest, repair the canoe & my feet & then go to the falls & back on foot.

Cut a great pile of spruce boughs & spread them deeply over the sharp rocks, & slept very heavily—too much mountain mutton.

Monday August 16
Up early & skinned the head & stretched the hide as well as I could on a paddle, with salt over it. I did by best—all I could do. Carved as much meat off the skull as I could & set it back in the river. Made mutton stew—also stewed raspberries—bathed, shaved & put on clean things. Canoe proved to be in an appalling shape owing to sharp rocks, & took most of the afternoon to pitch. Feet & legs about as badly hacked also.

Baked bannocks & sorted out my things to start for the falls, allowing for three days & two nights away. Shant be able to carry any blanket—scrambling up & down mountains & through the bush on these hot, dreamy afternoons, so I must rely on a good fire at night, as in the bush in wintertime.

Tuesday August 17
A day of disappointment. Had breakfast & bandaged up my battered shins & had everything rolled up & ready to start—the canoe carried high up on the rocks & safely tied—only the grub to cache so that it would be safe from bears & wolverine. The [place?] & the trees were all against me. I had hoped to be away before nine. As I [sic: it] was I worked like a navvy, had lunch & worked again until three until I realised that it was hopeless to try to make a safe cache in that camp. I took some chocolate & my rifle & climbed the hills disgustedly, hoping to get a bear. I saw a moose a long way off & the heat became so drowsy among the pines that I lay down on the needles in the shade on a sunny hillside & dozed & listened to the roar of the falls—perhaps four miles away—that I may never see.

Reasons—I cant leave my camp if I cant make my food safe from the animals. I am not at all sure that I can get my canoe across but would try if I had to do it. Having got across there may be another 5 miles of this swift water & sharp rocks & I have only one canoe, one pair of shoes & one pair of feet to go nearly 1000 miles with before winter catches me. Also—& particularly—I wish to look up the Flat River & at least one of its creeks before I finally turn for the Liard as, although there is gold in the water here, I feel convinced that a certain amount comes from the Flat & its creeks, & gold comes before falls much as I want to see them. Also I want to get that skull back to Faille on the Flat as he has a large tub in which I can boil the rest of the meat off & sterilise it.

Wednesday August 18
A warm, hazy, windless day of soft sunshine. I noticed a few young poplars in a low place by a creek with their leaves already gold.

I turned south and came down through the rapids at racing speed—in two hours run down I undid the work of two toiling days. I found that running a canoe down fast water is more difficult than I thought, but I was lucky & lived to learn. Some dont. But there are several things I must ask Faille if I can find him. Had lunch at the top end of the portage & by five o'clock had all my things & the canoe portaged through the woods & laid on the sands of a lovely bay—a relief after that roaring upper cañon with its jagged rocks. Here a man can walk as God meant him to & less like a wounded animal. There was less of a circus this time when I upended the canoe & got it on my head & altogether I am becoming a successful voyageur in the oldest way that Canada has known. But I regret my defeat when within sound of the falls—if only I had had more time—or less weight with me. I bathed after I had finished the portage—the afternoon was very hot & drowsy & the mountains very dreamy in the heat & smoke haze.

Thursday August 19   Midday
Same sort of day as yesterday—still & a sunny haze. I loaded up & ran down to the mouth of Flat River in a little over an hour with hardly any trouble—except once where I almost got into a whirlpool & had to track back a short distance.

I entered the Flat by a snye of the Nahanni—very shallow & I rasped the bottom of the canoe twice in the little rapids. The Flat is a little clearer than the Nahanni, & about the size of the Tees at Dinsdale, only faster in places. A short distance up, I believe, it becomes impossible to travel. Not a sign of Faille, to my intense disgust—not even a dog track. I slipped down a little way towards the mouth to look at two blazed trees & see if there was any message for me on them, but it was on old camp—possibly some Indians last fall or winter. I fired my rifle & shouted & the only answer was the cry of an eagle & the everlasting murmur of water. Finally I decided that he would have gone upstream, so I turned that way, tracking & poling, & in a mile I found his camp—some things lying at his landing on the shingle—a little shack almost finished—a tent with his stuff in it—his bed under the trees & the dogs tied up—which last were pleased to see me.

So I have had lunch by the waters edge—mutton & barley stew, tea, bannock, cheese—the kind that Carpenter got for me—& chocolate, & now I am going to unload. I must wait for Faille as we must do something about that skull pretty soon, although I have it in a fly proof sack & soaked it with a strong solution of Condy's & salt. *Faille* said if I got a head he would bring it out for me next May—I cant take it as I didnt bother to get an *NorthWest Territories* game license—about £15—& I am a resident of Alberta. *Faille* can take it under his trappers license. Also he wants to go down in his big canoe in a week or so to bring up some stuff he cached at the head of the Splits—& he wants me to go with him & load my canoe inside his, which will make travel faster for us—though the Lord knows it seems to me to be one riot of speed coming down the Nahanni. This suits me as I should be on the Liard by September 1—the poplars are turning to gold now. I shall leave my heavy stuff here & go on up the Flat & do some prospecting in the creeks until it is time to leave.

A wonderful view down the river—the green water with touches of gold beside it—the deep green of the spruce above & the pale blues & grays of the mountain tops in a cloudless, hazy sky. A hot day of early autumn—days that make me always think of horse chestnuts & conquerors.

Faille is away in his canoe—whether hunting or not I dont know.

I bathed & shaved & *Faille* appeared, walking, with his rifle. He had shot a caribou a mile up stream & had come back for his axe & the dogs, leaving his big canoe by the dead animal. He was very hungry & so ate the rest of my stew & went away. I did various things & at twilight he came back with a canoe load of meat & three positively bulging dogs. We had supper & talked till eleven—a most interesting man—a trapper from the age of 14. I arranged with him to make you up & match a collection of fur for a lovely stole, if he is lucky on the Nahanni & the Flat. Eight marten or eight mink or two otter or a silver fox or a fisher—in that order. Very kindly he is going to bring out my rams head & skin—I shall send them to that place in Picadilly—isnt it Rowland Ward? will you look & see

& tell me?—& we shall have a head & horns that will beat all at Foresters Lodge. They are not too large for the flat—a moose head, of course, would fill the place completely—also it is so common & a mountain ram is a great treasure. *Faille* admired the horns greatly & hopes his will be as good—when he gets them.

In return I am leaving him my prospectors pan & pick for his use in the spring—they will be useless to me after I leave the Nahanni as the Liard is well travelled & I must race south to beat the winter if I can.

Of course the horns & furs will not see Edmonton till next June as *Faille* cannot get down through the cañons until then, when the first rush of water & ice has gone out, & even then he must wait for the ice on the Great Slave Lake— which will make it perhaps July.

Friday August 20

I intended to set off up the Flat but it looked like rain—the first day the sun has not shone since leaving South Nahanni Post. Also I found too much to do.

Breakfast—porridge & cream—caribou steak—currant bannock & honey— coffee & stewed figs. Then I boiled, stripped & disinfected the rams skull, took out the teeth & packed it ready for *Faille*. He cut up all the caribou we could not eat fresh, & made a rack & smoked it. I baked & cleaned my rifle & pistol & got together food for the Flat River—& mended two paddles & a shirt.

We talked late that night—about animals, the war & foreign countries. *Faille* was taught to read & write by an old Scotsman in the Minnesota woods—is well read, has seen France & England, but will argue at any time—& prove—that the Earth is not round & that there is an undiscovered hot continent hidden away in the South Pacific.

Saturday August 21

A dull cool morning. We got up at five & started life on Norwegian Logging Cake & rice pudding.

Then *Faille* went to work on his shack & I loaded up & pulled out up the Flat. The canoe, relieved of all the heavy stuff, paddles & tracks like a dream.

We talked last night of the falls that I had missed seeing. *Faille* wants to see them as they must be a great wonder—he also wishes to survey the river up to there for his spring trapping. So, if I dont find anything to keep me on the Flat I am to return in four days or so & we set out together with *Faille*'s big canoe & the dogs & nothing but our food & bed rolls once more into that hell of rock &

water. Together in a big canoe we may do it—though it seems in a way fiddling while Rome is burning as today I notice even the mountain sides turning to gold where the poplars are, & we had intended to leave for the Splits & I for the South on August 27. However, I can stand cold fortunately, if I should be caught.

Also I want to have another look at the second creek between the Flat & the falls. It has come to be known as Murder Creek—ask me to tell you of Phil Robertson & the two McLeods—& up it is supposed to be coarse gold. The furs for you & the ram's horns for the flat depend on Faille retaining his life through a lonely winter—cut off from all help & all white men. Nobody has tried to stay in for 7 years—such is the tale of murder, suicide, starvation & Indian killing.

If I find gold up here it may alter my plans—I might stay later & go straight out—as in that case I shall come back to it next year properly equipped. I should stay in here now for the winter only that if I didnt appear you would worry.

I made good time today—10 miles I thing [sic: think] up the Flat from Faille's shack. A cool, misty morning & I came along slowly, finding a little gold in the sands & trying each creek carefully to see if it brought any from the mountains. I lunched on a spruce point, facing a curiously twisted cliff, & with an eddy & beach of black sand below the stones. Just before lunch time the sun started to come through, slowly & mistily, & the clouds fell apart & melted into a soft blue. Everything took on colour & as I ran the canoe's nose into the sand I saw a glitter. For two or three yards every other grain in the ripples was pure yellow gold & there it lay & shone like good farm butter as I dried in the sunshine & ate the tenderest caribou steak in all the world. I swore with excitement—it proves my contention that much of the Nahanni gold comes from the Flat, one reason, if you remember why I turned from the falls, though I did not know then that Murder Creek was near. It had just collected in that one spot—a little coarser than any I had yet seen & in far greater quantity, but still only fine gold. It has, I think[,] come a long way—the Flat is 100 miles in length—perhaps from the mountains that border the Yukon, some of which I can see from here. I found gold all along this afternoon—if I find much more I shall, in any case, try to get Gordon & come in very early next year & track it down—there is a fortune somewhere, both here & on the Nahanni. Let it be mine.

As I ate & watched that yellow stuff, I wished that I could come home this winter just for three weeks or so, & see you & try my luck at getting engaged— & then come back here & have one damned good try for the gold for all next year. Either alone again or with a real man like Gordon—no more little counter jumping bounders like Dennis—& a proper outfit & engine—not a waste-of-time lift on Cousins scows.

What do you think? Have I enough money to ask a girl to marry me even without the gold & would a girl wait a year for me? I know which girl I like best [now?] & I dont suppose she will remain single for ever—I invested 700 dollars in Winnipeg Electric before leaving Edmonton & there will be all my income since then, untouched[,] to invest. I should like to have a home some day & not always to be a bachelor, much as I love this life in the mountain west. Remember—this is only a long letter to you written bit by bit & it wants answering.

This afternoon was a dream of amazing beauty. I headed west into the sun & the glittering water—wading, tracking & paddling. A lovely haze, like that of an English summer, gave a softness to the country. To right & left were the cliffs & pebble shores, the green & golden forest, & sometimes the bare grass downs of the foothills—the winter range of the sheep, that far down south would be the winter range of Dick Brown's horses. Behind, the mountains of the Nahanni—ahead, the blue mountains of the Flat & the Yukon border. After that bellowing hell of the upper cañon of the Nahanni, the Flat was a dream of peace & beauty. It has its rapids, but there were long & lovely reaches where the trout jumped & little brown waterfowl nested—& always the splendid chocolate, black & golden butterfly & the one of pure gold.

As I sat here finishing supper I heard a branch snap on the far bank & there was a great black bear walking along. I lay watching him over the sights of my rifle but did not shoot, as why should I try to kill the beast simply in order to say I had shot a bear. I couldnt use the skin or meat, nor could Faille as he would not know for perhaps a week that I had shot it. I am rather out of sympathy with the pot hunting big game hunter. Unfortunately it was too dark to take his photo. He saw my camp at last & scampered away up the hill—pausing now & then for breath & wheezing noisily like an aged gentleman.

I am writing this by the firelight & cooking—must have used about a cord of wood to make a blaze to write by. Bed now—a lovely starlit night. Good night.

Sunday August 22
I lay for a little in bed last night, watching the Aurora. It was doing all sorts of things—first it made the Sunshade & stood up in long spokes, quivering. Then it broke that up & curled into the Question Mark & lay still right across the sky. Next it waved across from N.E. to N.W. in long ribbons, & when I fell asleep it

was all over the sky in weird blobs and patches—putting out the stars with its pale green light.

I was aroused suddenly by a heavy plunge & sat up & reached for my rifle, thinking it was the bear back & swimming across in quest of bacon & honey from my canoe. Nothing landed & the plunging went on at intervals close to me, so I went off to sleep again just as the moon was rising, red in the mists. It must have been a beaver or an otter watching my fire. The beavers had been at work cutting down trees where I had camped.

A lovely morning of haze & sunlight—too much haze as I cant see the far mountains properly & I want to know what they are like. I have come about 5 miles I think & am lunching by the river on a glorious stew of caribou, beans, barley & wild onions, & cheese[,] figs, bannock & tea. All this game makes sweet & tender stews—also the stew is incredibly rich as we are prodigal with it when it is plentiful.

The valley has widened to a great dale & the river bawls over the stones & boulders between the quiet reaches. More trees are turning & the hillsides have a glow of red from the fruits & little plants. The gold continues in the sand—if I can come again & trace it to its source this will have been a most valuable reconnaissance—it can be no more as time is too short now, & lucky to have been that much. The whole idea I had long had but I only decided to carry it out when Dr Stott advised a cessation of farm work & a rest in England for the summer.

I told Faille this & he said that to battle a canoe up the Nahanni was a quaint idea of rest, but that, as I was the colour of an Indian, no doubt all was well.

If I come back I shall try to get Gordon & if we can trace down the source of this yellow stuff I'll give you Edenhall.

I shall go on up the Flat today & tomorrow & if I seem to get no closer I shall turn & go with Faille to look at the sands of murder creek & the falls.

I saw a cow moose just before lunch. It never saw me, but walked out of the bush about three hundred yards ahead of me onto a shingle bar—drank, splashed a little, walked by the river for a while & turned again into the woods. What great animals they are.

A warm, still afternoon. I made good time—the river valley is still wide but it is getting faster & with more rapids.

I am camped on a point facing a great, scarred mountain side with a few spruce here & there growing amongst the rock slides. The water here is very still & gentle but above & below are rapids. I am having my supper beside the fire—

7:30 & the sun has gone behind the mountain. Marmots are piping amongst the rocks over the river—otherwise no sound but that of the water.

At 5:30 I was poling up a riffle when I heard a sound on the shingle near me. I looked up & about 70 yards away was a great bull moose walking to the river to drink—on the same side as I was & behind me—a lovely shot. I ran the canoe on to a rock, very quietly laid down the pole & stepped out into the river to get my camera from the bow. He was not in the least afraid & we stood looking at each other. I took his photo twice—side & front view—it reminded me of the playing cards in your desk at home. I said Good-bye & went on my way but he stayed stock still in the water looking after me for a long time until I turned the bend. The animals here dont seem to know men—I was right when I said at the gateway of the first cañon that A River came out of Eden.

I am very fortunate to see these things & these wonderful places. I shall never forget this summer, all my life—it will be a great treasure to me, such as few are privileged to have—only vagabond scamps & neurotics (?) who obstinately persist in going Where the Strange Trails go down, as the western novelists say.

By the way, when I said Faille was getting you a set of marten, they will be, of course, a present from me. I didnt mean to foist them on to you to pay for. I have a good mind to get a fisher or something also for the girl who pleases me—you must be sure & tell me what you think of my suggestion of last night.

I can see that I am not going to have time to get far into the mountains of the Flat. Tomorrow night will almost certainly be my furthest west, but if I come again with Gordon there will be no turning—we will plumb this matter to the bottom.

Dont show this letter to anybody—read out bits if you want to but remember that it is a letter & that in it I have made some pretty personal remarks about some people & have said things that are secret to you & me.

Monday August 23rd

At 4:30 a squirrel ran clean over my face & roused me to start the day with a burst of bad language. There always seems to be one squirrel round a camp—& later on a pair of whisky jacks. I lay & watched the sun rise in the mists & then got up, had breakfast & broke up my camp. As I was washing I saw a caribou come out of the woods about 500 yards away, drink & walk back—the first I have ever seen. A very pretty animal—smaller, more graceful & lighter coloured than a moose.

I went on up the Flat, watching the sands & the creeks. I have seen enough to convince me that this gold comes from further up into the mountains than I am able or have time to go this year—but I know that it is here. I came to a big creek of clear, glassy water coming in on the left. I did not want to leave it untried but to test it thoroughly I had to get well into its valley & above the flood level of the Flat. So I turned up it & tracked & pulled the canoe up rapid after rapid & am now camped & having lunch where the rapids are becoming too numerous to make a further advance by canoe worth while. I cant find any signs to make me thing [*sic*: think] that this creek brings the gold in to the Flat River—a fleck or so, that is all. However, I am going to leave the canoe here & trust that nothing will get into it, & go ahead on foot this afternoon. Then when I have seen all that I can I shall come back here to sleep & start off for Faille's early tomorrow, with a view to a second try for the falls the day after.

I went ahead a long way—enough to satisfy myself, as far as was possible, that I was not on the track of the gold.

I came back to camp & bathed in the warm, clear water & had some chocolate, & decided then & there to make a long day of it & to turn & run for Faille's camp. It was a glorious afternoon—the sunshine seemed to go clear through me & the valleys & mountains stood perfectly silent in the soft haze—except for the sound of water & a little warm breeze. I sat barefooted in the canoe & let her fly down the creek. In that glassy water I could see the stones slip past beneath me as I ran down the rapids & in the deep pools the shadow of the canoe glided over the gravels 20 feet beneath me down in the cool green water. In half an hour I was down to the Flat, having heard the canoe grind twice over the boulders in the fast water. The same thing happened at the first rapid on the Flat & after that I was more careful & lowered her down two of the worst places by hand. I was perfectly happy—few people know what that means—some never are. The perfect day—the sense of power & speed—the gliding swiftly past the cliffs in the still reaches, & then the roar of water ahead—the canoe gains speed, flies down a hill of water into the waves, through the foam & out into the calm below—it is a splendid way of travel.

Four & a half hours it took me—I reached Faille's in the dusk with the shadows over the valleys, having come, I think, 25 miles. The last rapid but one above Failles I couldn't remember—& couldnt see. I stood up as the canoe slid down the hill & saw a barrier of white foam & uproar across the river—with the suspicion of a black gap on the right. I put the canoe at it hard & we seemed to hang in air for a minute—then a streak of spray and foam & we were in the eddy below. *Faille* made me supper while I unloaded—I was very hungry.

+

*Hell's Gate Rapid, called "Figure-of-Eight Rapids" by Faille
and "Rapid-That-Runs-Both-Ways" by RMP.*

Tuesday August 24

Up at 5:30 & a busy day. I laid up & pitched the canoe, washed all my clothes (two of everything, & mostly in tatters) baked & cooked & generally niggered. F*aille* finished his shack—we lit candles & ate rather a marvellous supper as a house warming. Am awfully tired & must go to bed as we leave for that upper cañon once more at seven tomorrow. The falls & Murder Creek this time—no turning back.

Wednesday August 25

After supper 9:30 p.m. Camp at mouth of Murder Creek. It would have been a perfect day but for the N.W. wind which drove the smoke of the great fire on the Yukon border across the country in a heavy brown pall which obscured the sun—occasionally it shone through it a ball of red. The air was full of wood ash & one got terribly thirsty & sore eyed. Very trying & the close atmosphere made the sandflies bad this afternoon. Now the wind has dropped & the air is clearing.

Was wakened at three this morning by the wolves. Saw tracks of lynx, fisher, wolf & marten on the sand where we had lunch. Worked hard & fast & shot the figure of 8 rapid, that I had to portage, in Failles war canoe—thrown out into the whirlpool at the first try—at the second driven against the point, but I grabbed a rock & held & we pulled her through into the upper whirlpool by hand. We hope to be at the falls tomorrow evening. I am tired & sleepy & am just going to look for a level spot & unroll my tarpaulin & sleeping bag & get down to it. Faille is talking hard all this time—as a man talks who wont have much chance of talking for another six months, except to himself. The creek water a lovely sparkling blue—it cuts away back into richly forested mountains, & there, according to tradition, it the coarse gold. No sound but that of a rapid away below.

Thursday August 26   Falls
Fine clear morning—smoke & ashes gone. Worked up through the cañons with much swearing & damning & lunched on a spruce point just beyond the camp where I killed the sheep & turned back. Both wet & we lit a big fire to dry & warm. Crossed over & tracked up over the rocks—*Faille* steering, I tracking. We heard the roar of the falls simultaneously & shouted. I was first round the bend & saw them first—I hauled on the track line & pulled *Faille* into view. They were within less than half a mile of my last camp—their thunder had been choked off from me by the deep twisting cañon & the mists that I had seen in the early mornings were their spray floated down the valley. A sight worth travelling to see—counting the cataract above [,] the drop must be 200 *feet* or over & they are split in the middle by a great tower of rock. We went up over the portage trail & came out onto a little hill & there lay the upper Nahanni stretching on between low forested banks, calm & beautiful like a great lake, on into the evening. Beyond was the sunset, & the mountains of the Yukon set against it. *Faille* showed me where the whisky jacks hid blueberries for their winter feed & we also fell to on blueberries, hips & haws, cranberries, raspberries, evergreen berries & such flotsam. Took photos & back to camp for supper—it rained a little at night & the spray drifted over us.

Friday August 27   Return to Faille's
Up early & cooked breakfast before calling Faille. He had withdrawn completely, tortoise like, beneath his tarp & I couldnt tell which end was which. Shot down through the rapids & lunched at Faille's. I set up my camp & made bannock & collected my stuff, ready to leave & he finished his shack & put his gear inside. We had supper inside by candle light—a tremendous supper.

I have just contrived to remember two names which have been bothering me—Despoina, out of Maurice Hewlett's "Rest Harrow" & Brillat Savarin the French epicure of Bourg en Bresse. I am so relieved that my memory still holds.

I am very sorry to leave these mountains for the Liard & the south but summer wont last for ever.

Saturday August 28   To the first splits

Early mists gave way to the most lovely morning of all—never have I seen such colouring of greens & grays, sunshine & soft clouds as in the upper cañon. We ran down 40 miles about altogether—it was all too fast. Had lunch at the great gateway & I took a photo of Faille ahead in his canoe, going through. I paddled my own canoe down as it was just too large to go inside his. I would have put it in, of course, to help him, but I was glad it wouldnt go as I wanted to say that I had taken my own canoe unaided 130 miles up the Nahanni & back. On the Nahanni & Flat alone, I shall have travelled 350 miles.

We found an old camp & scow in the afternoon—a number of men had worked there but it was deserted—perhaps for two or three years—& everything left.

It was like coming through fairyland—later it turned colder & the shadows fell in the cañon. We came out in the evening into the upper splits—the beavers were at work & we saw several. Camped within a few miles of the lower cañon. Very hungry & ate a large supper. I slept under a big spruce from which I could see the upper mountains with the northern lights playing over them.

Deadmen's Valley

to

the Twisted Mountain

Sunday August 29

When I woke up under the big spruce tree everything was wet & shining with dew & a thick mist hid the river & canoes which were only a few yards away. I got up, dressed, pulled a few dry spruce twigs for kindling, stepped on a sharp snag with my moccasined foot & fell down the mossy bank on to the stones below—crashing my hand in exactly the same place as I did in Kensington Gardens on the morning of Marigold's party. I lay there & groaned & swore until I felt better—the dogs cheerfully wagging their tails the while. Then I lit the fire & I called Faille & the sun came over the mountains which began to appear through the mists. For a time there was a glory in the sky & then suddenly the mists rolled

+

The South Nahanni River near the Hot Springs, 1927.

back & river, mountains & forests flashed out in that raving blaze of colour that only comes after rain. We ate an enormous breakfast & started at 7:30 towards the cañon.

All through till midday it was like a morning in fairyland—my last. We slid through the great mountains & down rapid after rapid—hardly talking, sometimes a long way apart, watching the green, gray & purple of the canyon sides with the soft clouds moving over the walls & pouring down the gullies. We shot the bad rapid by my cache—twice I felt the canoe graze rocks & I swallowed hard for the second time on the Nahanni as I put the canoe at the last fall. She leapt over, buried her nose in foam & shipped half a bucketful & her stern dropped plumb on a rock. I sailed into the eddy praising the saints—particularly the Holy St James of Compostella.

My cache of bacon & milk was safe—not an animal had bothered it & I picked it up before we started again.

We made the hot springs at the lower gateway for lunch.

I believe Faille made a dam & sat in it. I went up to where the hot sulphur water ran over stones in a shallow stream, & lay there in the sun with it running over me. The Indians had come there to bathe for generations past & had cut many of the trees & all the brush for fires, so that there was a beautiful meadow of wild hay round about. The moose seem to come there & there were fresh bear tracks by the stream. I saw a humming bird amongst the flowers.

The afternoon turned cold & windy & we ran down through the Splits without incident to Faille's cache at the twisted mountain. Got there late & immediately made our beds & put up our shelters as it looked like rain. Had supper in the dark & talked a long time.

Monday August 30
It poured during the night—an excellent arrangement as we were safe in bed. A very misty morning, early. I baked enough bannock for myself for a week, pitched the hole the big rock had made in my canoe, shaved & chored round generally. A lovely, sparkling afternoon—some wind but not enough to hold one back. I had an early lunch & left at one for South Nahanni Post—we said Good-bye & for a long time I saw Faille & the dogs standing on a point of rock until I rounded the bend. I travelled hard without stopping for six hours, through & out of the Splits & into a calm, silent reach under Nahanni Butte & within three or four miles of the Indian village. The utter silence is the strangest thing of all after a month spent with the sound of water always present. As I ran down I turned now & then to look back at the distant walls of the cañon & all the mountain world that I was leaving—I shall never forget it. The evening looked like storm but it held off. A bear came into camp probably around two a.m. I crawled out from under the net & tarp & put a cartridge in the rifle & at the sound of the bolt it paddled away, upsetting the frying pan & wash bowl, & I went sleepily back to bed.

Tuesday August 31st
Put to sea in thick mist at 8:25. The mist lifted & showed a gorgeous place under the Butte & a lovely day. I passed the Indian village & stopped at what I thought was Le Fler's shack—the trader. Nobody there & I asked three Indians if he was back. They said he was so his place must be by their village. I couldnt be bothered to go back as I can get all I want at Fort Liard 80 miles upstream. There should be letters for me there too—havent heard from a soul since May.

I hit the trail hard—pretty easy water & I travelled till eight & came 17 miles up the Liard. River very low & from 7 onwards I was looking vainly for a place to land & camp.

Wednesday Sept*ember* 1st

During the night it clouded over, blew & finally poured & is still pouring. I got up once to make the canoe safe from wind. Didnt have the tarp up but had it wrapped round my sleeping bag so when the rain came I just pulled it over my head & slept on till 7:30. Then I got up, cut poles & made a shelter under which I consumed large quantities of porridge & milk, bacon & bannock & am now writing. I wait for opportunities like this as sometimes I get days behindhand with this letter owing to hard travel or something. It is a pity as if I could write when things happen I could tell you much more vividly about them. This is the first breakfast in the rain since I started in June. I shall wait & do various odd jobs till midday & then start anyhow—get soaked if necessary. But I think it may stop raining—in any case one cant wait for rain at this time of year.

12:10 p.m.   What an unspeakable day—its worse now, & I am going to have lunch, having done all I can think of.

1:45   Had lunch & cleaned rifle. Still raining but I am going to load up & go.

Travelled about 9 miles—it rained most of the time but was fair while I made camp—on a beach opposite a mountain side.

Thursday Sept*ember* 2nd

Breakfast time. It poured during the night & when I got up, but is not raining at the moment. In any case I am going on—I am exactly one third of the way to Fort Liard & should be well over half way by this evening as I am not going to have anything hot for lunch. The wood is too sodden now to go to the trouble of making fire three times a day.

Went on & tracked up the shallow Flint Rapids. Still raining & wet up to the knees. Came unexpectedly about 3:00 p.m. to Arthur George's shack, a trapper from the Cadotte River near the Battle whom I knew. He & his wife were there isolating themselves in this rich fur country in order to give their son a good education & to get enough money to start a sheep ranch & apiary. They made me stay the night & entreated me very kindly.

Friday Sept*ember* 3rd

Still misting a little. The Georges gave me beans, bannock & cheese & told me to spend the night with their neighbours "the boys" 18 miles away. I made good time up the Little & the Flutch rapids—close to the mountains again—& reached the boys at six in the evening. Eppler & Mulholland—trappers—they took me in & fed me & I slept warmly on the floor by the stove.

Saturday Sept*ember* 3rd

It began to pour in the night & by breakfast the roof was leaking. We had breakfast with the rain plopping on the table & later found tarpaulins & covered half the roof—so we had rain in one half of the shack & fair weather in the other. Kept the stove roaring to dry the water as it fell. It never stopped—the sun has not shone for four days now & it has rained solidly. I am getting close to British Columbia.

Eppler & I slept & read old Saturday Evening Posts—Mulholland cooked & sat on his bed & shot mice with a .22 rifle.

Later we argued long on the merits of king & president. Every 3 hours or so we had dinner, to vary the monotony. I expect us all to be very bilious.

Sunday Sept*ember* 4

As you see I lost a day in the date somewhere.

A lovely morning. I was up first & down to my canoe loading up. Then I came back & lit the fire & Mulholland is now making breakfast—a good one by the look of it.

Travelled all day & made good distance south. The wind was fair so I ripped up a grain sack & put up a mast & sail which helped a good deal but made me lose my temper a [lot?]. The sun soon went in & the N.W. wind brought down cold looking clouds—the further I went the faster the water got & I had to wade a good deal & get wet. At five I passed an encampment of Indians—couldnt find a camping place & went on till after seven looking for one. An overhanging willow removed my remaining pair of glasses into the Liard—I now have two pairs of spectacles left. Temper got worse & by supper time I was incoherent absolutely but supper, a warm fire & bed made me whistle a little.

Monday Sept*ember* 5

As soon as I got to bed it began to pour & is still lashing—this is about the fifth day. I lay warmly & listened to it—but it made me get up later. I was comfortable

& the thought of making fire with wet wood & cooking held me down. It is now nine. I have had an enormous breakfast to keep out the damp & as Fort Liard is only about 14 miles away I may as well load up & go—& get wet. The rain may never stop so it is no use waiting. That lovely month on the Nahanni when the sun always shone seems like another life.

Tuesday Sept*ember* 6   **7:30 a.m.**
Just finished breakfast & am sitting by the fire in sight of Fort Liard—perhaps 1½ miles away—waiting for hot water to wash in before going in. Didnt wash yesterday—too wet & miserable. It has rained for 7 days now—everything is either wet or damp—one gets quite used to it. I sailed furiously yesterday up river at a fearful speed & kept remembering Parker's famous sermon "The Lord blew with his winds & they were scattered." I was nearly scattered—twice—once in swift water & once when I took the wrong channel at the mouth of Muskeg River & hit a shingle bar. It was awfully cold—blowing & raining like the Deuce—& I was there jammed in the shallows in the middle of the Liard—half a mile wide, fast & rough. Got off, however, & had lunch before a fire but couldnt get very warm being too wet. Expected snow & I see it this morning all along the tops of the foothills over the river. Here it rains as usual & during the night poured whole water.

However, in to the fort I go—there may be letters there for me & in any case I have a sack of stuff there, including mittens—see end of volume. Also I want some things from the Bay. Looking forward to letters—I do hope Cousins has left them there—I may sleep at his camp tonight—it is 8 miles beyond the fort—quite enough in this weather—& the last shelter I shall get till the Forks of the Nelson—50 miles away. I am 210 miles on the way home now from the falls of the Nahanni—my furthest point north.

Reached Fort Liard & found Cousins' men there with their sawmill set up & working. DeRosier & his wife welcomed me & asked me to stay with them for the night. I accepted & hauled my gear into their warm shack to dry. They had letters for me & so had the Bay & the old priest at the mission—Père Gouet—all dated in May before you knew I was coming up here. I was awfully glad to get them.

A lovely day now of sun & blue sky—everybody here is most kind—two people are baking real bread for me & one making me a sack of doughnuts. I am living on the fat of the land & have been given butter, honey, milk, beans & apples so that I have bought all I need & only spent 33 shillings. I believe the fact that I reached the falls of the Nahanni & travelled 300 miles alone on the Nahanni & the Flat has something to do with it as that has long been the ghost country of the Liard.

Am away tomorrow—just going back to the mission to talk to the Father, who has kept my letters & extra food all this time for me. A Parisian, & in the Territories for over 30 years—once away to Rome & Paris.

Letters from Gordon, Marigold, Rafaelle & Edwin—he as usual says "remember, we are now middle aged & take care"!!!

Wednesday September 7

Lunch on a shingle bar two hours travel from the fort & all my stuff is lying about drying in the sun—some things got damp in the weeks rain. A gorgeous morning—all light, & the colours much the same as in your little prints of London. I am now about 15 miles from the Yukon & British Columbia borders & tomorrow I should be out of the N.W.T. where I have seen so much since I left Fort Smith. Looks as though it might rain later—a stray mosquito or two about. The river is running straight down from a blue mountain, snow capped now, & is pretty fast—wind against me.

I said Good bye & left Fort Liard laden with winter clothes, grub & letters for Fort Nelson & the Forks of the Nelson—50 miles up, & my next post. Saw the Father on the point, waving & looking after me for a long time. Must load up & go now. I have my letters to read while I eat—everything sounds so civilized—I have no doubt whatever that you were not sat on at Ascot. If Faille can get you the marten we shall lead the world.

9:10 p.m. & am writing by the firelight—camp made & a good supper eaten. I made amazingly good time this afternoon—only one bit of trouble—a fast cut bank with sweepers—just below here. Must be 13 miles or so from Fort Liard. An afternoon of unusual beauty. Long reaches of calm, quiet water with wild fowl— fresh mountains coming into view, snow capped—a sky of bronze with clouds like grey goose feathers & an arch round the sun—a sky of winter storm & yet warm & soft. Autumn everywhere—it makes me think of conquerors & hot roast chestnuts, tobogganing in the Waldy's field, & coming in all muddy from the garden to my soldiers or to those books of adventure in the north west that Uncle John always gave me—like "Murder Point." Perhaps he wanted me to come out here.

A great harvest moon rising over the mountains & lighting up the snow. Moths & the smell of wood smoke & dead leaves.

Going to read my letters again before going to bed. I will be a good boy another time but remember that I am so obstinate that I cant be bullied into it by anybody.

I knew that a long time alone away from cities would clear my mind on this matter. I should never marry anybody I didnt love—why suggest it? I got to know *Marigold* at Wheatsheaf that week end at Alan Portman's—that, our days at Oxford & Lynmouth & our visit to Amy & Boucher[.] I enjoyed most of every-thing during my time at home.

If I can get home this winter it will be only a little while, as you will see from the end of this book that there will be much to see to & we must be watching the ice on the Great Slave by my birthday.

Thursday Sept*ember* 8th   Lunch time
Lovely day—clear & a little windy at times. Made good distance but haven't much idea where I am or how far I have gone—possibly not so far as I think as the river winds so.

A perfect afternoon—river wide & calm & I made very good time. Am camped by a trappers shack in the spruce trees. The man is away & the door locked but it makes an excellent camping place. The moon, almost full, has come up over the hills & is shining through the great trees & is reflected in the quiet river. That, my camp & fire & the lights of the Aurora make a beautiful picture with the two cabins & their moose antlers & the high set cache behind. It is as light as day—a perfect evening.

Friday Sept*ember* 9th   Lunch time
I must have camped last night in the Yukon—I am now two miles past Rivière la Biche & well into British Columbia. I should be at the forks of the Nelson tomorrow evening. A splendid morning—intensely clear & sharp & pretty hot. I lay in bed & watched the sun rise & rose with it. Travelled for nearly four hours when the midday wind began to bother me so I put in here to a hot sheltered spot & bathed, spread out all the stuff to take the damp out of flour etc., changed my things & washed t'others & cooked. The wind has dropped now & as soon as the rice is done I am going on—but I could stay here a long time & cool my bare feet on the stones.

The country is beautiful, soft wooded hills—no mountains—& clear streams. The Liard is clear & green—very different from the mud we had to drink out of it lower down in July.

Saturday Sept*ember* 10th

Another perfect, windless afternoon. Went along past a deserted Indian village—they are all out now, fishing & hunting for the winter—& round a great bend. I met the first man I have seen since Fort Liard, a fellow called Thomas—owner of the shack by which I camped—paddling a Chipewyan skiff down stream. He had been away up the Beaver—apparently a good river & navigable for about 70 miles, last 30 all trouble—& was going home. The fire I saw from the falls of the Nahanni was at the head of the Beaver. Beyond, I think, personally. I said I was about 16 miles from the forks & hoped to be there this evening. He said my map was wrong & that I was nearly 30 miles away & it would take 2 long days. Either I am mad or everybody else in the country is—they all seem to me to overestimate distances. However, I shall know by tomorrow who is right.

This is seven o'clock. I have had breakfast, washed & packed everything & am just waiting for the mist to clear so that I can see what I am up to, as I can hear the Liard chuckling to itself over some stones & Thomas said that the fastest bit of water between here & the Nelson is just round the next bend by a wooded hill. This mist settled down while I was eating. I was up before sunrise but the sun is well up now & [setting?] the most vague & dream like colours through the mists onto the river & the forest.

I found an old powder horn where I slept—the powder gone & the strap long since rotted away. The first recorded journey of white men up the Liard is 1789—but there must have been others, lonely voyageurs, before then. Perhaps some Scotsman from the Hudson's Bay—or more probably a Frenchman from old Quebec or exiled from Versailles.

Lunch time   Havent come very far. I crawled on through the mist till it lifted & then spent most of the morning working my way up the bad place—not dangerous like the Nahanni but very hard—a swirling mass of swift green water rushing between steep banks with fallen trees. Then I struck a beautiful reach, almost like a lake & from here on Thomas said it was good going up to the forks. I have raised new hills into view this morning & away down to the south west along this reach the main mass of the Rockies has come into sight—three ranges, blue in the distance.

Amazingly still & clear—not a sound. The morning has been cool with a bronze, winter sky. Now the sun is coming out & if the sky stays clear it will be hot.

+

RMP engaged in a characteristic activity.

Sunday Sept*ember* 11   7:30 a.m.

A cloudy morning & the wind has gone back in the night into the north east—it may bring snow this time. I have just had a large breakfast & am ready to go—having shaved, washed & treated myself to my one remaining new toothbrush.

I travelled 5½ hours hard yesterday afternoon & got into camp very hungry. Must have eaten too big a supper as I was wakeful.

My friend Mr Thomas was mad—not I. This is written on the north west bank of the Liard, opposite the mouth of the Fort Nelson River up which I have to go about 200 miles. Thomas probably underestimated my travelling powers—I may not be good for much in this life but I can move, & in addition I get as obstinate as three mules & a Scotsman under these conditions. Wish you could see me—brown, wiry, & tattered. Thomas would notice my glasses & probably set me down as a travelling poet & correspondingly incapable.

Yesterday was a lovely afternoon—one of the golden days of the year, silent, blue & sunny & with every shade of red, gold & green in the bush—that rich smell of earth & forest in the warm air as one moved along the bank.

The Liard is very fast here & is bad from now on up. I shall have some trouble getting in to the Nelson, but once in I believe it is a nice little river to travel. I am glad to be off this great Liard where the winds sweep across & one can see for miles ahead. It is 4 miles up to the Hudson's Bay post of Nelson Forks for which I am carrying mail. I may hit them up for a lunch—must away now as the wind is rising & I want to be in the Nelson before anything starts up.

Landed in the Hudson's Bay post just as the rain started. Stayed for lunch & as it poured I am staying the night. Lots of new bread, honey & fresh moose meat & I might as well have a little out of the Company besides dividends. David Hooker, whom I met in Simpson, in charge. Teddy Trimble whom I met in Fitzgerald is here, & also Maloney, a trapper—formerly a gold prospector from the Yukon.

They say that the Nelson River is easy, & that if I can average 15 miles a day on the Liard I can make Fort Nelson in four sleeps—maybe sell my canoe there & go on on horseback to the Peace. Sold my old rifle in Fort Liard for £8-10\-.

Eight Indians—Slaveys—whose camp I passed yesterday at midday came in this afternoon. They sit in the Indian room & talk & smoke, look at everything & buy a little, camp outside & will leave again tomorrow. Asiatics, set in a cold, hard country. Wherever I go I am much questioned about the Nahanni. People hint at gold on the Flat—there have been many rumours for many years—I say nuffin. I noticed that the old priest was curious to know what I had been up to on the Flat. Still pouring—I am sitting in bed in the Bay House, writing. Unless it is raining absolutely whole water I shall go on tomorrow.

Monday September 12   Lunch time

A fine bright morning after the rain. Had breakfast & waited while the Indians made their trade & letters for Fort Nelson & the outside were written for me to carry. The Indians left for the Liard—I left up river & the others will go after lunch, leaving Hooker alone again.

The Fort Nelson seems a good river to travel & I ought soon to cover the 100 miles between here & the Fort. Great flights of geese are passing over, honking, heading southwards for the winter. I go in the same direction & I expect the first snow is not far behind—warm & soft though the day is. The yellow leaves are blowing from the poplars & floating past down the river.

How each river has a beauty of its own? The Nelson here is about the size of the Thames at Hampton Court—calm & quiet, not let loose upon the land, a mass of green destruction like the Liard, nor yet a bonny, bellowing fechter like the South Nahanni. The banks are not lumbered up with dead & uprooted trees, but are even & regular & beautifully forested down to the waters edge, & beyond are the low hills of a gentle valley, covered with birch, poplar, cotton wood & spruce—green & gold.

About four o'clock came down a sudden deluge—I proceeded unmoved, being now in *British Columbia* where it has as much right to rain as in the Lake District.

It cleared & I crossed the river & paddled alongside a cliff for over an hour. It was curiously rounded by the river & bored with holes. Every kind of fern & moss & lichens of all colours were on it & high above[,] the trees of the forest hung over. High hills began to rise to the south—I shall be into them tomorrow. The day went out in a blaze of golden glory such as I have rarely seen. The last minutes of the sun lit up the cliffs & forest in a mass of red & gold & this was reflected perfectly in the still water—a glorious sight & I have never seen any like it. One feels that it is a great privilege to have seen the beauty of these rivers. Later the western sky took on ripples & feathers of red. The glory left the east bank & it became blue & cold, & in the west the tall spruce stood out like spires against the sky—like the spruce of the "Magic Forest."

I am writing by the firelight. It is clear & cold now & utterly still. The moon is up & the mists that come after rain are rising from the river & spreading over the hills in silver clouds. I think tomorrow morning will be cold & misty but the day should be clear, sunny & hot. One can travel fast on this river—easy going, a relief after the wildness of the Nahanni & the great strength & speed of the Liard.

I am anxious to know what you think of my plans to take one of the Christmas special excursions home from the West. I believe that on the Flat River is the gold, & if Gordon will come I can get at it. But if we go it will mean a full year in there & I shall not see you or Marigold. Is it right & possible to get engaged & then go away into the mountains? I believe if a girl was fond of one she would wait a year—it might mean horses & a car & all that makes life good to live—all except this—the open life, that no money can buy. I wonder if she likes me.

If only you could see this silver night by the river—or even one tenth of all that I have seen this summer. It all looks so cold & barren on the map, & when you get to the heart of it you find humming birds, wild bees & tiger lilies, fruit, a warm sunlight that strikes right through you & colour & loveliness without end. And so to bed, first setting the porridge.

Tuesday Sept*ember* 13

Lunch on a shingle point opposite Maloney's shack—one quarter of the way to Fort Nelson. Early morning very cold, damp & misty—warmer now but still rather a dull, wintry sky. I can hear the cranes passing over head every now & then. Travelled $4\frac{1}{4}$ hours before lunch. River a little faster.

Wednesday Sept*ember* 14

Just finished breakfast. It froze hard during the night & I found the canoe all rimed out in white frost. The sun is just clearing the mists & it looks like a lovely day—the first real fall day. Yesterday afternoon was warm & sunny & I travelled for over 5 hours, & today should see me over half way to the fort. It snowed on Battle River a year ago yesterday & I have, in my three previous Septembers in Canada, never seen it go so late as this without snow, so every warm day of sunshine now is a day snatched from the winter.

Passed two camps of Indians yesterday afternoon but nobody in them—all out hunting, & canoes & everything left behind. I was wondering—did you snatch that £60—that I found for you from the Income Tax people? Be sure that Mr. Brodrick gets it for you & claims it in the future.

Lunch time   Travelled 4 hours—lovely hot day with a tang in the air. Not a cloud, not a breath, not a sound. I notice that the birch turns before the other trees—a hillside tree mainly. Should be at the halfway creek in another hour or so.

After supper. 10:15 p.m.   I passed the halfway in 45 minutes—my reckoning of distance is getting pretty good. Two more full days, if the weather gives me a chance, should put me in sight of the fort. There was a shack at the halfway—I think Teddy Trimble's—& another later on—both empty. A hot afternoon—but at four I saw the first sundogs of the year form & take their stand, one on either side of the sun. Then a great arch built itself round the sun, & long grey wisps of cloud came out of the north—the forerunners of snow & yet no wildfowl have gone over south today. Half an hour after sunset it began to freeze & is freezing hard now. I stopped at seven by a little stream & cleared the ground on the point & built a winter camp—the frost doesnt bother me but I hate the rain like any cat. The moon is up &, with the stars, is reflected in the river below—the moon with a halo round it, & a little breeze blowing out of the north. It may be as cold tonight as you ever have it in London & yet I was hot in the afternoon sunshine & only a couple of weeks ago saw a humming bird by the springs. I am not sleepy & am sitting on my spread out sleeping bag by the fire doing odd jobs—I must go to bed soon as I want to be up at five, if I can face the early morning cold with that much resolution.

Thursday September 15

Up at 5:45. Quite a hard frost but I slept warmly by the fire under my lean-to & was very comfortable. Travelled three & a half hours & stopped early for lunch. I seem to go better & faster after lunch these days & so am going to try a long afternoon—feel weak, empty & evil tempered before lunch. A lovely morning—cold in the shade but hot here on the bank. In about two to three hours I should see the wreck of an old steamer—that is the 75 mile landmark & about 25 from the fort.

Evening   Saw no wreck, so I may not be so far on as I thought. A sunny afternoon, & now warm & cloudy, no frost. A comfortable camp in the spruce & a good fire going, so all is provided for. I hardly expect to see Fort Nelson tomorrow now. The river is getting faster, here & there a little rapid, & a lot of very awkward sandy points & shallows where one cant paddle or track & the pole sinks deep at every stroke.

I thought you would never have taken Mrs Fenwick & Kathleen to Margaret Marks. Wasnt it rather a mistake.

I am so wondering if you went to Boucher's wedding—I do hope you did as I am very fond of him.

Friday September 16th

I found the wreck—only a quarter of a mile away & within sight of camp, but in the dusk I could not be certain that it was not a pile of driftwood & dead trees. It was by a rapid—an awkward place—& looked very forlorn. Somebody had hung the lifebelts up on trees in the bush.

A warm, sunny morning but a foolish, blustering wind was blowing which, though it helped me in some places, bothered me in others & made me fume & swear. A wind ruffles the water & makes it all look alike so that one cant spot the shallows & swift water. Also it makes a light canoe very difficult to steer as it can whirl it about like a cork. A wind seems to me sometimes such a silly, pointless, swaggering thing—I regret to say that it reminds me very much of Edwin & Mr Fenwick when they start to shout & bellow at waitresses, servants, railway officials & others who, by accident of birth or lack of money, have the misfortune to come beneath them.

I rounded a bad bend about midday & was looking out for a place to lunch when I saw a grey scow tied up to the far bank. People were on shore lunching & they called to me to come over. It was the Hudsons Bay scow taking Corporal & Mrs Barber of the British Columbia Police, two Bay men & another down to the Forks. Their rudder had smashed so they thought the best thing to do was to eat while they considered it. They filled me up with venison pasty & lemon pie & tea & I dished out a few letters that I had for them & gave them news. They had had no mail since January as the Liard River had mislaid the Nelson mail somewhere on her trip up here in July. Mrs Barber had lived in Knightsbridge & had not been to London for 6 years, so I had to give her all the news of London that I could think of. She was grieved at Cyril Maude's leaving of the stage & Charles Hawtrey's death.

At two we parted—they down river, I up. A lovely afternoon—the fifth in succession now & all different—& I came a little over 8 miles & am camped about ½ a mile above the Satanei or Snake River, within sound of it but on the opposite bank of the Nelson. At its mouth is an Indian village—deserted now, as the hunting parties are out. The night has cleared & the stars are out & I think it is going to freeze.

This may be my last camp with this canoe. It has carried me alone for 600 miles & I am only 12 from the fort. Barber tells me that the Nelson above the fort to Fontas & the Sikanni Landing is fast & shallow in the autumn. It may snow at any time now & I have no wish for any water wallowing when snow is on the ground. So I shall hit the trail on foot from Nelson to Fort St John—200 miles or more—going by way of Fish Lake & the Bay outpost of Sikanni Post—a trail hard to find but shorter than the one I intended to take. It is going to be a tough performance but I think I can do it if I can stay on the trail, which is not well marked. I shall take all the food I can carry, a rain coat, blanket & my pistol & may the Lord defend the right.

I may take it easy to Fort Nelson tomorrow & stay the next day there resting & arranging things. I have about £35-worth of gear to sell or leave with the police to sell for me when the Indians bring in their fur. Also I think I strained my right side a few days ago, giving a monumental shove & twist on the pole. I cant think what else it can be & each time I use it it gets worse, so that today it began to hamper me. However, to Nelson it must take me. Am going to wash now & go to bed—the water having boiled.

They tell me there is a telegraph at St John so in a couple of weeks I hope to be able to cable you & take a load off your mind.

Saturday September 17

8:45 p.m. after supper, by the fire, camped within sound of Fort Nelson.

Mist in the early morning. Up at six, shaved & tired my hair—like Jezebel—ready for my arrival at Nelson. It grew slowly, like a flower, into the very perfectest day of all—the valley lay green & gold in hot, clear, cloudless sunshine. I travelled 3½ hours & then stopped for lunch & bathed & put on clean things & started again at two & went ahead till six.

I didnt travel my fastest as I didnt want to force my side muscles too much. They are easier I think, but twice in fast water I had to use them to the full which didnt help them.

Even so it is further to the fort from the Satanei than I was told, or expected & there are little rapids at intervals. I could have got in this evening but I dont like to come into a strange place at dusk with a load of stuff—not with Indians, breeds & dogs around—all thieves. Camping places round the forts are much used & are dusty & dirty—I dislike them. There are only two white men in the fort at present, I believe, & I prefer eating my own good grub & sleeping in the cool, clean woods on a perfect night to being invited to eat & sleep in a stuffy shack—which one cant very well refuse. I want to get in in the early morning—make my camp, cache or sell my stuff & be ready to get out on Monday early.

The fort must be round the next bend. At six I heard shots, the barking of dogs, cow bells & yokelish hallooings & bellowings as of one who would call home his cattle. The cow bells sounded strange. I have been away so long in the land of dogs & canoes that I had almost forgotten that there were such things as barns to be cleaned, horses chased & cows milked—chores generally. Back to the land of the living again & to our dumb friends—it all sounded very pastoral.

The first time I heard the cow bells was in July of 1920 at Les Brenets in the Jura—seven years ago, & one of my happiest years.

I feel very comfortable & at peace with the world—well fed & no worries & I have cut balsam boughs & laid them beneath my sleeping bag over the thick carpet of leaves—a good fire, my lean to shelter up & a candle to write by—& absolute silence.

By the way—have those people downstairs wearied of their hideous wireless yet? or the Fenwicks?

I have just re-read a few of the Nahanni days. I do hope the pencil lasts & that you can see to read them—that is if they dont bore you, as they are all much the same—got up, travelled & went to bed.

Sunday Sept*ember* 18th
At Fort Nelson. Met Sutherland & Gunnell. Cold & north wind.

Monday September 19

Hit trail for Sikanni Post. With pack of 45 lb. Camped at edge of muskeg damned tired & had to dig well in moss for water. Shot partridge.

Tuesday September 20

Camped in poplar bush on hill, clean done to the world. No water.

Wednesday September 21

Camped by stream—not so tired—getting used to it but not much grub. Met bear on trail last night. Shot partridge & squirrel with revolver & stewed up berries & hips & haws—it all helps. Hope to meet Chehtaneta & his Indians tomorrow at Fish Lake & get meat. Trail hard to find in places—not much idea where I am or how far I have gone—it was 90 miles to the Post from Fort Nelson. Going to bed. Raining. Ill tell you the details when I get out of this mess.

Thursday September 22

Rained & misted all day except a little at midday. Camp in the forest in the hills somewhere. Reached Fish Lake—no Indians—trails forking all over the place— hope I am on the right one as I have only enough grub for two days left now. Saw no partridges, & spent 3 hours this afternoon trying to make sure of the right trail from the Lake to the Post. Have done my best & must stand by it now. Rain makes things miserable & mist makes it hard to get an idea of direction. Between 60 & 70 miles now & never a man—Indian camps & houses at Fish Lake but nobody there. Going damply to bed—sure to sleep sound anyhow, beside a good fire.

Friday September 23

Worst day since March 21[,] 1918. Snowed in night & all day & is snowing now. Trail hard to find & ended in an empty Indian hunting camp after 15 miles. Half way back to Lake now—only hope snow doesnt blot out trail & that I can find Indians & food.

Saturday September 24

By Gods Providence the snow stopped at breakfast time & a little Chinook blew—heaven's wind for me. I got back to the Lake at noon, wet & chilled. Not a human being in sight—only the cold hills & the gray, cold lake. I decided to break into an Indian shack & get food & shelter & [fag?] it somehow until somebody should come who could put me on the trail. I managed to get into three poor little dwellings—not a damned atom of grub—not even a bean, only a little tea & some candles. Nothing for it now but to pull out early in the morning back for Nelson—65 miles on half a pound of cheese, 3½ biscuits, tea & a little sugar, ½ lb of pemmican, ½ lb of raisins, 1½ candles. The last of the rice & bacon I shall have for breakfast.

I decided to stay here in this little shack—dirty I'm certain—for this afternoon & night to rest, dry & warm & pull myself together for the toughest effort of my life—I must go all I can & get to Nelson before my strength fails. The snow is the trouble—one needs more food, the walking is bad & in places I am liable to lose the trail—in which case I shall try to head N.E. across country & hit the Nelson River. Count on me to do my best—I will say a strong prayer & if the cold land gets me you know you have all my love—& give my love to Marigold. I dreamt, last night out in the snow, that she & I were arm in arm trying to come down stairs three steps at a time—I explaining that this was the way Powell & I used to do it at Rossall.

Isnt this shocking luck? & carelessness—I was told the way was easy to find & that Indians were at the Lake. I am only 25 miles from Sikanni Post & warmth & food if only I knew the way. I shall cache a lot of my stuff in a tree a little way down the trail from here to save weight, but my bedding I must have in order to sleep warm as I cant warm myself by eating.

I have shaved & combed my hair & eaten a little—now I am going to sleep—I hardly feel anxious because I know you love me & it seems a protection somehow. Every now & then the Chinook roars—good luck to it, but the frost is fighting it hard.

Sunday Sept*ember* 25
A Chinook day—wet as the devil but warm—snow all slush. I am sitting by my fire in the woods having just had my apology for a supper, made my bed over the snow & cleaned my teeth. I travelled well—9½ hours on foot—& two more days like this will put me in Nelson—hungry but all right—if only I can find the way. Bits of todays trail were hard to find but tomorrow afternoon will be the worst. Both knees raw with wet cords rubbing on them but otherwise excellently fit—& tolerably sopping. Night night.

Monday September 26

Travelled 9½ hours again & crossed the big muskeg safely. Chinook again—it is saving me but one wades all day in moccasins in slush & peat moss—sometimes up to the knees. I shot a partridge this morning & had the heart & liver for lunch & have just roasted the whole bird on a willow spit & torn him limb from limb with my hands & teeth. Tea, a little cheese & raisins completed supper. I have 20 miles to go at least—over wild country—the cow trails to Collier Law in midwinter are highways to this. I dont feel tired yet—I must have been in splendid condition after the Nahanni to stand this—& am used to being hungry. A brush wolf followed me a long way this evening—I have heard that those animals can tell when a man is up against it. I have two thirds of a biscuit, 1 ounce of cheese, a little pemmican, tea, a twist of sugar & a handful of raisins left. The stars are out & it is freezing hard. I am going to make up the fire, put on dry socks & my wool hat & go to bed. Unless I hurt myself or the wind brings snow out of the north I shall be in Fort Nelson tomorrow night—warm & full & dry—& we shall eat together of Scott's lobster salad yet again. When the first storm of the winter caught me grubless in the cold foothills of Fish Lake, light & laughter & pretty things looked a long way away to me. This Chinook & that partridge have almost put me within reach of my tails & my stove pipe hat again.
Good night.

Tuesday September 27

Just going to roll into my blankets on the floor of the Hudsons Bay house dining room at Fort Nelson. Lord—how I have eaten—a memorable eating & the like of it has not been seen, no, not in all Israel, since I lost my appetite at the age of 22. Four moose steaks with fried potatoes, corn & Worcester sauce, two bowls of cornflakes & tinned cream, toast, butter, brandy, pineapples & tea. Opes I shallnt be sick.

11:30 p.m. & the radio is playing dance music from Atlantic City to a hunting party of the Sikannis.

Wednesday September 28th

I travelled well at first yesterday morning but tired after two hours & 50 minutes wallowing in the muskeg & through the tall timber & so stopped by a little stream in a cold, snowy hollow & made tea & ate the last of the cheese, pemmican & biscuit—a very little bit. Went on again but soon tired again even though I had cached my tarpaulin at my night camp to lighten my load. I didnt feel so hungry but one weakens at last after nine days in the open on a [bare?] four days food, 4 partridges & a squirrel. Ones footsteps become less accurate & you trip where, with full strength, you step over. Logs get in your way, you curse swamps & mud holes childishly, willows whip back at you & you slash back at them with the axe in a rage & all nature seems to fight you. It always does in this country but, well fed, you can dare it & beat it.

Then it rained & finally poured—I dribbled on limply & sorely, both feet strained by the forced pace, down the banks of the Fort Nelson River, & at last came to the point within sight of the Fort between the Muskwa & the Nelson. My hands were very numb & I slugged the heavy pack down under a big spruce & fumbled with matches to light a fire on the extreme point. I put horse dung on it to get a good smoke & then fired my pistol twice & waved one of the famous red handkerchiefs on a pole. I saw a canoe put out & in about forty minutes I was in the Bay house—food, dry clothes, warm duffles & mucklucks instead of slush round my feet & all the people I knew watching my feats of gastronomy.

I had travelled 20 miles by four in the afternoon that day, & in all had come 65 miles in 27 hours on foot, sleeping out two nights in wet snow on two pounds of food & a partridge. Not so bad—hard to kill.

Archie Gardiner was there—the only man who knew the trail. Had he been here before I should have been now on the Sikanni Chief River, as I was never off the trail, even in the deepest snow. But where it had seemed to me to end in the hunting camp, it really went on. The Indians had built a horse corral across the trail & the milling of horses in the long grass by the lake, with the heavy fall of snow, had thrown me off the scent into the bush where no trail was. Hard luck, but I'm glad I havent made a fool of myself—in fact they seem to regard it as an achievement getting back at all—& fortunate as news has come by the river that the Post as Sikanni may be abandoned.

It is worth it to meet with northern hospitality—life is one long meal. Breakfast today with the Bay, lunch at Gunnell's of the *British Columbia* police, coffee at the Bay & I am just going to supper with corporal & Mrs Barber of the police—whom, you remember, I met on the river below.

I have had a bath & dressed my raw knees & rubbed my ankles which are swollen & painful with moccasin sickness. I must hurry & get them better as I want to hit the trail again in two or three days & get out to the Peace.

I wasnt sick & that brush wolf was an optimist.

Thursday September 29

Topping good supper at the Barbers. Mrs Barber is English & had made a pudding & pie specially for me, because Cousins had liked it when he was here last winter & she said "I knew you were a friend of the Colonel's."

She is a little like Mrs Muncaster & I think must have been at Knowle, Dorchester House in Park Lane & Drayton with the Sackvilles. Her mother was one of the old Buckinghamshire lace makers from the Chilterns & she showed me some lovely lace that you would have loved.

Barber was educated at a little village school near Hereford & last winter, on patrol on the Fontas, he gathered up & buried the bones, cleaned by the wolves, of a newcomer English trapper who had been out of grub & trying to get in to the Fort, but had weakened & lost the trail. Months later when the reports came through[,] he found that he & this trapper had sat together on the same bench in the village school, as little boys.

I was up at 6:30 & went over to Sutherland's tent & almost ate him out of house & home for breakfast. A cheery, sandy haired boy was there—Henry Courvoisier—also a stout Frenchman—& I found that on the snowy day when I was in the Indian cabin at Fish Lake he had upset his canoe in a rapid up the Nelson, lost everything except flour, baking powder & lard & had reached the Fort the day before I did, twice swimming the snow cold river. We felt a bond of sympathy & said "Isnt life hell?" & grinned. "You cant spell my name" he said. So I spelt it & I said "—& thats the most famous brandy in the world." He was delighted—I was only the second man in the north to do it. "My folks dont come from Quebec," he said. "They was great folks in France once & was driven out into Switzerland in some old religious war—I cant tell you when it was because I aint had the schooling, but my dad can—he came from Caux, if you know that place. But its a good name & we sure had power in France at one time, & here I am an ordinary, doggoned trapper, & if you meet Charlie Brant, my partner, in Fort St John, tell him I've upset five hundred dollars worth of grub into the Nelson & to freight in some more."

Archie Gardiner is going out after a horse & to hunt moose on the return trip. I have made a bargain to ride one of his horses with him out to the Sikanni Chief over the Fish Lake trail & pack my gear on one of his pack horses—for five dollars a day. Well worth it to me as it will save me that 90 miles of wild, wet walking & I shall have the company of a cheery fellow & the only white man in the Fort, besides myself, who knows the trail. I may buy a pack dog from Dave Hooker, who is up from the Forks, & pack him on from the Sikanni.

As soon as we can we start—he has matters to arrange & I my feet to mend—two muscles a bit strained. I dont wonder a bit—I certainly drove them to their utmost. Have you ever read "Youth" by Joseph Conrad? Do. I felt like that when I had changed & was eating after I got in. My weariness fell off & a vein of humour fell on me & between mouthfuls I told a few stories of the trip against myself that made these men here roar.

Barber had brought along a flask with about three fingers of brandy in it for me from his house. "You dont seem to want it," he said. "I expected youd be frozen & faint—but anyhow youre very welcome to it for friendship's sake." "Your very excellent health" says I, & completely ruined his brandy supply for him. As a matter of fact it was a kindly thought—it certainly drove the blood back into its old appointed courses.

The snow has all gone & I can see the Fort Nelson River from my armchair by this window, flowing peacefully past the foot of the knoll, with the last golden leaves reflected in it. Outside are whooping & the jangling of horse bells. One, Belly Full, a chief of the Sikannis, & all his kin have ridden in. A degenerate, low, Mongol type, these Indians of the north—not like the riders of the plains round Calgary. I am glad they are dying out—they make way for the white man. Do you remember Buffalo Bill's show & "Oh Mummy—Indians!"

They have some moose here at the Bay which has gone gamey & cheese which has moulded a little—delicious—nobody will eat them but I—all afraid, bless their Canadian upbringings.

I may go to Edmonton now after this delay before going to the Battle. I want more clothes, which I have in my trunks, & Peace River is a silly, expensive place to buy anything one already has. Also I must see Gordon & my bank, & cable you. No need for you to give my love to Marigold—not this tide—one more storm weathered. Isnt life fun? If you think it wise for me to come home it will be in December—& I refuse to spend Christmas at Foresters Lodge Home. I must have tons of money in the bank by now.

Give my love to [?] & Peggy—I was thinking of them last night. I am going out—I must have exercise or this armchair life will ruin me.

Friday Sept*ember* 30
A lovely, lazy, warm day of sunshine. I have done little but eat at various little houses, doze in the sun on the veranda of the Bay House with a book of Maurice Hewlett's, fit a new axe haft & make my final arrangements for pulling out with

Archie Gardiner—a quarterbreed of the Crees—as soon as his sons come back with horses & moose meat—Tuesday, perhaps. I am still pretty lame where I twisted my ankle, but am well fed & getting restless. One should be on the trail these fall days & not hobbling round Fort Nelson. Sitting in this dreamy sunshine it seems almost impossible that a week ago today I was camped in the foothills on the side of Fish Lake Mountain with the snow drifting onto my blankets & as much food for four days as I could eat in one square meal.

Sutherland tells me that the split mountain on the Nahanni that Faille & I called The Gateway is known to the few who have seen it as The Gate. So we were not far out in our naming of it. I do hope my photos are undamaged—I have taken every care of the films but they have suffered cold, heat & damp. My camera with the remaining roll in it dangles at the tip of a young tamarack on the trail one mile this side of Fish Lake—or did when I last saw it.

Saturday October 1st

Up at 6:30 & away to breakfast in Sutherland's tent on hot cakes, bacon, butter & golden syrup, all mixed together in one glorious mouthful, & coffee. Sutherland pulled out about 9:30 for his trap line beyond the Forks of the Nelson on the Upper Liard, taking my old canoe, his big one & an almond eyed wife & daughter. I came back here to buy a box of chocolates for his little girl & missed his departure so now have a box of chocolates on hand. Am just heating rain water for a bath—the last, I expect, till Edmonton & am going to dress my knees & rub my ankle—all healing fast now. Lunch here & supper is to be for me at the Barbers' at 6:30. How kind people always are—I find the world full of friends. I must write a couple of letters this afternoon—the first for months—to Marigold & Amy.

Heard of Dennis' life at Simpson after I got rid of him. He wont be welcome back in the north—things that one would not expect from any gentle, or educated, man. But then he is neither gentle nor educated—still less a man—& these hard bitten folk up here read him clean through & sized him up very soon.
Frost last night & sunshine again now.

Sunday October 2nd

I am writing in the big sitting room of the police barracks—very warm & comfortable. Milne & Hooker have just left in a power scow up the river to open up the Bay outpost of Fontas & the Bay house here is closed for a few days. So I was invited by Mrs Barber to stay here until I leave, & have some English cooking—

which involves Yorkshire pudding, scones & afternoon tea—really I shall soon be hopelessly out of training.

My ankles are mending—it was what they call snowshoe sickness, through having the thongs of the moccasins too tight & splashing along all day in half frozen water & wet snow. However, I cant grumble though I should have been in Fort St John by now—a maddening delay, but I have learnt a lot from it, & everybody here has been so kind to me—I am simply living off the country.

I was up until three this morning, after playing bridge here, checking the Hudsons Bay accounts for Fontas for the wretched two—Milne & Hooker—& making coffee & toast as it was a cold night. I found several mistakes which helped things along. We were all violently disturbed along of a stew of moose, rice & vegetables which had gone a little sour.

Bright & sunny today but a north wind which is getting colder. I have thrown away my worn out summer clothes & bought good wool—wish I was away over the trail with Archie as I expect we shall catch some hard weather. I may have a lot before me before I see Edmonton.

Still a little lame.

Monday October 3rd
Horses in & we are leaving in three hours. Archie's sons killed, & the moose steaks are cooking now with Yorkshire pudding & fresh green peas. A little snow fell in the night but it is not snowing now although the day is grey & cold. My first bit of luck for some time—Corporal Barber has suddenly to go to Fort St John so he is hiring another horse & riding out with me to the Sikanni Chief, paying half Archie's wages & half the packing fees. From the Sikanni onwards we walk together for 200 miles with two of the police dogs carrying our beds & food—I paying for half the dog feed. Excellent, as he knows where the water, camping places & shacks are & can give me friends at Fort St John who will house & feed me if I have to make any stay there. But I dont intend to if I can possibly get straight on to Peace River or overland to Grande Prairie & the Edmonton train. I am still a bit crooked but am off today if I have to have a ladder to get into the saddle.

Camp at the first lake on the trail—just where I ate my last handful of raisins last Tuesday. Very different now—we have just had a splendid supper—the night is cold & dry & I have my full outfit of bedding down by the fire. I can hear our horse bells down by the lake—I have a good horse but not a patch on my beloved Urchin. Just dressed my knee which is healing fast.

Camp five miles out—ate roast dried moose meat Indian fashion. Powdering of snow at night.

Tuesday Oct*ober* 4th
One dog went home carrying the dog feed & two raincoats—tother went sick & temporarily mad & very nearly got a bullet from me. One horse headed for St John & delayed us an hour. Night caught us in the big muskeg—perfect hell, horses continually down. Ate a tremendous supper & camped by the Loon Lake Creek.

Wednesday Oct*ober* 5th
Woke up under snow & it snowed a little on & off all day. Lunch at Round Lake & we now have our beds spread by the fire under a big spruce tree at Balsam Creek about $2\frac{1}{2}$ hours from Fish Lake. The moon has just set, the stars are out in a clear sky & it is freezing hard—we should have sunlight tomorrow. We hope to find the Indians tomorrow & get meat & fish & reach the Sikanni Post the day after.

Thursday Oct*ober* 6th
Camp at Long Lake about six hours from the Sikanni. A very hard frost last night—we found lakes & streams frozen over, but the day has been lovely, all sunshine, & tonight will be warmer. Saw grizzly bear tracks in the snow a few miles back.

Friday Oct*ober* 7th
Up at 4:30 as it looked like snow & had a good breakfast & sat round the fire until daybreak. Then we hunted up the horses & started. A cold north wind sprang up & from the top of a high hill we could see the snowstorms spreading over the country. It snowed for an hour or so & then it blew a Chinook & the sun came out & drove back the winter once more. We reached Peffer's post on the Sikanni Chief River at about 12:30 very hungry. The Indians are here & they brought us moose meat, killed yesterday & sat round us while we ate. I have a photo of Archie & Barber, Chief Bigfoot, Belly Full, & Chuhnaneta who were here waiting for a pack train of 16 Hudson's Bay horses due here today with supplies for their new post. A great bit of luck for us to come here on this very day—Barber has gone off to see what arrangement he can make so that he & I can ride back with the train to Fort St John. I was shaving & had my stuff all over the place under the trees here

+

Autumn 1927 travelling companions and Dene: (l. to r.) Chushnaneta, the Sikanni Chief,
Corporal Barber, Archie Gardiner, and Belle Feuille.

or I would have gone with him. I hope we can get out with them as it will save us walking & packing our gear for 200 miles. Archie is flat asleep here in the warm sunshine—in two hours the Chinook has changed things from a snowstorm into summer, & I see that there are even wild bees round the jam.

Archie here is, as I told you, one quarter Indian—a grandson of a General Gardiner, son of a Mounted Policeman & a connection of *Field Marshal* Earl Haig. He tells me that the proper Indian pronunciation for the Nahanni tribe is Ná-ániké—"The people who speak like ducks"—their language being different from the Slavey of the Nelson & lower Liard Indians.

Saturday October 8th

We camped last night in a very clean well built Indian shack, & were just having supper when the two owners came in leading a pack horse with a freshly killed deer on it—so we fell to with renewed vigour on the meat. The Bay have hired the shack as a ware house until they can get their buildings up so I went down the bank & opened up & cleaned out Peffer's bunkhouse, & we have moved in & are very comfortable. Last night it snowed, rained & froze in turn so we were just as well off under a roof as outside. Today is like summer again. The Bay has hired all the Indians & their horses to pack the stores over from the old cache to the new building site & warehouse so there is a great clatter & bustling about. The *Hudson's Bay Company* have had bad luck with this post—their first attempt burned down & their second was washed away by the river although the Indians saved & cached most of the stuff. The remainder of the Bay horses have come in under Angus Beatton, three parts Scotch & one part Beaver on his mothers side. We leave with him for Fort St John tomorrow, hiring two saddle horses & a pack horse for 15 dollars & providing the food for the three of us.

Barber, who is as clumsy round a cook stove as they make them, has just succeeded in cutting a finger & thumb to the bone & I have just bathed, disinfected & dressed his hands—bad cess to them as I now have the baking to do—Archie being hopeless.

Sunday Oct*ober* 9th
A dream of a warm, sunny morning. I have washed & shaved & fixed up Barber & am now writing, sitting on a log in front of our shack in the sunshine—my blankets airing on some fallen trees. Archie has just left for Nelson—he had waited a day for Peffer & his pack train but they have not turned up & he could not afford to lose another day of this Indian summer. We leave after lunch for Dead Horse Lake on the St John trail, & soon I should be telegraphing to you & on my way in to Grande Prairie & Edmonton.

Evening   Camp at Dead Horse Lake. after supper. A moon, almost full, shining out of a clear sky. We rode four hours & twenty minutes, up out of the valley of the Sikanni & into a country of rolling hills, muskeg valleys & jack pine ridges. From the top of the Sikanni hill I saw, away to the west against the sun, the high mountains, snow capped now, the view I like best in all Canada.

The day was gloriously warm, & I'm glad to be outside again—I dont seem to sleep so well now in houses.

We have six horses—three saddle—two with packs & one with an empty pack saddle—& Im certain we are going to have trouble with them.

Monday Oct*ober* 10th

We were up at 4:30 & had breakfast in the frost by the light of the moon. By dawn we were riding away south east, in single file over the narrow pack trail, into a rolling brulé country with jack pine ridges—very much like our own moorland. The stars went out—the sky changed from dark blue to mauve, & then in turn to green & gold & pale blue—& then the sun came up, clear as a flame, & set the frost crystals glittering.

It was sharp at first, but by ten I had my jacket, hat & gloves off & tied behind my saddle—another day of warm Indian summer. We hit the main wagon trail to St John & lunched by the Conroy Creek—now we are camped & sitting round the fire by Spangler Lake, in the jack pine, the horses belled & hobbled & turned loose in the wild hay.

A gentle Chinook wind & a full moon in a cloudless sky—we put up no shelter on nights like these (or most others, for that matter). I simply roll up in that sleeping bag that I once used on the drawing room floor & know no more until rain falls on my face or the sun shines, or other disturbance comes along. We have come 30 miles today.

Tuesday Oct*ober* 11th

Camp at an abandoned Hudson's Bay post on the North Pine River. We have had supper & cooked inside the old living house & it is now nine o'clock. I have my bed laid down under the trees outside—it is such a lovely night & I have perhaps only three more nights left to me after this before I reach the outside world & have to sleep in a shut in room—I havent slept in a bed since May & a week tomorrow I may be in the Macdonald Hotel in Edmonton with my own bathroom & a Japanese boy to answer the phone.

We were up at 5:40 today & left camp at 7:15 & have come 24 miles—in places the trail was simply unspeakable. For over an hour we worked to get a packhorse out of a swamp hole in the muskeg & finally pried him bodily out with long spruce levers—I really thought his ribs would give way. Towards evening we met a horse that Charlie Brant had left in an awful state. An ill fitting pack saddle had left his back raw & festering & the ravens were feeding on him as he grazed. Barber shot at him with his revolver but missed & he ran away into the pines, so he has paid a breed five dollars to go out & shoot him, & will bring the matter before a *Justice of the Peace* at Fort St John.

A lovely day & the Chinook still blowing—if anything, harder. A wolf is howling in the bush as though his living depended on it & all the dogs are accordingly making the night hideous in reply to him.

Wednesday Oct*ober* 12
Up at 4:30 & started at 6:40 & came 28 miles to Keye's old cabin—the floor having rotted out we are camped outside, the lean-to put up as there has just been a sharp shower. We bought a little stuff at Peffers store at Niq Creek, which we reached at nine, & lunched at Windy Point on Squaw Creek. The worst of the trail is over now—this afternoon we had good going over open moorland country, with tall yellow grass, dwarf willows & blueberry bushes, & occasional clumps of jack pine & swamp spruce. Dry ridges & hills of poplar & jack pine in between. Twice, very far away I saw the high mountains, blue, like clouds, in the west. The Chinook still holds, & has blown all day, except for three hours this morning, when the cold east wind sniffled across & mastered it & made us button up & think of snow. A smoky, gusty fire—I cant really see to write. Moon & stars are shining in a clear sky & it is very warm.

Thursday Oct*ober* 13th
The Chinook blew all night & it was warm & clear. We were up at 4:30 & had porridge, moose steaks, bacon & cheese for breakfast & were away by 6:35. I watched the sun rise as we rode—it was mauve, old gold & pale green at first & then all these gave way to a flaring yellow & up came the sun with a dog on each side of him, to shine all day & help the warm wind. We are well into the Peace country now & the thick bush & muskegs of the north have given way to the parklands & rolling open hills that I have so often told you about. We no longer wallow in half frozen moss & this morning we came to the first real prairie— Squaw Creek Prairie—unfenced, untouched—only one old trappers shack by the stream. It was like coming home again to hear the song of the wind & to see its ripples in the tall yellow grass after the silence of the woods, mountains & the great rivers. It is the change from the north to the west.

We only went 23 miles, as one horse is sick & is holding us back, & we are now in Martin's cabin on the south bank of the Blueberry River, just the three of us round the stove by candlelight & the door open onto the moonlit river, hay flats & barn. There are big stacks of wild hay outside, smelling sweetly, & my bed is laid down between them. Tomorrow we reach the open prairie & the first farm—the ruffed partridge has given way to the prairie chicken—coveys of them were rising before us all day long.

From a hilltop north of the Blueberry I could see, very far away to the south east, some low, blue hills—I think perhaps the western edge of the Clear Hills.

Friday October 14th

I slept outside on a little knoll above the Blueberry—it froze sharply & I found hoar frost on my pillow & over my sleeping bag in the morning. Angus roused me when he came out to feed the horses—I thought it seemed early & the moon was still high but I got up & we made & had breakfast in the cabin. Then I looked at my watch & it was 4:30—Barber having misread his watch in the moonlight & got up at 3:30 instead of an hour later. So we sat round the stove a while & finally hit the trail at 6:15. It was still freezing—the sun rose through cloud streamers of pink & gray, mauve & green & shone all morning through a film of cloud. Before sunrise the whole country, in the yellow light, was a study in monochrome—all shades from biscuit to the darkest mahogany & very beautiful.

After a stretch of open country we travelled through 5 miles of big timber with mud holes in the trail—hidden from the sun by the trees & cold. Then willows, & then the parklands again & lunch at Holdup Creek where, 18 years ago, a trapper held up his partner at breakfast time with a rifle & took their joint catch of fur & hit for St John. The other, however, knew the country better—beat his partner in by a short cut & had a Mounted Policeman waiting for him.

There was an Indian baby's grave at Holdup Creek—I took a photo of it.

This afternoon we travelled down a lovely, shallow, grass valley—we might have been in Sussex but that a big bull moose crossed the trail just ahead of us & climbed the hill into the trees.

At last we saw buildings & oats in the stook, fences & two men stacking & are now camped in Clay Martin's shack, having come over 20 miles—Fort St John tomorrow.

Saturday October 15th

I am writing, sitting up on a camp bed, by the light of a lantern, in the cooks galley of Harry Weaver's scow at the Fort St John Landing at the foot of the hill. Outside the lap-lap of the Peace River running fast here over a riffle.

We hit the trail at eight this morning & after riding for some hours we topped a high grass hill & saw below us the farm buildings & the laid out grain fields of

+

A typical scow running on the Peace River.

the settlement of Fort St John. The great dale of the Peace ran from east to west beyond it—over the river, to the south, the blue hills that lie beyond the South Pine—to the west the snow mountains beyond Hudsons Hope.

In half an hour we were at the Bay &, after some business there, rode on to the police barracks & unpacked & sorted our stuff. We were hungry & went over to some people called Finch & demolished roast beef & stewed plums with real cream & fresh butter. The telegraph office was half a mile away & I was going there after lunch when I heard that Harry Weaver was due in at the landing, four miles away, with his last cargo of the season before freeze up. So I seized my pack sack, said good bye & bolted—I need not have made such haste as he was delayed & it was six o'clock & I was sitting round the fire with all the teamsters & home-steaders when we saw his searchlight round the bend.

For 13 dollars I am going with him & Woods up to Hudsons Hope & back to Peace River—& so the journey is ending by a series of strange chances as I had originally planned it.

We had supper in the little galley here—fresh moose that they had shot near Dunvegan, potatoes, onions, tomatoes, fresh fruit & cream—all the things I like best.

This will make me a few days later in Edmonton but I shall see the Hope & 250 miles of the Peace. There is a telegraph office at the Hope, so on Monday I shall be in touch with you.

A thunderstorm broke at supper time—there was much uproar, a deluge of rain & flash after flash lit up the great valley.

Sunday October 16th

This morning we unloaded 12 tons of stuff for Fort St John onto the beach— every mortal thing that a settlement can need from flour & chocolate bars to lumber, stoves & radios. A lovely morning but gray now—we lunched heartily & put to sea at two & are now ploughing up the green, swirling Peace. Great grass hills form the closely shut in valley on each side—brown & red in their autumn colours. The poplars are leafless now & only the clumps of spruce remain green. We may reach Peace River on Wednesday or Thursday—I hope that ice, snow & winter storms dont smite us before then. The St John schoolmaster, Holland, also a prisoner of war, is travelling with us to the Halfway River—we should tie up at Cache Creek tonight.

It seems to be my lot to head continually west towards the mountains.

Monday October 17th

A year ago today since I left Battle River in the snow in Slim Jackson's sleighs to go with Gordon to Dick Brown's on the Red Deer.

We came to Cache Creek in the dark last night, about 7:30, & tied up there— a party of the settlers waiting as usual on the beach for their mail & supplies. Two skiffs with outboard petrol engines were tied up there & we were told that they belonged to General Sutton & Mr Humphreys—a provincial surveyor of British Columbia. General Sutton is an Englishman—retired from the East to Victoria & with engineering experience in the Argentine. By all accounts he must represent some big interests as he has made this trip in from Prince George, over Giscome Portage & down the Crooked, McLeod, Parsnip & Peace Rivers with a view to extending the P.G.E. railroad through the mountains, linking it with the E.D. & B.C. & so opening the Peace country to the Pacific coast. So my Battle River land may soon increase in value if this is true. The General & his party were sleeping up in the settlement.

This morning we were up early & unloaded our freight on the beach & were having breakfast when Sutton's gang appeared—Sutton, Humphreys, a man journalist, a girl journalist, the Bay manager from Hudson's Hope, a practical prospector & four men to look after them—all correctly attired for the far west in fringed buckskin jackets, red scarves, khaki breeches & field boots. The lady journalist in purple & white wool with tassels here & there & a monstrous pair of fleece lined, buckskin thigh boots. I talked with the prospector who had heard I was from the Nahanni & was at me immediately—said good day to the General & took stock of the outfit—garbed as I was in moccasins, stained cords & a shirt torn up the back—all that is left to me. The funny part is that in all probability we shall all be staying at the Macdonald in a weeks time—& probably I shall be the best dressed of all.

If you remember, I very nearly came in over Giscome Portage a year last July with the men from Fort Grahame—& now I am finishing a long trail that exceeds my wildest dreams of that time.

The General had a very poor undersized moose head in the canoe that he had shot himself. In the other canoe was a set of moose antlers that he had <u>bought</u> from a trapper! On the Nahanni I have watched, without shooting, better moose than he has probably ever seen.

They went away down river & we came on upstream. We stopped at the Halfway River to land the schoolmaster, & lumber & crates of apples for a man with a large family of rosy cheeked children—who kept a silently watchful eye on the apples. Just after lunch we came to the homestead of a man called [Ardill?]—Irish—more children, more apples & presents of fresh vegetables & moose meat from Harry Weaver who seems to be the universal godfather of the upper river.

The river gets more & more beautiful. Now & then we can see ahead of us the great snow capped saw line of the Rockies & the valley becomes deeper. It is a great river, blue green like the sea—smooth & fast. We are 700 miles up from its mouth at the Rivière des Rochers that I passed with Dennis that hot day in early June. The day is a glory of sunlight playing on the red, purple & russet of the hills—it seems unusually good to be alive—but then it seems that almost every day. But it never grows old, & on each day of this western sunshine you think—This is better than all the others.

We are driving on towards Bullhead Mountain & Hudson's Hope & should be there tonight. We fried fresh eating apples & eggs together in butter for lunch—excellent.

Tuesday October 18th

About five o'clock yesterday we came through the lower gates of the Peace, where the river makes its first cut through the mountain rocks. A great view opened up—pile upon pile—from the green of the nearer cliffs to the red brown of the further hills, & beyond the deep blue of the first ranges. Last of all came the snow mountains &, curling above them, the white & blue storm clouds that hung so often on the Pacific side of the summit, but rarely cross to the eastern slope. We came to Hudson's Hope in the cold blue of the evening, with the sun setting in a sky of winter copper, fending off the cool wind with hot coffee. We anchored, washed & went up the road to Mrs Gething's "Trail's End Coffee House" where we did good execution. The place was agog with General Sutton & his railroad. Mrs Gething showed me a Vancouver paper with a map of the proposed extension which puts a line, as far as I could see, almost slap through my homestead. I always maintained that I had a good eye for country. I may see more of that party as they are also to stay at the Macdonald.

This morning we unloaded, shaved & cleaned up & I cabled to you—I do hope you are at home when the cable comes. There was a white frost in the night—the morning mists soon cleared & the day is one of warm sunshine & flying white clouds—a spring day—& a tearing, roaring, warm Chinook blowing through the mountains, which should melt a good deal of snow, raise the river & make it easier for us to get down. We hope to leave tomorrow & be in Peace River on Friday.

After lunch I took my camera & walked out west along the portage trail to the head of the Upper Gates where I am now writing & lazing in the warm wind & sun. The Peace makes its second cut in the rocks here & has cut them into a wide, low canyon with curiously shaped rock islands in the middle—spruce topped. Between these it bawls & bellows over rapids & its green is flecked with white foam—not at all the Peace that I have known below, but like a vaster & more powerful Nahanni. The boats cannot come beyond the Hope—the total length of the canyon is 21 miles & the portage road is 14 miles—& navigation on the upper Peace is mainly by means of skiffs & canoes. I can see where the foothills shut in on the river but I havent time to walk on to the actual canyon—not very spectacular, I believe, except by reason of the great size of the river. It is the gate to a mountain country rich in game & gold & other minerals, which I hope to see some day. I will now take a little snooze on this warm grass slope, before the sun sinks too low.

Wednesday October 19th

This really is the most perfect day of all—better than all that have passed. I mean it this time. A hard frost last night & a sky of cloudless blue today—utterly clear. We left Hudsons Hope this morning & are now flying down stream between the Halfway River & Cache Creek. As we left the Hope I wished that I had just one more film left—that was the last of 80 that I took yesterday at the Upper Gates. But there, this morning, was that view that I love best of all in the west—the blue foot-hills & behind them the great snow peaks flashing in the morning sun against a blue sky—the whole picture made more lovely still by the Peace & the hills of the cañon in the foreground. A perfect, warm October day, & the whole thing reminds me of that pleasant week at Dick Brown's on the upper Red Deer just one year ago.

The mountains are dropping out of sight—perhaps for the last time this year. We hurry on towards Peace River, making calls at little, lonely places, winding up accounts & leaving the last freight & parcels of the navigation season. The water is clear & cold now—just waiting for the north east wind to freeze, & with the falling of this warm Chinook & a change to the cold wind it would be possible for the Peace to run with mush ice in two days from now.

We have just hooted to warn the Cache Creek settlers—we load 150 sacks of wheat here. I'm very glad as we have just made a walloping meal of moose, fried cabbage, pemmican, tomatoes, onions, rolled oats, brown bread & butter, strong tea, tinned cherries & fresh apples & cream & I want some work to do. If only I could bring this appetite into a city with me.

Thursday October 20th

Reached Taloy Flats last night & cleaned up & spent the evening up at the house of the storekeeper, [Davis?].

Frost at night & when we woke up the snow was falling out of a grey sky. We washed very hastily in cold water & fled up the bank into the warm shack of the ferryman, McKnight, whose wife fed porridge & cream, eggs & coffee to us.

By the time we got further away from the mountains & down to Rolla Landing the snow changed to rain. We had by this time a miscellaneous load, including wheat, furniture, vegetables, skis & a cow—Buttercup—& her calf. Butttercup exceedingly depressed & lowing continuously, while the calf bawled kind of monotonous but highly persistent.

Woods left the ship at his homestead, to trap for the winter & at 3:45 Harry & I started on the long run to Dunvegan—I being now both passenger & crew.

The rain stopped & it grew colder, then warm again. We both froze & talked in the conning tower & at six I went down & brought up tea & bread & butter & we felt strengthened.

He ran on without stopping until 10:30, in order to get me into Peace River for Friday's train. It was dark, moonless, misty & cold & he steered by his knowledge of the river & by the searchlight—a remarkable performance as the Peace is fast & shallow at the Many Islands, the Montagneuse & the Narrow Gut.

At ten I went to the cook house & made coffee & bowls of hot porridge. We tied up at Bear River & went to bed much fortified—Buttercup still hollering.

Friday October 21st
The last day. 10:00 a.m.

I forgot to tell you that on Thursday afternoon we took long range shots at a big black bear but missed him.

We were up & away at 6:45 & I had breakfast ready when we made Dunvegan at ten to eight. We got rid of Buttercup & her offspring & left her owner struggling on the beach while we shoved out & drifted down river during breakfast. It was a pretty morning, half mist[,] half sunshine—utterly silent until Weaver broke the stillness with his violin—an after breakfast habit. Moose steak & onions formed the menu.

We are now thrumming on towards Peace River—the last lap. The valley is narrow & deep—bare grass hills on the north shore while the forest covers the south slope. Low clouds hang on the hilltops & it is coldish—everything being open & no fire on board except the gas cook stove which we only run at meal times.

Reached Peace River at ten minutes to three after crossing a wonderful stretch of water by the mouth of the Smoky. Warm sunshine—I just caught the bank & then had a hair cut & shampoo. Later met Radcliffe of the Alberta Provincial Police & sat over beer with him in the club talking. Train left at 7:30 for Edmonton & I am just going to turn into my berth—between sheets for the first time since May.

Saturday October 22nd
Woke up with an awful headache—the result of sleeping inside & the noise of the train, I suppose. A lovely day. General Sutton & Bryan, the member for North Vancouver, on the train—both interested when they heard I had come from the Nahanni—the "mystery river" Bryan called it—a journalist by profession. We are

nearing Edmonton, that I left five months ago—I can see the lights now, away to the south, & in a few minutes I shall have completed the circle—journey's end.

Sunday Oct*ober* 23rd

I slept last night in Gordon's camp bed on his verandah—in the clean frost again, & feel better for baths, my clean clothes, milk, eggs & a comb of honey to breakfast.

We are all three going out to lunch at the Macdonald—& then Gordon & I are going to get busy over maps & decide on our plans for tackling the north next year to run down that gold. He will come with me & I shall be home to see you at Christmas & tell you everything. Tomorrow he & I leave with his car for Drumheller & the Saskatchewan border—camping by the way. We shall be back about Friday & then I shall deal with my mail & we leave for the Battle.

I am the better for the trail I have made—in every way. A little stronger & heavier, more obstinate, quicker to think & act alone & able to do without things & to drive myself on against my own will.

I know the way in to the gold rivers—& I have seen very great beauties in a wonderful mountain world.

This is how I travelled—as near as may be

	Miles
By train, Edmonton to Waterways:	296
By canoe, with Dennis to the Demi-Charge Rapids on the Slave:	250
On the Canadusa to Fitzgerald:	37
The portage trail to Smith:	16
From Smith to the head of the Liard rapids on Cousin's scow's:	584
Alone, by canoe, to South Nahanni:	55
On the Nahanni & Flat Rivers alone:	310
In Faille's war canoe to the Falls:	40
Alone, to the Forks of the Nelson:	150
Alone to Fort Nelson:	100
On foot, alone, beyond Fish Lake & back to Nelson—the hungry trail:	160

By saddle & pack horse with Barber & Archie Gardiner to the
    Sikanni Post: 90
Riding with Barber & Angus Beatton from the Sikanni Chief River
    to Fort St Johnon the Peace: 200
On Harry Weaver's scows to Hudson's Hope & back to Peace River: 290
By train, Peace River to Edmonton: 310

A total of 2888 miles.   2888
Of this I travelled 905 miles in my canoe, & 775 miles alone.

I hope this very long letter wont bore you & that you can read it without hurting your eyes. Please keep the little book safely—I may need it for reference later—& at the back end are a few notes & two useful recipes for camp cooking that I picked up this summer.

Love from
Raymond

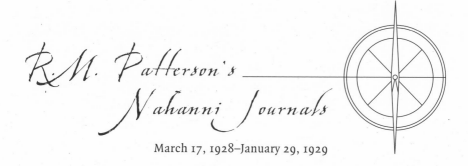

R.M. Patterson's Nahanni Journals

March 17, 1928–January 29, 1929

[Patterson returned briefly to England that winter, where he proposed to Marigold Portman before sailing back to Canada in early February. In company with Matthews, a team of Alsatians, and supplies for a year, Patterson left Edmonton by train for Spirit River. From there, with the assistance of a wagon and four horses, they made it to Finch's store in Fort St. John in mid-March, where they transferred their supplies to sleighs.]

1928

March 17th Saturday

Started from Finch's store with the dogs & ran three miles to Hansen's where we picked up Clay Martin. Took the Charley Lake trail & lunched by the logging camp. Strong Chinook blowing & things became very wet as we headed up the creek. On the bare hillside sleighing became impossible & at four p.m. we made camp in a clump of fire killed poplar.

March 18th Sunday

Chinook all night & pretty bare going up to the head of the creek. Lunch under the spruce in the warm sunshine & heard from Gordon the story of the gun at York Factory & the "fleas in my iodine." Suggested scouring out the copper tea pail but *Gordon* said it was an antique, made at York Factory in the eighteenth century & had never yet been cleaned. Thought of all the bearded voyageurs who had drunk tea from it & decided not to clean it. Headed through the bush in the afternoon & over the divide to the Montany, doubled up & relayed the sleighs to Holdup Creek & finally made camp in the Big Willows.

March 19th Monday

Still Chinooking & the trail devilish sloppy. We bumped & clattered through the Blueberry timber & then hit an absolutely bare prairie over which we dragged heavily to the Blueberry River. The hay meadows were bare & the streams running with water over the ice—a hot, cloudless day & we shaved & washed & fed the dogs, &, now, at six p.m. on a March evening, lie in the hay pile, barefooted in a blaze of sunshine. The dogs also asleep in the sun, the Chinook dying down a little & now & then the hum of an insect in the air—an amazing winter evening for the frozen north. I think we shall probably roll out our eiderdowns later on & sleep outside in the hay—not in the stuffy shack.

March 27

Made camp at Kenei Creek on the Sikanni Chief River & sat down to wait for spring & open water.

April 25

River ice moves on the Sikanni. I got one ruffed partridge & Gordon a mallard & a partridge.

[Finally having reached the Sikanni Chief River after struggling from Fort St. John in Chinook conditions, they spent most of the next month waiting for the Sikanni Chief to break up. When that occurred, they moved their cargo by canoe and raft down river, into the Fort Nelson River, and then on down the Liard River to Nahanni Butte.]

May 26 Saturday

We left La Flairs post at South Nahanni late in the evening, after supper. A still, cloudless, perfect evening after a day of wind & the little engine drove the three canoes over the water at a good pace. We went up the little snye, past the Indian village & past the Hudson's Bay outpost—MacNeill at the door with his dogs, watching us. Round the shoulder of Nahanni Butte, where the rock comes down to the water, & on into the calm reaches to camp at the mouth of the little Bluefish River. I slept on the point between the Bluefish & the Nahanni & in the night a beaver played by the canoes.

May 27 Sunday

A fine, cloudless morning & we had our tea & porridge & were on the river by 5:15. After some miles the water became swifter & by ten o'clock we were at the

+

Jack LaFlair's trading post at Nahanni Butte.

foot of the Splits—debating whether we should make a cache there & leave one canoe. We decided to try to reach Faille's cache at the Twisted Mountain with all our gear, & so went on. We took the right hand channels & had the full force of the river against us where it swung round two dangerous cutbank bends, full of sweepers & cross currents. The wind began to blow & the sun went in & Gordon began to realise the fearful desolation of the Splits that had been so impressed on me the year before. I went ahead on foot to reconnoitre the second bend—a right angle turn with lashing sweepers & swift water. Decided to try it & we got round it somehow with the engine all out & the water lapping into the canoes. We jammed once on a bar & the engine stopped—things looked rather blue but away we went again & got out of the current into a small snye which promised a safer way round. Had an inspection of the engine & found a nut off the new collar & the bracket fractured. Things looked very desperate, but we made some sort of a hay wire job of repairs & went on to the head of the snye where we made camp early—about five—feeling that ill luck had hammered us enough for one day. The Twisted Mountain is in sight—if only we can get this unwieldy, dangerous outfit there we can lighten it at Faille's cache & travel like Christians.

May 28 Monday
During supper it began to blow & rain—as a day, it forgot nothing. Rained like the deuce in the night & we slept late as a gale is blowing & we could not think of

leaving shelter & tackling the main river. The river had risen & the canoes were six inches deep in rain water. So we had breakfast, pitched the tent & brought in our stuff & baled the canoes & soon lunch time will be upon us—moose steaks, the last of the moose that we got at the mouth of the Nelson. I become impatient at these delays & only wish we could get on into the mountains—but we can do nothing today with the weather like this.

Later
A glorious, cool, rain washed evening. The rain stopped about three & we laid things out to dry, cooked, washed & mended the sail. I went up with my field glasses to the head of the snye, where it opened onto the main Nahanni. The tops of the higher mountains were covered with freshly fallen snow & the last of the rain clouds hung low in the valleys & on the hills, with the sun breaking through & bringing out the clear colours of the unburnt forest. The fast water of the Nahanni rushed & swirled through the islands & bars of the splits, & with the help of the glass I picked out tomorrow's course which lay up a stretch of fast water & into a little snye that I travelled last year. And in the middle of the river, by a young poplar on a bar, I could see two stakes that I had driven to hold my mosquito net in an old camp of mine. They had stood there since last July— through the freeze up, the winter storms & the going out of the ice—& from them today I got my bearings.

May 29 Tuesday
Cloudy & coldish. Broke up camp & started out at seven—dogs on opposite bank of the snye. The snye became shallow & the engine stopped at the entrance to the main Nahanni. I jumped out into the water which was fast & cold & tried to pull the whole outfit over the bar but it was too heavy for me. We tried poling but the current was too fast & the canoes lodged on a sweeper—[at] what time the idiot dog, Quiz, got himself into trouble under the opposite bank & distracted the attention of Gordon who is foolishly sentimental over the pot hounds. Also the engine was racing so finally we drifted back down the snye & spent weary hours tinkering with the shock absorber. At last we decided to abandon the engine & the big canoe, & to make a cache of a thousand pounds or so of stuff & go ahead with the two smaller canoes. So we shall travel as the Lord intended men to travel in the north west—by pole, trackline & paddle & such strength as we have—& the devil take me if ever I fool with an engine again in a wild country.

+
RMP beneath a typical cache.

We crossed over & made camp among the spruce & unloaded most of the gear which was very wet & sodden after being over three weeks in the canoes. In the night it rained.

May 30 Wednesday
I picked a place where four spruce of the right size grew close together in a square, & I cleared the brush & felled the big trees that stood around so that squirrels might not jump from them onto the cache. Then I set to work & cut off the trees about ten feet from the ground & built my platform up there, & ringed round the trees with tin to keep the field mice from climbing up. It was cool at first & sunny later on & the good smells of the bush & the moss, & of wood chips, were very pleasing. I was rather proud of that cache as I had never made one before—& it was my own child, as Gordon is not in sympathy with tools & wood, & worked around camp—sorting stuff & packing the engine. At lunch time I was most amazing famished—swinging an axe & handling logs makes one hungry.

In the evening I went up alone to the point on the main river. There was a wonderful light of sunset abroad, touching the foothills where the rain clouds hung & lighting up the snow mountains towards Fort Liard & the rushing channels of the Splits. I wish *Marigold* could have seen it with me.

Thursday May 31st

A day of sunshine & showers, & thunder in the offing. We worked hard, drying & sorting out the stuff & putting the things to be left behind up in the cache. We pulled the big canoe up the bank & laid it up under a big spruce—& thank God to be rid of it—from now on will travel lighter. Rather a mosquito evening & I'm writing this in the fire smoke—bed time now & I hope that by tomorrow we'll be nearing the Twisted Mountain.

Friday June 1st

Another day of disappointment. We loaded the little canoe & then launched the 18 *foot* freighter & started work on it. Gradually we realised that it could not take the load we had intended for it & still be handled by one man "waking the white ash breeze" on the Nahanni at its present stage of semi high water. At last *Gordon* suggested that I take the little canoe & a load of traps & such stuff as would not perish & could easily be cached, & push ahead as far as possible—to the Flat River, to see or meet Faille & suggest a partnership, or even to Irvine Creek. We had lunch on it—the bright spring sunshine coming down through the big spruce & black poplar & lighting up the little snye. I agreed—I love the trail & *Gordon* cant handle a canoe worth a damn, so I'll do my best. He travels fastest who travels alone, & I'll remember that for the rest of my life—barring *Marigold* whom I couldnt do without. *Gordon* is the best & kindest of men—& the most good natured as he can stand being with me. But the Lord knows he dithers hopelessly at times.

So I sorted my gear & baked bannock & we had the joy of seeing Rouillé & MacNeill go by on their way to South Nahanni from Rouillé's trap line on Jackfish River. Now only Faille & ourselves are on the river. I wonder whether Faille is still alive or whether the ill luck of the Nahanni country has taken him also.

Saturday June 2

There was a fair amount to attend to & I didnt start until ten on a gorgeous morning of hot sunshine. I crossed from the snye to the sand bar & up that, &

then back across the main current to the second snye. It wound & twisted through the trees with all the tricks of a little river—now sighting O'Brien's Mountain & now Nahanni Butte. From it I came to a big, fast snye, running between cutbanks, which gave me a lot of bother. This split into three, & I took the centre snye & so came out into the main centre stretch of sand bars of the Splits. Thunder had been sounding, & in the middle of that desert of stones & water the storm came on me with a lash of rain. I waited there an hour & finally made a dash for a possible camp. I tied up in a little snye & had supper in the rain washed sunshine. A good camp & not too far from the Twisted Mountain. Give me weather & not overmuch water & I may reach the Hot Springs, but I'm afraid I cant pass the canyons now. Too late—what a fool I was not to travel light & alone. A red sunset under heavy clouds & the mosquitoes busy—so it looks like rain. The limestone patch has gone from view & I am almost opposite the snow covered hill, with the Long Walls through the trees. Bed now.

Sunday June 3rd

Started at eight of a sunny morning & tracked to the head of the snye—then took the centre of the river among the shingle bars. All went pretty well till towards midday when I came amongst stranded trees lying on a submerged bar with a very fast current running through them. My waders swamped & filled & I could hardly hold the canoe—much less pull it round one particular sweeper. So I took the axe & cut the tree away & then managed to lug the canoe up the riffle—the track line obligingly tangling itself in a driftpile. Wet to the waist by this time, & the Nahanni water is very cold, even in the hot sun, at this time of year when it is still fed by the winter snows. So I decided to paddle over to the mouth of a snye & have lunch, & change my things the while. The current was very fast & I missed that snye, but managed to get into the next one—thank the Lord, as if I had been swept past that a whole two hours work would have been ruined. After lunch I went up some little & annoying snyes & reached a broad & very fast current running under against the mountain below the mouth of Jackfish River. A thunderstorm was blowing up &, as my only way led up a submerged bar in the middle of the river, I am waiting in the spruce of a big island for the wind & rain to blow over—not wishing to repeat yesterdays performance. From here I can see far up the valley, beyond the outpost hills where the Splits narrow down &, I think, to the mountains of the lower canyon. Wonder if I can reach them on this half flooded river.

And here I made camp—a rotten afternoon & many mosquitoes.

Monday June 4

In the morning light I found that I had to turn back & take the snyes behind my island. Hard going on a hot morning, &, as I cut my way through the over-hanging trees under a steep bank, the axe—our big building axe—flew out of my hand into the river. I hung on the end of a line tied to a tree & fished for it as long as I could stand the cold water but no luck, so I went on. Lunch on a bar in the hot sun & then on, round a long stony point—swept back once half a mile by a very fast current. From 4:30 to 6:30 it rained in torrents & I sat by a roaring fire, sheltered from the gale by some little poplars. Then I crossed & tracked up the far side & made camp & had my supper under my tarp with the rain pouring down. Very close now to the Twisted Mountain & opposite to Jackfish Mountain which still has snow on it & appears & disappears amongst the clouds. A torrent runs down it in a gorge through the forest, flowing out of the treeless sheep ranges at the summit—through the glasses I can see its waterfalls. Up Jackfish Creek is the coal which Cousins is to come & see—I think, with this fast water to contend with, that it will stay there for many years.

Tuesday June 5

In the night it rained & I didnt get up till nearly seven. I had breakfast, shaved, washed my hair & cleaned my rifle—really all this cleanliness was in order to delay starting, because, frankly, I didnt like the look of it at all. Almost all the bars are submerged & the water travels at a great speed, swirling dangerously round driftpiles & great stranded trees. I saw that the canyons must be, by this time, impassable, & that at my present rate of struggling, fighting travel it was not worth even trying to make the Hot Springs—& probably impossible. So I decided to try to land the traps on the Twisted Mountain & camp there for a while. Then I loaded up & started.

A lovely, blue morning—even the greens seemed merely shades of blue in the clear mountain sunshine. I had hard going & was swept back down a side riffle. Hauled the canoe up again & had it swept under a stranded tree & half swamped—a nasty place. I had lunch opposite the mountain with the fast main current of the Nahanni in between. Through the glasses I could see the big swells in the fast water coming from the first rapid at the shoulder of the mountain. It was wide & very fast & I hardly dared to cross—however I risked it & made it with about ten yards to spare above the driftpile I had feared. I landed in the eddy below the rapid & close to the rock & found a good landing place & an old Indian camp with a trail along the bank.

So I made my camp & cached the traps & drew the canoe up into the trees, safe from floods & logs. Camp is shaded by birch, spruce, poplar & alder & is white with sweet smelling fruit blossom. A wonderful view over to Jackfish Mountain & up the creek with its jagged peaks—& away up the Nahanni beyond the outpost hills to the mountains of the canyon—black clouds against the blue & a yellow, angry sunset beneath them. Thunder has been about all day & the mosquitoes biting as they only do when rain is near.

Wednesday June 6

A sunny morning. After breakfast I set off through the bush to Faille's cache. Cool when I started but it soon warmed up & the mosquitoes—the little, grey stinging devils of the moss—rose in swarms. The bush was thick & the going hard & steep over rocks & moss & across little hillside streams with deep cut valleys, & the mosquitoes & the heat of clothes tightly buttoned on their account made one irritable & played out. I reached the cache after about a mile & a half of this & lit a smudge hurriedly—glad of even a smoky relief from the pests.

No sign of Faille & nobody had been there since last August—the branches of my bed lay untouched after nine months. So I made a little blaze on one of the trees of the cache & left a pencil message for Faille, in case he should come down that way, & then made my maddening way back to camp.

After lunch I took my glass, camera & rifle & put on a head net & thick gloves & set out for the peak of the Twisted Mountain—also called O'Brien's Mountain because some years back a trapper of that name was found on it by La Flair, frozen to death—possibly abandoned by his partner to die, though this was never known for certain. But O'Brien merely died on the mountain—he never lived or made his habitation on it, & so it shall always be the Twisted Mountain to me because of that tremendous upheaval in the strata.

The slope faced south & a little west &, but for a little space of bush, had been cleared of the old forest by fire. There was bare rock in places & a young growth of poplar, spruce, alder & jack pine. Then there were grassy slopes & marvellous stretches of rock garden with tiny, delicate flowers & plants—& through all this, in the blazing sunlight, there were little blue & little purple butterflies, great gold & black butterflies, & butterflies of every shade from the palest orange through red to the darkest brown. There were the first of the wild roses, bluebells, great yellow daisies, purple orchids, the little flowers of the rocks, the white fruit blossoms of gooseberries, saskatoons, strawberries, bearberries, all manner of currants, raspberries, the kini-kinik, cranberries & the multitude of the northern fruits that blossom in June & are ripe in August under the blasting, day long sunshine.

I sat at the very peak with the drop of the precipice on my left. Below lay the maze of the Splits with their snyes & winding channels. Opposite lay the jagged valley of Jackfish River & a great marshy lake over against the mountain. One could see the Liard & the calm waters of the Nahanni, &, at the same time, the gateway of the lower canyon—the place of the hot springs. A wonderful view, & I sat & watched the piled up hills through my field glasses—in the distance, here & there, the black masses of thunderstorms. I was down to supper at seven—heard the putter of an engine & saw Starke & Stevens camped below me on a bar—life didnt seem to be all jam & honey for them, hauling on their scow.

Thursday June 7
Starke & Stevens seemed to be in difficulties so I went down & gave them a pull on the track line & they struggled up to my camp. They had lunch with me & offered me a lift, in return for my help, as far as the Hot Springs. So again I hope to go ahead a little. They had met Faille on the Liard on his way to Simpson, to return immediately, so we must have missed him in the Splits. He had lost two dogs, drowned—had lost many of his traps, frozen in overflow & had no great catch of fur.

In the afternoon it lashed with rain & we decided to camp where we were for the night.

Friday June 8
With block & tackle we hauled the scow up the Twisted Mountain riffle & the rest of the day was spent mainly in cutting brush along the banks & in pulling madly on the line—the engine refusing to shove the scow up the smallest riffle. The Lord help them higher up—not for worlds would I take an outfit like that up a fast mountain river. A sunny day—mosquitoes damnable. Camp on the down-stream point of a little island & a little target practice after supper.

Saturday June 9
Another day of sunshine. A good breakfast, some hard hauling & then suddenly the engine brisked up & we made some progress. At midday we sighted a cow moose & calf, swimming the snye in front of us. We let loose an appalling volley

of excitable shots & fetched them both down in the shallows. The calf was dead but the cow rose & struggled to the bank where she stood, as we thought, ready to die. So we didnt shoot again, & suddenly, to our intense disgust, she moved away into the trees—mortally crippled but a loss & a waste unless we could find her. We crossed & landed & while Starke & I lit a smudge & skinned the calf, Stevens went off to trail the wounded cow. The thick bush, a maze of moose tracks & the thousands of mosquitoes were together too much for him & he returned to us with no news of the cow.

Followed a lunch of calves liver and bacon, a bannock baking, washing, shaving & a boiling & salting of the meat. The mosquitoes seemed roused to a frenzy & Stevens retired beneath his net while Starke & I sat in the fire smoke—he telling me tales of the Klondike trail of '98, of Fairbanks & the golden beaches of Nome, & the Omineca country. We lit also on the habits of animals &, in particular, on the migration of the Barren Lands caribou.

Sunday June 10

A damp stuffy night & what an unspeakable mosquito morning. Rain was in the air & devil a bit of rest could we get from the damned insects which hummed round us in their thousands. I wore a headnet & sweated prodigiously in that & with thick gloves on in the damp heat. The two mosquito months of the year sap ones energy & wear one down thin & lean. They pester, torture, suck blood & give no rest—many a white man, since Canada's history began, must have fallen & died in the northern bush, clean worn out by their attacks or else driven raving mad.

We made a little distance with difficulty & much cutting & hauling on the line. At midday the thunder started & the rain came down & we travelled no more. Now I am writing in bed under my net—its a little cooler but the mosquitoes still thrum outside the bar & I think there is more rain to come.

Monday June 11

A bright & fresher morning & I see that a field mouse has nibbled holes in my mosquito net—bad luck to him. We made some fair distance in the morning but spent the whole afternoon coming up the snye beyond the low point. The breeze fell & the air moistened & the mosquitoes became maddening—worse than ever before. As for the travel it was simply bull work—Swede work. The water was too fast & shallow & we strained & hauled & jagged the scow up by line & block &

tackle—cutting the overhanging trees away from the banks & sweating & cursing at the mosquitoes in the bush. These two arent river men—not canoe men & artists with the delicate paddle, such as Faille. There's no sport in this—simply labour. They merely bull their beastly outfit up the Nahanni by brute strength. And they'll need it all, & more, when they reach the canyons.

The cod line & some roots got tangled round the propeller & Stevens stripped & went into the ice cold water to set things to rights. I well knew from experience how cold it was. He came out numbed & had to lie in his eiderdown to warm.

Colder now & raining hard. I have my lean-to up, pegged down & tied to a tree & am going to lie comfortably in bed & read. There are hardly any mosquitoes—they come out in vicious swarms before a rain, & it must have been the approach of this rain that made them attack us so this afternoon.

Tuesday June 12

Nothing much to report. A late breakfast & start & possibly two miles gained in the morning with one stretch of half a mile on end of cutting & tracking with the mosquitoes savage. We passed an old cabin & cache &, set back in the timber, a baby's grave, set up on two trees, well made, with a wooden cross & covered with a white canvas. Further on, a canvas covered cache.

After lunch we tracked on up to the head of a fast little snye & there the propeller fell off & was lost. Heaven help those who tackle God's own wilderness with an engine. So here we are—camped on the big windy bend, almost between the outpost hills, & repairs to do tomorrow. A ruffed partridge is drumming in the bush & close to my bed the fast water of the Nahanni is hard at work, eating away at the bank & cutting it into the river by yards at a time.

Wednesday June 13

Up late to a grey, sunless day. New propeller keyed on to the shaft & all ready to hit the trail again. In the evening a two year old moose calf clattered out of the trees & into camp. He saw us—not twenty yards away—then jumped into the water by the scow, swam a little way down the river & came round through the bush again—clean through camp, across the snye & away into the spruce timber. Their tracks are everywhere—only yesterday, as we had breakfast, a moose calf grazed & nosed about on an island about one hundred yards away. He took a keen interest in us & it seemed that he would have come across but that he feared to swim the fast water.

Thursday June 14th

Another grey, damp day. We began life by cutting our way all round the windy bend with the mosquitoes in swarms about us. After lunch things went better & by poling hard we made perhaps three more miles & camped on a bar just below the camp from which I sighted the jagged canyon walls last year. The rain poured down & I made up my bed in a desert of wet, glistening shingle—the only thing I could find to fasten my tarpaulin & mosquito net onto being a big stranded spruce.

Last Sunday a bald headed eagle flew over us at lunch time—the first I have seen up here & a magnificent bird.

Friday June 15th

No rain & as the clouds lifted off the mountains the sun returned to us & shone nobly—there was a roar of colour in the rain washed air—the season of flowers is on us, the wild roses are opening & there are more of the big gold & black butterflies. The mosquitoes lie low a little, for they hate the hot, clear sunshine. I thing [*sic*: think] we have climbed about 3½ miles—may be more. It was all through the low valley that lies between the outpost hills & the ranges which now stand out blue in the west & close to us, with the last remaining snows all rose in the late sunset. A sweet evening—the sound of the Nahanni all round this island, & the thrum of a mosquito hawk which always reminds me of Battle River & those long June evenings with the Urchin raising the black dust of the trail beneath me. Now & then the wind brings a whiff of sulphur down the valley from the springs.

I'd like to take M*arigold* into the mountains—to Anceindaz & the Cerdagne, & eat the jolly food of 1920 once more in the mountain rest houses. And drink the black beer of Sion & eat the pleasant, dribbly pears of Randa & Zermatt.

Saturday June 16th

Up till lunch time we didnt do so badly. I was up early & roused the two sleepers, & we hit the river at 7:30 of a lovely morning of sun & breeze. And all went fairly well until, at midday we came to the point & head of the last snye just below the hot springs reach. There was untold hell toward. We jammed the scow twice on the point of the island & fought & scrapped with the thing in the cold, fast water until we got it down the snye head. We then spent the almost five hours that remained to evening working the damnable scow out of the snye by means of block & tackle, pole & sheer brute shoving—always in the water & building our deadmen on a submerged bar, out of poplar logs & boulders.

We got the scow out when the sun was low & the water glittering in our eyes, & ran for a point of the rock, swung out to cross the river, missed passing a fast snye head on the opposite bank, crashed into a log jam, & ended up, after an afternoons toil, about ten yards ahead of where we had lunch & on the opposite bank.

When we landed we found a little, two months old moose calf curled up on the shingle, partly hidden by young liards. His mother's tracks were fresh in the sand—she had left him there where the wolves were not likely to come, & he lay there very obediently & dead still, except for his anxious eyes, until I was within ten yards of him. Then he could stand it no longer & rose & tried to cross the snye but misliked the swift water. So he clattered past Starke & away down the island.

From here I can see the canyon gateway, split in the rock against the sunset, & the old shacks perhaps a mile & a half away up the reach. But there are mosquitoes now & no wild fruits to eat, & the Nahanni is rising still & swinging past in a muddy swirl of fast water that makes travel impossible—very different from those golden August days of last year—only the loveliness is unchanged, excepting its spring colouring.

Sunday June 17

And so at last Starke has come to the conclusion that he is uselessly bulling his way up the river & that he may as well camp here & wait for lower water. Also he says, damn him if he would ever tackle the South Nahanni again with an engine of any sort—nothing now is any use but a two man Yukon poling boat. I still hold to the canoe, as in the beginning—& I think that for many, many years this will be a little known river. So back in the spruce I set to work this morning & built a triangular cache—well made & at least 11 feet off the ground. In it I put—1 sack of dog harness—1 sack 50 lbs. whole wheat—1 bale 40 lbs. rolled oats—1 bale 56 lbs. Smiles porridge & 5 lbs. rolled oats—1 box candles—my top boots, rubber boots, shoes & 1 moccasin rubber. On the ground below are the stove & two sacks of traps—in all a good 340 lbs of weight on its way to the Flat River.

I did it alone—it was hot work & I had to wear my face net because of the mosquitoes which were thick in the bush. Then I sorted things out, cleaned various things, washed some clothes & ended, just before supper, with a glorious bath on the point in the sun & the breeze—changed into clean summer clothes & so came as near to godliness as this country will allow. A gorgeous day & a beautiful evening but one cannot stay out to talk & watch the mountain sunset. The mosquito is king in June & we are driven under our nets to read & write.

At midday a loon passed by, floating down with the current & treating us to his weird call.

Monday June 18

A very hot day & I made it a laundry day & a day of general cleansing—consequently a hell of a day, but its over now & all my things are clean & in order. The river has dropped nearly two feet in the last two days, so if the drop holds & tomorrow is fine I shall go down in my canoe to the Twisted Mountain & try to bring up this far the traps & things that I left there. Upstream travel at this lower stage of water will be easier, as the current will be slacker & many bars & beaches will be uncovered. This may be the beginning of the big drop as the snows are light in the mountains this year—the Lord now save us from heavy rains.

Starke & Stevens hauled their scow out of the water, preparatory to cutting her down in width—the better to tackle this fast river.

Two moose appeared today on the bar by the sulphur spring that flows from the painted cliff, &, this evening, either a moose or a bear far down river on the edge of the bush. A wonderful game country.

Tuesday June 19th

Two moose were bathing in the river at breakfast time—on the first riffle below the springs. Soon afterwards I loaded up my canoe & set out. I reached the Twisted Mountain in two hours & twenty minutes—a glorious, blue morning with white, bumbly clouds hanging over the hills, & I shot downstream without a care in the world—all lifted away by the breeze & the flash of the sun on the water. The wild roses are coming out now & the banks are one mass of flowers, with the butterflies among them.

About a mile above the riffle I passed a moose—perhaps 150 yards away & standing cooling himself in the water. As I wasnt going down to Gordon & the dogs I had no use for the meat, so I just whistled to him & he looked at me very soberly & without moving.

I had lunch & loaded up the traps on the rock above the riffle, set off back at 1:25 & travelled till 6:45. I have the much dreaded Splits of the Nahanni down to a science now & my own particular trail though them, & I made a very good afternoon's distance without too much grief—except a lot of wading up riffles, & the water is warming up fast. A splendid sunset, but best looked at from under a mosquito net. I shall try to make Starke's camp tomorrow just to show them what hitting the trail really means.

Wednesday June 20

A sweet day. The breeze came up about ten & drove down the mosquitoes—the leaves tossed & glittered in the wind & the sunlight—there was a pleasant feeling of heat & a smell, under the banks, of conifers & wild roses—the hot smell of the bush & the earth, & hardly one mosquito showing of all the prodigious army sheltering in the moss & grasses from the wind & the hot sun.

Lots of the gold & black butterflies & also one new one—a splendid fellow in black & white. Came on a brood of nine chicks sheltering in an eddy—dark brown & with a band of white across the wing. One dived under my canoe as he swam to his mother, & scuffled madly underneath, unable to rise.

I started at seven & travelled ten hours—travelled well & am now camped about one mile below Starke's camp.

Thursday June 21st

A jolly morning & at 7:20 I started & poled on up, to find Starke having breakfast on beaver tail & Stevens still in bed. I put my gear in the cache &, at ten, I set off down river for Gordons camp. Didnt make very fast time as there was a strong head wind which spun the canoe like a cork, so, except in the tricky places & fast water, I let her drift most of the time. No mosquitoes owing to the wind & I had a glorious bathe, sunbath & shave at midday. In the afternoon I followed a maze of winding snyes that lay over on the Jackfish side of the Nahanni—it would take a lifetime to learn thoroughly all the channels of the Splits—an amazing stretch of fast, rushing waterways that extends for at least twenty miles on the Nahanni. I fished about for almost an hour in the snye in which I lost the axe when I went up but had no luck & so I pushed on down till Nahanni Butte came close to me again, & reached Gordon's camp at supper time. I think I had come about thirty miles, & the aneroid showed a fall in height of 250 feet down from the hot springs, but this may have been partly due to a normal rise of pressure.

Found a neat camp set amongst the tall trees & the wild roses—nobody at home but presently Gordon came up the snye with a reinvigorated engine.

He handed on the gossip—Astley had been up to Jackfish River prospecting for coal—poor Cousins' mill & lumber had burnt at Fort Liard the day we left— Faille was reported to have had a sack of gold, or what he believed to be gold, with him when he went down to Fort Simpson—Harrington is to make a police patrol to the Flat next winter—Father Gouet's cattle were wrecked on the Liard. The scow being left high & dry on a driftpile, while the cattle swam ashore & camped, very sensibly, in the nearest patch of green grass. Meanwhile, Alexander & the B—t walked to Fort Liard in search of help.

We decided to trust the engine to get us to the springs at least—nest the little canoe inside the nineteen footer, load up the 18 foot. freighter which I shall handle with the time honoured weapons of pole & paddle, & take all our possessions with us at one departure.

Friday June 22
A blazing hot day, all sunlight, & a breeze that made life bearable & kept the insect world down in the moss & leaves. We spent the day loading up & preparing to leave—everything is ready, including a shocking bad bannock that I baked in a hurry, & now dam me if the river hasnt risen a good five inches. She is increasing in power again, getting muddier & sending down drift logs & floating trees—all the signs of a flood & I thought the June flood was over. Maybe this hot weather is melting some snows far up at the head of the Flat—however, we shall see in the morning.

Saturday June 23rd
A very hot day, but with a breeze that lasted till evening. The river has now risen eighteen inches & it would be foolish to start with it on the rise—a rise that may be due to this heat melting the last of the snows. So we did odd jobs to kill time & in the evening *Gordon* took the big canoe & engine down the snye to try for a beaver. He saw two at work felling trees but couldnt get in a shot—I noticed that the engine was driving his canoe & load very well against the current when he came back.

Sunday June 24
The wind has changed from east to west & has driven back the blue smoke haze from Mackenzie River fires, so that it is cooler now & the hills stand out clear & sharp in all their colours like a day of early spring. The river has risen two more inches & is now hanging almost steady, so still we have to wait. I sharpened knives & axes this morning & drew spikes from the old cache, & now we are reduced to reading on this lovely afternoon. I never saw anything like the wild

roses here—they are everywhere, on bushes six feet high, standing out against the green in clusters of great even petalled flowers in every shade from red to the palest pink. They are well sheltered from the winds by the big spruce, have lots of sunlight & a very rich soil.

Monday June 25

We heard Faille's engine last night & he came to our camp for supper—& then we talked. From breakfast time today—Faille made the old Norwegian logging cake—till lunch, which he had with us, we talked again & heard his news, & then in the early afternoon he left us & set off on his way.

He had been a month on his way from Simpson, working his canoe with a ton load up the rapids of the Liard, & is now going to find new ground above the falls of the Nahanni—in the open, rolling, well wooded country of the calm waters into which he & I looked last August from the head of the falls. His last trap line on the Flat River was too much hemmed in by the mountains & on it he had only bad luck. Early snow & ice caught him barely ready—wolverine broke into his shack & stole three wolf pelts & so much of his grub that he almost starved. In order to get in the wolverine tore out the stove pipe & enlarged the chimney hole, &, having done this, proceeded to raise hell with all within. One dog was drowned & another ran away to the wolves. Faille slipped on a mountain side & was laid up for three weeks, during which time many of his traps froze in in the overflow & he lost much fur—also the game left the country &, being sick, he could not follow or tell where if had gone. Wolves & wolverine ate the fur from his traps—he fired at caribou, needing meat, & missed, not knowing that his sights had slipped up to 1000 yards—he had adventures with a raft amongst the ice—was wind whipped in the canyons on the way down—et alia—a full winter. And now he is trying again. We were glad to meet again—he has sent my sheep head out for me to my bank in Edmonton—one of the best of fellows.

A lovely day—clear sunshine & wind, & the river dropping steadily. Tomorrow we intend to leave for up river.

This country would be a paradise of mountain, forest & flowers if it were not for the mosquitoes—outside my net they hum unceasingly.

Tuesday June 26

A very hot clear morning & we loaded up & started. I went away first, poling the 18 foot canoe, & as I headed up stream *Gordon* saw a bull moose watching me all the way from the far bank. He—*Gordon*—followed me up the snyes with the 19 footer & the engine & did various peculiar feats of navigation, one of which might easily have resulted seriously. Sometimes I wonder whether he has any eye at all for the actions & dangers of fast water. After much bedevilment the vibration finally & irretrievably smashed the repairs to the engine—so thank God we at last know where we are. At the time I was about a mile ahead with the fire made & tea water boiling, on a sand bar, waiting for lunch. I boiled that kettle for four solid hours, wondering what had happened, till *Gordon* appeared dragging a canoe that was far too heavy for him. So we made lunch into supper & camped there & in the night it blew very hard. Now we are saddled with a useless engine, all the petrol & that great lump of a canoe—all of which results from not abiding by our original decision to abandon the engine.

Wednesday June 27

Started latish & made desperately slow going. The big canoe is really too heavy for one man to handle—we must simply try to get it to Faille's cache & leave it there. *Gordon* is still wonderfully unhandy with a pole—but I suppose not too bad, considering that he never punted in England. In the afternoon it rained & in the evening we had a lot of work & trouble around a driftpile—what a day. Also my pole finally snapped as I was poling the big canoe—it had been sprung since Starkes scow bent it against the bank.

Thursday June 28

A strong cold head wind, clouds low on the mountains & a little drizzling, misty rain. I had to make a new pole, so I rooted up a good straight piece of drift & at the same time walked through the point with my rifle to see if I could stir up a moose, as we need meat badly. Now it is afternoon, the pole is finished & *Gordon* has gone a-hunting—too wretched a day to travel, always soaked & in the river half the time, if one can avoid it. I worry sometimes a great deal—I have taken this year from *Marigold* & everything seems to be turning against us so that we can achieve nothing. The luck must turn soon.

Friday June 29

A morning of soft mountain clouds, turning later to sunshine & breeze. We headed for the island of Trinacria, beloved of the Greeks, over against Jackfish Mountain, since I had decided that it was better for us to build a new cache there

& not to try & reach Faille's cache at the Twisted Mountain. So we camped at my old camp of June 3rd & had a much needed supper. Then I began work on the cache, choosing & peeling my trees & felling those close by from which squirrels might be able to jump. We unloaded the big canoe & worked until nearly eleven.

Saturday June 30
A sweet summer day—clouds low over the mountains & then wind & a clear sunlight. I finished the cache & we laid up the engine & our unspeakable Noah's Ark—we launched & loaded the little canoe—cached our extra grub & I made a new pole, having smashed my second in an awful effort to turn Noah's Ark into the right course.

At five we hit the river & slipped through the snyes behind the island & camped on the main river at their head—a lovely place & a lovely sunset behind the hills over a mile of calm, shallow water. After supper I mended a paddle that I had a split over Quiz' head when he moved in my canoe at a critical moment, & now I am safe under the net with the mosquitoes roaring outside. For once we have done in a day all that we set out to do.

Sunday July 1
Sunday always seems to be with me what Corporal Barber would call "one sweet scented son of a female dog." It has been a lovely day—sun & a south wind which made the mosquitoes lie low—& there you have its one redeeming feature. Also we have travelled some distance & are now camped where, last year, I saw the bear swim the river—at Lone Spruce Island & well beyond the Twisted Mountain. But we had trouble in the wide splits with the dogs—the damned animals have no sense & swim wildly in all directions. Gordon worries & keeps a-hollering to them when all his attention should be on his canoe, & we lose a lot of time. Also, this evening, Poilu made a very bad crossing & was carried miles down stream & *Gordon* was late to camp through having to go after him. Never take dogs on a trip if you can avoid it & above all never anybody's pet dogs.

Gordon is miraculously slow in handling his canoe—the little one—& I have to teach & explain to him the very simplest things concerning it. Seems slow in the uptake & uncommon clumsy, but I think he tries hard—he may be a slow learner.

I came very near to drowning & losing my canoe this afternoon just above the Twisted Mountain. I jumped for a steep bank of shingle with the track line in my hand—the stones gave way & the canoe whirled in the fast water & pulled me back in. I was being hauled downstream, up to my neck in water & clawing at loose shingle for a hold. However, I hung on to the line & the canoe & somehow wriggled back to the bank & out—a damp affair & it made my temper very short for a while.

Monday July 2

A very hot sunny day & now a much cooler evening—possibly as we are getting higher into the hills. We are camped within 8 or 9 miles of the hot springs, at the head of the windy bend & have travelled a fair distance. But we lost a lot of time in a little snye—the river has dropped so much that places which were deep when I last was here are now almost too shallow for our canoes.

Gordon did the unpardonable thing today—fumbled his track-line as he was climbing over a log jam & lost his head & his canoe at one & the same time. Luckily I was close ahead of him & could turn my canoe & pursue his downstream & catch it before it could come to harm—otherwise half our outfit would have been lost, together with our small canoe. If I had known that it was an utterly green hand that I was bringing as my partner then I should have come back alone as the Nahanni will not give him many more chances to display his clumsiness. Yet such a pleasant companion & we get on so well. But—coupled with the zoo—what a drag on the wheels.

Tuesday July 3rd

Another blazing day—by the time we made camp in the evening I was pretty well dog tired. We travelled for nine hours &, as the main course of the Nahanni is from the west, for the last hour or two the glitter of the sunlight on the water was in our eyes—a very tiring thing. Ones eyes also smart in these summer months from the smoke of smudges & the honest sweat that mixes with the citronella & mosquito oil & runs down into them. And a beard—there seems to be no time these days to shave—& tattered shoes, torn on the rocks, & soaking rags of clothes, wet all day hauling the canoes up rapids & riffles—this is not the romantic West of pictures & stories—of chaps & taps & latigo straps—of scarlet shirts, Stetsons & lumberjack boots—but simply the North where in summer one fights heat, bulldogs & mosquitoes, in the winter the frost & the storms & in the spring cold water, slush & rotten ice. But I think that the golden days of the fall make up for it—a sweet, clear stillness, soft sunshine, wild fruit, & the golden leaves glowing over the clear green of the rivers.

The Painted Cliff.

We have made camp below the springs & opposite to my cache & Starke's old camp—not a bad day. I gave *Gordon* some more instruction in tracking—he improves apace & I feel more hopeful. To save our souls we cant sight a moose, & for this work we need red meat, & lots of it. I handle the heavy 18 foot freight canoe, being the more experienced of us two, & when I get hold of a moose or bear there's going to be a memorable eating. In the meantime we eat vast quantities of porridge.

Wednesday July 4th
Up late, at 6:30, & the sun blazing like a furnace—the river & the mountains seemed to quiver in the fierce heat. Today was to be something in the nature of a holiday—one needs an occasional spell away from the fast water, the wading, & the handling of a loaded canoe. So we had a lazy breakfast by the river & then tended our various cuts & hurts. Ones legs become hammered & scarred on the sharp rocks & in the bush & only yesterday I nicked my ankle with an axe—& all these heal very slowly when one is everlastingly in the water.

Then we slipped across to my cache on the far bank to see that all was in order & to get my packsack of clothes & my pistol. About eleven we moved on upstream & came past the painted cliffs, where I had a drink of the sulphur water that trickles from the rock. The dogs had a hard scramble & swim round the cliff—in fact Poilu, thoroughly spoilt all his life, gave it up & made the summer noonday hideous with his yells until he realized that we had no intention of helping him—whereupon he also got down to it & came up to us as we had lunch under a point of rock from which, out of every crevice, grew innumerable flowers.

We crossed & came to the place of the springs—a joyous stench, as of rotten eggs—streams of clear hot water flowing into the Nahanni—cleared spaces of old Indian camps now overgrown with wild roses & wild fruits—swarms of mosquitoes, & the cliffs that form the gateway to the Lower Canyon closing gradually in, mysterious in the haze of afternoon, with the downy seed of the poplars floating lazily from sunlight into the blue shadows like so much thistle down. We crossed to the old cabins on the left bank of the river & there fell upon wild strawberries—enormous, red, & with that sweet smell that reminds one of old walled gardens in England & of irate gardeners in hot pursuit. There were gooseberries ripe & wild onions & a promise of many raspberries to come—the fruit of the wild roses was reddening & there were clumps of marguerite daisies—& everywhere a little mauve & white flower that smelled like heliotrope. And one trod on wild thyme that crushed very sweetly, as it does in Sussex or on the rock islands off Fort Chipewyan. A bathing place of the moose—in the black sand were the tracks of many cows & calves. So we camped there, where the stones & the bank sloped gently up into the tall spruce & there we settled our final plan.

Without the engine we cant do what we set out to do—trap & winter on the headwaters of the Flat River—as we should be all summer moving the outfit in there. So we shall make our base beyond the canyon, in the Second Splits or Dead Man's Valley as it has been called since the killing of the McLeods,—possibly on the Meilleur River. *Gordon*, who is the trapper, will stay there & build our shack (God help us this coming winter) & hunt & cut the trap line & seek out the haunts of the fur. I shall go on alone as far as I can travel up the Flat & try to find the gold that was found & lost again ten years ago. I shall take the small canoe & travel light & as fast as possible with my rifle, a little grub & my prospecting outfit & shall only return to the Meilleur River when the snow falls & the waters begin to freeze. In this way each of us will do the work for which he is best fitted—*Gordon* will see to the trapping & I shall tackle the river travel &

+

First or Lower Canyon of the South Nahanni.

---

the search for gold. So I shall hit the trail alone again, I hope—save maybe for the little bitch, who is very attached to me & who answers variously to the following appellations—Ma'm'selle, Mrs Blimp, Mrs Doin's, & Mrs Wallop-her-tail-then.

Thursday July 5th

I decided that, with this height of water against us, we could not get between the sheer cliffs by the shingle island in the canyon. So I left *Gordon* in camp, airing the loads & hoping for a moose, & went down to our cache 25 miles below, in the Splits & opposite Jackfish Mountain. I had a head wind most of the way—came down in 3 *hours* 50 min*utes* travelling time—& the aneroid showed a drop of 125 feet. I took all that we need from the cache & left it, I hope for a year, to guard the derelict engine, the petrol & the big canoe, & am now camped at my old camp of June 5th. I should reach the springs in about two days from here & with the river falling, as it is, we should then have a better chance in the canyon. This makes my ninth time over this stretch of the Splits—I shall know it now like the palm of my hand.

A hot, breezy day—all sunshine.

To remind myself—the next time I'm in Hatchards, in Piccadilly of blessed memory, I want to get—Casanova's Escape from the Leads.

F.C. Selous' book on the Yukon

Hanbury's "In Lands Forlorn"

Casanova's Memoirs (they had an edition, very well bound—unfortunately its appearance coincided with a state of abject poverty on my part.)

From the springs to Jackfish Creek the aneroid showed a drop of 125 feet.

Friday July 6th

Up at four to a cloudy sky with thunder in the air. I had breakfast & was on the river by six & made one devil of a long days travel, as I sometimes do when alone. I was on—& in—the water for 11½ hours—had lunch at eleven, supper at five & finally camped in the bay at the foot of the poling reach at eight in the evening. I never realised how dead tired I was until I had made tea & changed into dry things—then my feet felt suddenly leaden. Wading in the water on & off all day is deadly tiring but owing to the stimulus of the cool water one doesnt notice it until the evening & the next morning. Also the day was very hot, with rain in the air, & the mosquitoes, wherever the water was slow & the banks wooded or mossy, were maddening.

Just below the Twisted Mountain I fired three shots at a moose at about 400 yards range. The river was rising owing to thunder rains & sending down drift, & at first I paid no attention to the moose who was swimming & looked very like a drift log. He landed in the willows & trotted swiftly over the bar. I hit him with the third shot & he lurched forward—then plunged into a snye & disappeared.

Saturday July 7th

Thunder still all round & a day of fierce, tiring heat. I reached the cache at 2:30, lit smudges & worked away for a couple of hours putting my load up aloft & covering it up. While I was doing this the river changed from green to a muddy brown—the result of some violent rain further up. Then I poled on up to our camp by the springs & landed, absolutely dog tired. I slept in the tent—there was no rest at all. The dogs were restless, the rain lashed down, the mosquitoes hummed & it was awfully stuffy.

Sunday July 8

Decided to have a day's rest as I have been continuously on the river for a fairish while, & I woke up scarcely rested. A day of sun & thunderstorms with wonderful cloud & rain colourings in the mountains. I had a hair cut & a thorough clean-up—the most refreshing thing in the world. Also some rifle practice with my telescope sight at a black rock across the river, at which I made some pretty shooting, receiving a kick on the forehead from the sight that made my head fairly sing. I fitted a haft to a big axe head that *Gordon* found in one of the old cabins. He has been gleaning & has picked up besides, two chisels, a prospector's shovel & the Fourth Canadian Reader which contains many oddments such as the 'Inchcape Rock' the 'Death of Nelson' & extracts from Pickwick Papers.

A misty, rainy evening & the mosquitoes savage. I have my bed & bar pitched outside where there is air—cant abide that stuffy tent.

Monday July 9th

A clear sunny day with the clear colours that come after rain—& a new & most gorgeous butterfly, pale orange & blue. We loaded up the canoes & pulled on into the canyon mouth, & at last the walls closed in on us & shut out the lower country. Below the first rapid we found Starke's scow anchored off the shore, only half loaded & no sign of her owners. We found them camped above on the great flow of rock & loose stone that comes down from Lafferty Creek—the scene of the fake gold rush of years ago. The stakes of the worthless claims are still showing—Starke told me that he had followed the creek up for some distance & that, though it is merely a seep through a desolate valley of stone where it enters the Nahanni, further up there is a good body of water, running in a tremendous cleft in the rock that is almost a tunnel. He panned ten pans of gravel but in only three of them did he get the faintest colours.

They had been unable to get up the first rapid & had been there eight days waiting for the water to fall & getting only this rise which still continues & is making the river muddier & faster, covering the bars & sending down the drift. We gave them our useless engine grease that we had brought for them & in return they gave us dried moose meat, salt, an axe & a magazine—we seem to have become snappers up of any odd trifles these days. Afterwards we lazed on the hot stones, full of good vittles, soaking in the golden sunshine, talking, & looking on a world of grey & purple stones & precipices that might well have been some South African valley instead of the mountain west. Then we took our canoes & pushed on round the bend to my Last Man Camp of a year ago, & now supper is cooking over the fire by the waters edge, with the great cliffs towering above us, their tops yellow & gold in the light of the setting sun, their bases in the evening shadows with the rising Nahanni clashing & swirling against them.

Tuesday July 10th

The most perfect day of the summer so far—the sunshine pouring down out of a cloudless sky & a sweet breeze eddying through the canyons. The heat & the wind accounted for the mosquitoes, & all day we have lazed by the water's edge, bathed & done odd jobs, unable to go further because of the rise in the river from the thunder rains. We walked up through the bush to the next point & considered our chances, but I decided that we could only move with so much labour that it was not worth it, as the water reached its height & turned about breakfast time & is now falling fast, so I think that tomorrow will see us on our way. The cliffs here rise to about six hundred feet above us, & are now turning grey & mauve in the evening light—the sky above blue & rose coloured, & the trees that cling to the ledges a dark green.

Wednesday July 11

A fine hot day & we are making our way slowly but surely up the canyon. The water is still much higher than I had it last year, the load is heavier & there are dogs to look after & occasionally to carry in the canoes, all of which holds us back, but, even so, I think we have come up four miles of difficult water. We are camped on the island by the valley of the pinnacle with the fast water boiling past on both sides, cutting & undermining the cliffs which rise here to 700 or 800 feet—trees growing from every ledge, the gentler slopes & old falls of rock thickly timbered,

& the whole jagged canyon with its impossible twists & windings settling into twilight under a rose coloured sky.

Thursday July 12

About midnight it began to rain so I got up & covered everything that we had lying on the beach. Then I slung my tarpaulin over my mosquito net & went back to bed to sleep the sleep of the justly tired. We had breakfast with mist & rain driving between the canyon walls & then loaded up & tracked the canoes to the head of the island. The whole morning was spent in getting the outfit along the stretch of cliff that almost stuck me last year—I had a good deal of climbing to do & in two places we went ahead with the long line, floated it back & so hauled up the canoes. Finally I took the little canoe up into a bay of black sand—an old camp of Failles—& clambered back to *Gordon* over the cliff. We then embarked with the dogs in my canoe & poled, paddled & clawed hold of the rocks until we had it in the bay beside the other—& there we had lunch. We travelled a short while in the afternoon & then my pole smashed between two rocks—I seem to be unlucky with poles this year. So we camped on the moraine of a creek that runs in from the left bank of the Nahanni, below the old gold claim. The sun had broken through & lit up the canyon walls to gold, with the shadows a lovely blue—& overhead a deep blue sky with white clouds driving across before a strong wind. It might have been a May sky in England. I fashioned a new pole—& *Gordon* fished, & is still fishing. He has caught a brook trout & a coney—which is the "poisson inconnu" of the old French voyageurs. This is interesting since the coney is, officially, only to be found in the Mackenzie River & its system of lakes and rivers. It is ten now—twilight & a clear sky, but with a cool, gusty wind that may mean more rain.

Friday July 13

A tearing wind all night & a sunrise which turned the canyon walls to copper. A downpour started at breakfast time which lasted nearly all day & we had to move our camp a little downstream from the exposed moraine to a more sheltered beach. The wind made any attempt at travel impossible, the river was rising & the canyon walls were hidden in driving rain & streamers of mist & cloud. About five it cleared & I took my rifle & walked up the moraine & up the creek valley for an hour or so. It was a deep valley—almost a canyon—& a valley of tremendous stones, wooded at the sides & rising to the great limestone cliffs &

the high pastures of the wild sheep. It was cool in the evening shadows, shut off from the world & lonely—across one end, & very far below, the brown flood of the Nahanni swirled past—upstream the high hills stood out clear against the sky in their rainy day colours with the last wisps of cloud around them. In places the creek bed was dry, the water seeping somewhere beneath the overburden of boulders & there I found masses of beautiful quartz, some of them showing the blue & green stains of the copper that seems to be in all the ranges of the Mackenzie Mountains from Nahanni Butte onwards.

About supper time the water began to rise prodigiously, & we had to set to work & shift the tent & our gear to a higher spot, as the canoes threatened to float in at the door. So now we shall have to lie up again & wait for this flood to pass. Its high time we had a little good luck—ill luck has dogged us since we left Kenes Creek, & furthermore we fished for an hour in the rain today & caught nothing but a damned good wetting. However, *Gordon* found red currants ripe in the bush.

Saturday July 14

The glass went up last night & the morning was all pure gold—a gorgeous burst of colour. I took my pack & rifle & some grub & went again up the valley of the creek, followed it up for two hours & then turned to the right & went up the side of the valley to try to get out onto the open grazing lands of the sheep. I had a long climb over rocks & grass & loose screes of broken stone, where a false step might easily have started an avalanche of rock, & a mad scramble at the end, in the course of which I found an outcrop of copper & galena from which I took specimens. This landed me very near the top, but under a cliff up which I could not climb & over a dangerous scree of stone which I was doubtful about descending. So I sat still on my ledge for a time in the hot, still sunshine—no sound except the thrum of a little warm breeze, the rattle of a falling stone & the occasional chirp of a cri-cri. No sheep, no eagles—not a sign of life, but the very perfectest of summer days & a view of mountains piled range on range into the blue distance & a brown ribbon that was the Nahanni moving through its gorge, over 2000 feet below. Nobody could get me out of the mess but myself, so finally I tackled the job with prodigious care & got down somehow, & here I am by the creek again, having made tea & eaten & soon to set off down to camp again. The great cliffs make an amphitheatre of the place in the middle of which I sit with the creek running by from pool to pool, under & over the big stones. One side of the valley is in the shadow, the other lit up by the full blaze of the evening sun—& the smoke of my fire rises in between. It has been a very lovely day but I didnt get my sheep—& if I hadnt obstinately tackled the loose screes there might have been mutton for supper.

This valley reminds me very much of that of the [Liserne?] in Switzerland, on a certain Sunday of 1920.

To get me—Ralph Stock's "The Dream Ship."

Sunday July 15th

The Nahanni was in full spate this morning, but just on the turn for the drop. It was impossible for us to move against that tearing, heaving flood of water so I set out once more up the creek. It was a cool, fresh morning & I climbed fast, keeping an eye on the aneroid which I took with me this time, setting it at zero at the camp by the waters edge. I was amazed to find that in this clear, mountain air we had been hopelessly underestimating our heights. The main canyon walls just here are a good 1500 feet, & the topmost cliffs that rise almost sheer above the Nahanni are an easy 3000 feet or more above the river. I went far up the creek valley—in sunshine, mist & rain—until, at about 3000 feet above camp, I came to the end of the trees. The last little wood was of spruce—trees such as are found in the Barren Lands, eight inches or so thick at the stump & tapering away to a point at anything from three to seven feet above the ground—twisted, knotty little trees, always fighting the cold & the winds, & some of them even growing along the ground. The creek valley ran from here on up into the bald hills & the blue sky—a bed of great boulders with a stream of clear blue water running down, shut in by screes of grey stones & bare, rock strewn, grassy hillsides running up to the limestone cliffs above—it might have been in my own north country, or in Scotland, or among the stony Welsh mountains. There was even a little cold wind & here & there a patch of snow—but there were also the gorgeous black, white & red butterflies & the golden ones—& a few mosquitoes, but very few—the June heyday of that pest is over.

I began to climb, & at 4000 feet I came out into a wonderful country, such as I had never dreamed existed behind the canyon walls. It was the Southdown country of Sussex on a vast scale—not a tree or a stick, but simply the open pastures of the caribou & the mountain sheep of the north west—miles & miles of high, close cropped grazing land, stony here & there & with sometimes a great block of stone standing solitary, like a farmhouse in its fields. I went on for about three miles along under the ridges, searching the valleys & the prairies with my glass but I could see no game—for some reason this may not be their favourite range. At last I perched on a rock on the top of a round grass hill at a height of 4500 feet—the roof of my world. The whole green upland lay around me with the sunlight & the rainstorms & a cold wind sweeping over it. The country was rent into a maze of canyons & deep valleys out of which came the noise of water & the boiling cloud vapours. I could see the country beyond the Liard—lazy in the sunshine, Nahanni Butte—fifty miles away, the Long Walls, the Twisted Mountain, the whole range of the Mackenzie Mountains & a mass of mountains away towards the Yukon border. I sat there with a mountain world round me, lovely in all shades of blue in that clear blue sunlight, until the cold wind & the evening mists gathering drove me down from that flower starred country into the valley of the great stones, & from there into the trees of the arctic forest & back to camp on the Nahanni. I never stopped—four hours it took me & I came home tired & hungry, but with a day that I shall always remember.

Monday July 16th
A blazing hot morning & the rain flood almost gone from the river—so we loaded up & started & did our best, but met with illimitable damnation under a cliff & around a pile of boulders where the water, still high, swirled dangerously. However, we got round & finally camped in a sandy eddy, with the canyon walls still steeper & closer around us. Thunder showers soused us during the day but the evening cleared to a sweet sunset.

Tuesday July 17th
A hot, perfect summer's day, with a breeze & almost no mosquitoes—I think they are coming to an end, at least in the canyons with their cool nights. We started well but were forced to portage the whole outfit round two huge boulders where the full lash of the current made tracking hopeless & dangerous. Starke & Stevens appeared with their scow & passed us, & later we came up to them & we all camped together. It seems that life is not all pleasure for them—the Nahanni is giving them work a-plenty.

The Lord send it dont rain tonight as I only have my net up—no shelter—& it looks like rain. And I'm very sleepy.

Wednesday July 18
A hot perfect day & the mountain colouring very lovely with the pale blue heat haze in the canyon & the shadows, & the sunlight from the creek valleys cutting

across it. Starke set out before us but we travelled well & were level with him at lunchtime but on the opposite bank of the river—too far to call or be heard, but the smoke of our fires floated lazily out & joined in midstream. After lunch the water became faster & the hell began again. Far ahead we could see Starke & Stevens working like madmen in a riffle, black dots against the rushing, sunlit water—up to their waists & hauling their scow. Then through the glasses I could see them windlassing round a rock, & ahead of them, at the end of the reach, a white line of tossing water which I knew for the Cache Rapid which Faille & I had named last year—the worst place on the river & the head of the Lower Canyon. We came to a great rock with a roar of water round it against which we could do nothing & we were forced to portage the whole outfit—canoes as well—over thirty yards of tumbled stones. So it was not till after eight that we landed in camp in the little sandy bay at the foot of the Cache Rapid—very tired & with tempers raw. Starke was there—said he couldnt get up the rapid till the water was at least a foot lower. I said that we would be up the next day & I think he had his doubts. It was a lovely sunset & at 10:30, when the others were all abed, I walked up over the rocks & stood by the white, yelling water, considering it very carefully in the rose coloured twilight.

Thursday July 19

Early on a cool, bright morning I went ahead & reconnoitered the rapid carefully. It seemed to me that we could get up without portaging & by means of lightening the canoes only in the worst place of all. So I went back to camp & got *Gordon* & placed him on a rock in a strong strategic position—then I went back & paddled the little canoe up to him through the eddy. With *Gordon* on the line & myself in the canoe, paddling & fending her off the rocks with the pole we got her safely up & tied her in calm water under the cliff & well above the white water. Several times she took in water, & it was exciting work sitting there out in the rushing water trying madly to keep the canoe's nose in to shore & her body off the shark rocks—however, we worked carefully & achieved the rapid, & then went back— wet & hungry—for lunch. I was just finishing a plate of very tough dried moose meat when Stevens sighted a mountain sheep on the far shore, grazing some little way up the hillside. He went for his rifle & *Gordon* at once said—That's a good 400 yards—better let George get his telescope sight. So I fished the thing out of my canoe & fixed it to my rifle & lay down on a rock & fired. The sheep ran a few yards & then stopped, so I fired again & this time it crashed stone dead down the hill & onto the shingle in a cloud of dust. The next problem was to get to it so we finished our lunch, loaded up—& *Gordon* asked Stevens to give us a pull on the line with our big canoe. So they went ahead over the rocks & I took the paddle again & brought the canoe up to them. All went pretty well for a time, but Stevens, being more used to handling scows, was using more brute strength & less cunning & patience than a canoe demands. Suddenly, in the worst place & before I could straighten my canoe to the current, he hauled & had me nose out from shore. There was a lash & a plunge & a boil of water & I was reaching for my knife to cut the line & try to run the rapid, when the canoe hit with a crash in behind a big rock that stood well out in the fast water. Stevens still held the line & there I hung, gripped by the eddy, & about six inches from the most evil of all that tearing water. We all swore & shouted directions to each other at the top of our voices—& of course nobody could hear a damn thing for the roar of the rapid. I got myself out somehow from behind the rock & hit the rocks of the shoreline with a prodigious wallop—clean out of control—poor unfortunate canoe. But I was still above water & we finally reached the head & then made a frantic crossing to the far side, paddling furiously to avoid being swept down into the rapid. We tied the canoes & then set out to skin my sheep. To get to him we had to wade a fast snye which took us in over our waists & almost swept us off our feet. The day was turning towards rain, cold & miserable, & by the time we had skinned the sheep, fed some to the dogs, & had waded the snye once more with the rest of the meat in a sack we were two fairly wretched objects. So we made camp there on the island in the rain & put on dry clothes & warmed our innards with mountain mutton & strong tea. He was a yearling ram, & never was meat so tender or so well tasting—practically lamb.

My canoe was leaking fast after the rough handling Stevens had given it— & me—in the rapid, so I had to go down & bale it at intervals in the night. What a day!

Friday July 20
By the way—both my bullets hit that sheep. *Gordon* found the butt of one as he was skinning—the other came to light later in his soup.

It was a sweet, fresh, rain washed morning & we broke camp early. Just as we were about to move Starke appeared. They had crossed & come up the rapid & he wanted to know if there was any more trouble ahead. I told him that there was a series of strong riffles & he went on ahead to see for himself. We had a most difficult morning—I was on ahead practically all the time, wading & hauling my heavy canoe up hills of water, grabbing her by the snout & hauling by main force, out of my depth twice, soused to the neck, sometimes poling the canoe under cliffs, with the dogs in the thing to make matters worse—giving them a lift where they couldnt swim. After four hours the country opened out sweetly into that paradise of low wooded hills & clear streams, cut out of the mountains—the Second Splits, or Death Valley. I tied my long suffering canoe by the first creek & strolled across into the spruce where the old trapping camp & caches are, & there, wading in the tall goldenrod, I fell on great fat raspberries, gooseberries, red & black currants. *Gordon* appeared with a tale of the woes of Starke & Stevens—he had seen their unwieldy craft swept backwards over a rock & had left them damning & swearing in the middle of a riffle—their propeller dinging on the stones. A strong wind blew—too strong for us to travel—so we unloaded & beached the canoes & camped & saw to the multitude of things that always break, go wrong & need cleaning—& fed ourselves well, out on the sun warmed stones, on Logging Cake & wild mutton—the green water slipping by calm as glass & reflecting the last walls of the Lower Canyon.

Saturday July 21
A wind all night & a yelling gale all day from the westwards down this sunswept valley—utterly impossible for a canoe to take the water. We had the tent up last night for fear of rain & this morning, at five when I called him, *Gordon* sat up in his eiderdown & saw a sheep on the far side of the Nahanni. I wanted him to take my rifle & the telescope sight but he left the tent with his own Mauser, sat down in the sand, took three bangs & unfortunately missed. It was a long shot & he grieved that he did not do as I suggested.

After breakfast I went over the creek & demolished all the raspberries that had ripened overnight & examined the old caches. Along the sandy beach between the trees & the water there were fresh tracks of a moose & a bear.

Then we started work on the big canoe & patched, pitched & repaired her & now have her ready for the water again as soon as this gale will let us go. It is still roaring & the sun has just disappeared, yellow & angry behind a mountain. I am now going to devour what raspberries the day's sunlight may have ripened for me.

No sign of Starke—I imagine there is untold hell toward with that scow down on those riffles below us.

Sunday July 22

Still another day of sunshine & gale—if this goes on much longer its going to be a serious loss of time for us. About 2:30 this morning Quiz yelped & I looked out & saw three sheep trotting down the far shore—I took one long range shot & missed, gave Quiz three of the best for scaring game & went back to bed. Breakfast at six & I took a long shot at four sheep high up in the rocks at about six hundred yards—no luck. In the morning I climbed the round butte at the canyon mouth & found it to be 550 feet above the river. From the far side I could see all of the Cache Rapid laid out below me & saw no sign of Starke & his scow, nor smoke from any camp fire—God knows what has happened to them. The four sheep I could see very plainly, white in the sunshine & grazing on the ledges of the precipice on the far shore. To the west I could see far up the Nahanni—the river narrow & still by our camp & fanning out into many channels higher up, then swinging north west into the mountains of the Second Canyon—the valley a great triangle in the hills, well wooded & with the blue cloud shadows chasing over the forest. After lunch we stalked & fired at two sheep which had come down to the far shore to drink. I dropped one where he stood & *Gordon* wounded the other. Mine—a young ram with a fair head on him—fell by the water & lay for a while as if dead. Suddenly he gave one last kick, rolled over into the rapid & was swept downstream. Just the luck I had with a moose last summer—& I hate to lose & waste good meat. *Gordon* crossed in the little canoe & started on the trail of his wounded one & soon after I saw it come out from the trees & move slowly up the rock face. I was just pressing my trigger to fire when a shot sounded from the woods below, & the animal ran a few paces & then crashed down the face of the cliff into the bush. A young ewe—so again we have fresh meat in the sack, & on the fire.

If only this wind would drop & let us go, but there's another flaring yellow sunset behind the mountains, & wind clouds driving across a deep blue sky.

Monday July 23

The most perfect of all mornings & we launched the canoes & went on into the valley, westwards. We had lunch by one of the many mouths of Prairie Creek— the creek of the mountain sheep above all other creeks, according to the old Indians. A creek of utterly clear water which comes down from the high sheep pastures & rushes out from a cleft in the mountain wall to form a tremendous delta of stones before reaching the Nahanni. In the afternoon *Gordon* smashed his pole while rounding a sweeper & we were delayed while we hunted up a piece of drift & fashioned it into another. After a long crossing of the river from bar to bar we landed up in my old camp of last year—where Faille & I were held up for wind—wet, cold & weary. It looked like rain, & the mosquitoes bothered us—but nothing came of it.

Tuesday July 24

A dullish morning, & we trailed on towards the Meilleur River through a seemingly endless snye—finding the water very cold. Just before lunch *Gordon* fired at a black bear & missed it—with excuse as the bear was a snapshot on the run & I had not even time to get my rifle. The sun came out & the hills took on their colouring of blues & greens & we came to the delta mouths of the Meilleur River—a creek with a valley promising us much game & fur but with no building place or good canoe landing at its mouth where we could make our base. So we pushed on in the hot sunlight—feeling very weary, which I think must be due to the sudden chill in the water. We explored quiet, dreamy snyes & found them too shallow to give us a home, & we looked at every patch of spruce but found either no building timber or else a bad site & landing. At last we came to the reach that runs up to the gateway of the Second Canyon & the mountains began again to close round us. It was no use going further into that bottle neck so I called a halt & suggested that we turned back towards the middle of the valley & looked for our cabin site in a place that I had in mind—at the mouth of a little creek where Faille & I camped together on our way down river last August. *Gordon* agreed & so we made camp for the night, put on dry things & made ourselves a very excellent supper. During supper a moose swam out onto the shingle bar in the middle of the river, so we set down very hastily our porridge & raisins & opened fire. We hit it twice & then I dropped it—but not dead, so we went back to our porridge & then sat & smoked & watched the red sunset on the lovely canyon reach until the moose should stiffen—since a wounded moose, if disturbed, will get up & travel for miles through the bush, even on three legs, only to die in the end. Towards dusk we unloaded the little canoe & went over to the moose. She—it was a cow—rose & tried to tackle *Gordon* who dropped her dead with a bullet in the heart. We worked until it was dark, skinning & cleaning the moose & then left it on the bar, covered with the hide until morning, & went back to camp & so to bed.

Wednesday July 25

A perfect morning & after breakfast we went over to the bar, quartered the moose, brought it back to camp & loaded up for down river. *Gordon* took three of the dogs & I took Poilu & all the moose meat—a gory, ghastly load, piled high & not over safe in wind—my canoe looked like a butchers shop. However, no wind blew until we made the landing I had in mind—a fast journey downstream which took us 40 minutes. I found the big canoe with her awkward load & her water gripping keel difficult to handle well—thank the Lord it was the last time that that load was to take the water under my care, for this time we found our winters home.

Wednesday Aug*ust* 1st

Since I last wrote there has been a week of hard work, lasting well on into the evenings, & no time to keep a diary. The site that we chose for our home was a good one. It is on the south bank of the Nahanni & faces north but we can set the shack a little way back into the trees & get the sunlight by making a clearing to the south of it. There is good building timber & a good beach of gravel & sand with a good landing for the canoes, while, a few yards above us, a little creek of bright clear water flows in over a moraine of stones. We are well sheltered from the high winds & can see downstream over a long reach of river, & we have a wonderful view of the mountains & of both canyon gates. Almost opposite us Prairie Creek flows in with its clear fishing pools, & we look north over the Nahanni, through the Prairie Creek Gap & into a great amphitheatre of mountain & sheep pasture. It is well in the centre of the country that we intend to trap & behind us we have the low rolling hills & little creek valleys, all thickly wooded, where in the winter-time the fur should be.

So we landed & unloaded & soon saw that we were in a great game country for in less than one hour we saw five moose either swimming or coming down to drink, &, in the afternoon, two more. The next day we saw six moose & one grey timber wolf, & the day after, as we sat at breakfast, out on the beach just after sunrise, a bull moose swam close by, eyeing us curiously. After that we saw no more—probably because most of the days were spent in the trees, cutting building logs & working on the cache. Gordon set up a rack on the stones & smoked & dried a store of moose meat—& gave me a hand when needed. I took the cache in hand & it was finished on Saturday afternoon—an enormous cache, set on four trees, cut off about eleven feet above the ground, & big enough to hold all our gear & a big store of meat as well. So we put the stuff up in it & covered it over & I sorted out my outfit for the Flat River & laid that aside.

On Sunday night it rained & on Monday morning in the rain washed sunshine we took down the tent from where it stood on the dry soft moss under the spruce trees & set out to get our last load from below the hot springs. On the way we stopped at a place where I knew of wild raspberries—& there they were, great glowing fruit, on the sand bars & under the trees—we fed there on the sweet fresh fruit for an hour. We ran the Cache Rapid carefully & anxiously—I steering. We hit one rock a grazing blow in midstream through sheer carelessness—it suddenly appeared in a seemingly safe reach when we were craning our necks, marvelling at the amazing cliffs instead of watching the swirling water. And we had trouble with Galoom—so I christened the last rapid of the canyon because his waves lash in a narrow channel against the foot of the precipice, & when I first saw them in the summer dusk last year they seemed to be yelling "Galoom, galoom, galoom." A nasty, threatening place. A cold wind came up & we just got our camp made when the rain lashed down. I went over to the old cabins, where I knew the wild raspberries grew—& never have I seen such a sight. They cover the ground in a tangled mass &, even in the rain, from them came a glow of red, so many were there. While *Gordon* made the fire & cooked I picked three quarts & we had them with cream & sugar—a most civilised meal. In the night & next morning it rained & then—yesterday afternoon being fine—we went down to my old cache & loaded the remainder of our outfit & brought it back here to our camp at the springs. *Gordon* loaded the traps & odd stuff while I had a much needed laundry day. Then I made supper & an amazing batter pudding of flour, raspberries & lard—good & of a marvellous staying power. We have lived on raspberries, stewed, fresh & cooked in the porridge—they are here in such quantities that we make simply no impression on them. There are also wild gooseberries, strawberries & red currants, & yesterday, on an old Indian camping ground over by the springs, I found saskatoons—the first I have seen on the Nahanni. All these wild fruits grow best on burnt country or on the cleared ground of man's old camping places & habitations.

This is Wednesday morning & we are all ready to start back for home. But the rain started again in the night & is lashing down now—there are limits to what one can stand & this is beyond them. I only trust it doesnt bring the river to flood again.

Starke came up to our camp last Wednesday evening, camped there a night & passed on. They had damaged their scow in the riffle above the Cache Rapid

& had been forced to portage all their gear once again. They were no longer confident—they merely hoped to reach the lower reaches of the Flat River, & Stevens told me that with one more good ding on their propeller they were finished. They now have a wholesome respect for the South Nahanni River & mean to try again next year with a better & more suitable outfit—probably poling canoes or a Yukon poling boat. They made a wild chase after a swimming moose with their scow just opposite to our camp, wounded the animal & then let it get away into the bush. This completely upset Gordon & me for the evening as we particularly dont want wounded animals knocking about our country & scaring the game away.

And it rained all day—on into the evening.

Thursday August 2

A dull, horrible, cold day with clouds hanging low on the canyon walls. No actual rain all day but never a gleam of sunshine. We loaded up & started & have travelled a few miles into the canyon—all sorts of trouble & in the water over our waists almost all the time. A cheerless day. We are now in camp & in bed & again it is raining. I hope to redeem the day a little by having at least pleasant dreams.

To get—Seton Thompsons books on this country.

Friday August 3rd

Rather a better day with some sunshine but the river still rising. I passed the day in a helpless state, fairly crippled & laid low by that old rheumatism of mine—the result, possibly, of so many raspberries, of these wet cold days spent in a damp, cold tent & of the prolonged battle yesterday soaked in the cold river water. I was rather foolish to start out from the springs on such a day as I felt the attack coming on, but I wanted to make all the speed that was possible. And now here we are—away from the hot sulphur springs, away from our home camp & all our medicines, & nothing to do but lie up & await until it is the pleasure of this pain to leave me. Also we found ourselves almost without matches—apparently only three left, until I found a full box in my rain coat pocket—each of us having thought that the other had plenty. Gordon is most patient—& I feel furious with myself as time is so valuable to us.

Saturday August 4th

A cold night & a very pleasant sunny day with the river once more on the drop. Gordon brought me my breakfast in bed—on the Nahanni River of all places!—&

now it is afternoon & I am lying on my eiderdown on the warm sand between the trees & the river, keeping still in the hot sunshine & feeling much easier. It puzzles me why so many strong, fit men are content to work in banks & offices when physically speaking, they might tackle these wild places without let or hindrance—while those who make these journeys are often hampered by some weakness such as this of mine.

The splendid butterflies are out once more on this lazy afternoon—& hardly a mosquito. The first touches of fall are appearing—ripe fruits; here & there a golden leaf; cool, misty mornings; & the red of the hips & haws. Opposite me the canyon wall rises sheer, well over 1000 feet to the forest that grows to the brink. The clouds are driven fast overhead & there is the sound of the last rapid below us & of an occasional rock slide.

Later in the evening a plane droned over the canyon & disappeared—to our very great amazement & speculation. And then it thundered & lashed with rain all the night.

Sunday August 5th

The river still falling & I feel much better though still unable to travel. Breakfast in bed & I did not get up until the sun was well over the canyon walls. As I was washing on the beach we heard the sound of the plane again, but didnt see it. Then, round the bend, voices & the putter of a small engine, & into sight & to our camp came a canvas canoe—collapsible—& three men.

A Mr Fenley Hunter F.R.G.S. of Box 97, Flushing[,] New York, his canoe man George _____, & an Indian, Albert Dease of Dease Lake. They were on a trip up the Nahanni & over the falls—up the upper river to its head, then portage to the Gravel River & down to Fort Norman & the Mackenzie. Down the Mackenzie to Fort Macpherson & across the divide by the Rat & Bell Rivers, & down the Porcupine to Fort Yukon. Up the Yukon & out to Skagway & Vancouver. A long journey & possibly more than they can compass in this short season—so we may see them back this way. Hunter very kindly gave us some small luxuries & some medicine to set me to rights—& above all took letters for *Marigold* & the mater. He gave us news—the plane was from Upper Liard Post—flu is killing off the Mackenzie & Liard Indians by scores—&, most important, Sherwood & Poole Field mean to leave South Nahanni for the Flat with their big outfit about August 20. So we are fore warned. They had lunch & went on—I hope to be able to move tomorrow. And still it rains—with intervals of sunshine.

Wednesday Aug*ust* 8th

Nine o'clock of a cool, perfect August evening & I am writing by the camp fire in the little bay at the foot of the Cache Rapid. I breakfasted in bed again on Monday & the sun shone down through the mists & I stepped out of bed & into the canoe & into the river water, & since then I have traveled—despite a roaring summer wind that arose at midday on Monday & only died down this evening. It made the going difficult & the steering hard but we held to it—*Gordon* tracking, I poling—& have reached here with much wallowing & wading & the canoe badly leaking, but without any portages. I have just been ahead to look at the rapid—it looks wild in the sunset light—the lashing, green & white water with the blue mountains of our valley behind. However, I dont think we shall have the bother that we had last time—the water being much lower.

There are no mosquitoes—we have not had any for some days now—& tonight, for the first time since May, we can sleep without nets. Regret to be obliged to state that my river trousers below the knees had reached such a state of delapidation that today I was forced to take my hunting knife & make shorts of them. Hence legs much sunburned & likely to be more so as time goes on.

Thursday Aug*ust* 9th

A chilly, grey, windless, sunless day—& nothing but hard work & wettings for us. However, we have dealt faithfully with the Cache Rapid & its two attendant riffles & are now safely in camp in our old camping place beside the little butte. The tent is up & for the first time today we are warm & dry—though a little weary of a straight diet of coffee & quaker oats. Hunter is camped here also—resting, I fancy, after the fast waters of the Lower Canyon which seem to have something unnerved him & his party—though possibly only his guides, who question me closely about the Nahanni & appear to wish themselves safely at home on the Stikine & Dease Lake. They say that this is the worst water they have ever travelled & much worse than the Frances River, & all seem to have tacitly abandoned any idea of reaching the Gravel River. They returned here very late, after we had finished supper, having spent the day up Prairie Creek. They had seen six black bears, three sheep & one moose—& had failed to bag a single animal! They tell us that the open hillsides there are aglow with raspberries—never before had they seen so many.

For our part, owing to the dogs becoming scared & shifting suddenly in the canoe, we lurched & filled with water as we were crossing the head of the Cache

Rapid to the island. I managed to swing the canoe back to the shore we had left & Gordon jumped in with the line, was pulled downstream a way, & barely managed to hold her as she grounded on a rock—nose in air & tail completely under water— the waves washing over the load. A hair raising moment as in a few seconds I should have been backwards into the worst of the rapid—& in all probability everything would have been lost. Gordon semi impaled on a rock, but holding on very stoutly. I was half afraid that his chest was stove in. However, we unloaded some of the gear, baled & raised the canoe, re-loaded, made coffee & more porridge & then went at it again with awful caution & this time succeeded. But what a day—wading above ones waist in fast water, soaked all the time, chilled, never a gleam of sunshine & the canoe leaking like a sieve. That damned canoe with this load & Gordon & I & the dogs all in is down in the nose & utterly beyond our strength. Most dangerous & I'll be happy to have it home tomorrow & be rid of it.

Friday August 10
A sunny breezy morning & Hunter & I lay in the sun, going over & correcting his map of the Nahanni. He took the names that Faille & I had given—such as the Cache Rapid, the Twisted Mountain & the Windy Bend—while he named the creek of my three climbs & the high sheep pastures Patterson Creek. We talked a long time & Gordon talked with Albert Dease, the Indian, who thinks that freeze up "come pretty soon this country," that the wooded ridges of our valley will give good trapping—especially in marten—& that Hunters canvas collapsible canoe is no damn good. In fact both he & George Ball, the white canoe man, are scared of it & wish they were safely out of this. Then Gordon & I picked a pot of raspberries, loaded up & set out for home—I had named our creek Wheatsheaf Creek—which we reached about three in the afternoon, feeling very empty after a 3 mile battle with the wind & a lump of a canoe that needed baling about every 10 minutes. We unloaded for the last time with a sigh of relief & made a notable lunch to celebrate our home coming. Everything was as we had left it—some animal had rooted about amongst a few odd things that were on the ground but the cache had utterly defeated him. Jolly to sleep knowing that we havent got to rise & lug that monster of a canoe up stream again on the morrow.

Saturday August 11th
A day of sun & showers & we set to & laid out the wet parts of our swamped load to dry on the shingle bar. Far less was wet than I had expected & practically all

can be dried & saved. I had a much needed hair cut & a shave & shampoo & felt the better for it. Cleaned my rifle, sorted my kit, mended waders & wrote to the mater—a day of odd jobs.

Sunday August 12

Sunshine & rain once more. A lot of disgruntled men in England today, sadly attending north country churches in little out of the world villages. I wrote to *Marigold* & Mrs Portman—letters for Hunter to take out. When one cant see them the next best thing is to write to those one is fond of—its almost like talking to them. Then I went out to the sweet smell of the woods & set about clearing the site for our shack—and there was a great burning. Feeling that he must, in fitting manner, celebrate my departure, *Gordon* made pancakes & we overate grossly of them with lemon juice, butter & sugar. And I, not to be outdone, made my very best bannock which we ate, new & hot, with cheese.

Monday August 13th

I cleared away my spare gear, pulled my outfit out of the cache, fixed up my new pole & loaded the canoe. We had an early lunch & I set out on my journey on a cool sunny afternoon. I travelled 4 hours 40 minutes & made camp on the left bank of the Nahanni, about one mile from the mouth of the second canyon. I just got my shelter up & my bed made in time to forestall a fierce downpour of rain which made me put off supper till it was over & wander about the woods in my wet river things, eating cranberries. Not far below was the camp I made with Gordon & the bar where we got the moose. A little below that was McLeod Creek, where the McLeods were killed for their gold in 1904, & at my camp was a little cache, an old landing place & the broken sweep of a scow.

To get me:—Palmer Cox' "Brownie Books."

Old bound volumes of B.O.P. containing "The Star of the Settlement," "Colonel Pellimore's Gold" and "The Clipper of the Clouds."

Tuesday August 14th

A glorious August day—clear & hot & like the days of last year, though the water is much colder for wading. I travelled just over 8 hours & travelled fast—this little canoe & its light load handle like nothing at all compared to that Noah's Ark which has stolen so many of my summer days in toil. To fetch up the nose when I am tracking & so to make her track more easily I put a big stone in my seat—

which saves me much work & worry. I went clean through the Second Canyon & through the Little Valley, which looked as lovely as ever, & finally camped, well weary, on a sand beach just round the big bend of the river. A lovely, cold night & I slept without shelter or mosquito bar.

Wednesday Aug*ust* 15th
A clear summer's morning with a hot day to follow—the first, it seems, for long ages. I was up at 5:30 before the sun had cleared the mountains & was early away. I travelled 8½ ho*urs*, stopping at midday for a bathe & a shave & a laze in the hot sun. I find that about 8½ ho*urs* is my limit for this upstream work. Longer than that &, if I have been travelling hard & steadily, I become played out & might as well camp as hobble onwards. I expected to reach the Gate today, but found that I had completely forgotten a days travel of last year. I thought I recognised an old camp of mine, & then suddenly I came on the Library Rock which I thought was beyond the Gate. After that it all seemed new to me—there were two bad places, some long riffles & many islands—a day of long, steady tracking. I am now in camp with a sheer face of rock opposite, the last riffle sounding down river & a creek with a big valley & the usual moraine of rock, under which it seeps into the Nahanni, just above. Not far, I fancy, from the raspberry camp of last year. A day of splendid colours & a lovely evening.

Thursday Aug*ust* 16th
A warm cloudy night & I was up at 5:30 of a dull morning. I boiled a pot of meat & baked two bannocks before breakfast & was on my way by 8:30. After a hard stretch of tracking against a steady drag of water I passed the shingle island & came to the old raspberry camp. I stopped to pick a pot full & to eat. There were not so many as last year & they will soon be over—but the wild rose hips & haws & both kinds of cranberries are ripe now & plentiful. The glass had fallen very low in the night, &, as I picked, the storm broke. Crash after crash of thunder banging against the canyon walls, a flicker of lightning & a downpour of icy rain. I went on, bent on making a certain camp, in the tall spruce, by the big eddy below the Gate. A little fall & a long point of uneven rocks in the long riffle defeated me when in sight of camp. A dangerous place, I was cold through & my hands had no feeling left in them. I tried to warm them back to life but failed, & with senseless hands I couldnt attempt this risky bit of tracking. Thoroughly wretched, feeling very much badgered & alone & wishing I was at home in England, I slung my gear

+

Pulpit Rock, looking upstream.

out of the canoe & under an overhanging ledge of cliff where there was shelter, lugged out my canoe & lit a fire under the ledge. I warmed my fumbling fingers over the fire, changed my clothes & ate a hot meal, sitting literally on top of the fire. I felt better & the rain gradually ceased. A pale, watery sun rolled the mists away from the mountain tops—& I saw that they were covered with snow. No wonder my hands were cold. Feeling that I had had enough of water in any shape or form for one day I set to & portaged the whole outfit up to my camping place, made camp & went a-fishing—no luck even there, as I hooked a trout & he broke the gut & went away with my Indiana spinner in his mouth. So I consoled myself with a good supper, & bed by the fire.

Friday August 17

A wintry morning, with little, fine clouds & a storm ring round the sun. I climbed to the top of the Gate, far above the Pulpit Rock, from where I could look down sheer into the deep, green Nahanni. The sun came out—it was a fall morning & very soft & warm save for a cold breeze which blew now & then off the snows. I found low bush cranberries of a size that I had never before seen—& for the first time in my life I ate my fill of blueberries. No mountain goat were to be seen though I searched the hills with my glass. Twice the mystery plane flew over—& then fearful yells disturbed the peace—just as I was dropping rocks over the precipice to measure the height (5 seconds to the first pitch & 4 seconds from there to water). Hunter was having lunch on the beach by my canoe, so I hurried down to talk with him, wounding a spruce hen on the way but being unable to pick it up. Hunter soon went on—in a hurry to reach the falls & get back to Simpson—having given up his Gravel River plans. I told them of the Box Canyon portage just ahead, & this time we said good bye.

A cool afternoon & the water cold—if only a little hot weather would come to make things easier.

I saw that the creek which flows in at the far end of the Gate is a long one, with much water, running far back into the mountains.

Later on I caught a small trout in the eddy & had it for supper.

Saturday August 18

Chill & dull at six a.m. but by eight the sun had driven back the clouds & made that best thing of all—a perfect August morning. I loaded up & slipped through the Gate—still, I think, the greatest marvel to me of all on this lovely river. Last year I saw it in the blue, dreamy haze of a hot afternoon—today it was in the clear, fresh colours of a bright fall morning. The canoe slid over the quiet green waters that lie between the cliffs & again the place gave one the impression of a vast, silent cathedral.

Followed 4 hours of the steady damnation of fast, rolling water & of hard tracking & now I am lunching at the creek which flows in at the foot of the Box Canyon portage, & considering how to tackle the thing. I have the load out of the canoe & airing on the hot stones, & I think I shall portage most of the gear on this side & again risk the crossing & tracking the canoe from the ledge on the far shore. Foolish, perhaps, but I did it successfully last year & it saves time & work.

The sun blazes down—hotly, as it did last year—& new & gorgeous butterflies are abroad. Almost all the snow is gone & the mountains stand out very clearly, beautifully wooded on the lower slopes & shading up into bare browns, greys & greens against the blue of the sky. A good day to be alive.

Later   Evening now & the portage finished. I crossed safely & tracked my canoe up the far side, except for the worst 150 yards where the water boiled under the ledge at great speed & almost swamped the canoe. There I thought better of it & portaged, & the rest of the outfit I brought up in four trips on this side, packing it over the trail.

Down the valley I can see onto the Red Screes with their gorgeous colouring clear in the sunset light—the rest of the valley cold in the blue shadows. The Screes are purple, like the heather hills at home are now & against them stand out the delicate green of the mosses & the black green of the spruce.

Sunday August 19

A very cold night but again a perfect fall morning—the water still cold. I am lunching in the warm sunshine on the beach below the Green Island. Tomorrow I hope to be on the Flat River.

Travelled on in the afternoon for 5¼ hours & made good headway. Soon reached Mary River, a lovely, clear stream with a wide valley of its own running far back into the high hills. Beyond that the valley of the Nahanni becomes more open, with some islands & many long shingle beaches & quiet reaches of river. Much evidence of glacial action in the shape of enormous deposits of till. A gorgeous afternoon but the glass fell very low & it looked like rain in the evening. I made camp at the foot of a little island & put up my shelter amongst the spruce, & was up late by the fire baking bannock.

Monday August 20

Glass still low—one blaze of sunshine for an hour or two after breakfast & now dull & cloudy. I travelled 3½ hours & am lunching about ½ mile below the mouth of the Flat River & within sight of it. Beyond lies the hill between the two rivers with the tall spruce, where Faille built his shack last year, at its foot. The rush & swirl of the two currents meeting under a low cliff on the far shore makes a sound like that of a strong rapid. The crossing to the mouth of the Flat will be difficult.

Later   It was. I had to go on up the Nahanni & then come down backwards in an 8 mile current. One drive of the paddle & she passed from the olive green of the Nahanni into the still emerald of the Flat with a swirl & a surge that made her take in water. The Flat is very low—too low for easy travel—& the shallows are a constant nuisance. It was a warm, still, thunderous afternoon & the sand flies bothering. In an hour I reached Faille's old cabin. The place was deserted & the shack dark & chill inside. There was the litter of departure about & on the door a notice "A. Faille left here for the Fals July 8."

It seemed sad after the pleasant evening we had had together there & I felt sorry to think that we might never meet again. So I took my pan, pick & axe from the shack & went on—past the island & the little barrier rapid that I ran in the twilight last year—on for about 2 miles & then made my camp in the spruce by an eddy with an angry, storm sunset lighting up the hills.

Tuesday August 21

I decided to shave before breakfast & was just lathering my face when a moose came down to the little creek, about 300 yards up & on the far bank. He started to swim across & I dropped my shaving brush, grabbed my rifle & ran up through the trees. I got him as he landed at 200 yards range. I fired four shots in a standing position, three of which hit him, & he fell dead within a couple of yards of the water—most obligingly. So I went back & finished my shave & had my breakfast. Then I threw away very joyously the last of my old, musty dried moose meat & set out to make a job of the new one. Made an excellent job of him & now I am ready for lunch—kidneys & liver & thank the Lord for it all. The meat—all the best of it & all that I can use—is smoking & drying a little before I pack it away to carry with me. I have it lying in the sun on a little rack of spruce boughs with smudges round it. And a large potful boiling on the fire. A good morning's work as I was ready for fresh meat.

Later　went on until nearly seven—the hottest & most beautiful afternoon of this month, if not of the whole summer, but with that stillness in the air & the touches of red & gold on the hillsides that come before the fall & the early snows. I soon passed the Wish Pool & came 4 or 5 miles to camp on a shingle bar in the long, calm reach. A low cliff on the far side & rolling hills ahead & from here I can hear the boom of the falls of the Nahanni away to the northwards.

Flat River amazingly low & clear & I expect trouble in the rapids when I come to run down.

Wednesday August 22

Dawn in a clear sky but in the main a cloudy morning. Lunch time now & I have probably come at least 5 miles, having pulled up many riffles. An annoying river & much wading at this stage of water.

Later Came a good distance but beastly tired towards evening. A beaver slipped into the water just ahead of me under a bank—not five yards away—but was into his hole before I could steady the canoe & get my rifle—otherwise I should have had my long promised meal of beaver tail. Another beaver is playing some distance downstream from camp now. I can hear him smacking the water with his tail. I am not far below Caribou Creek—near the big earth slide, & I can see the lone round hill which marks the big pool on the creek. Opposite is a deep & narrow creek valley, well wooded & running back into high pointed hills. About two miles up river is the smoke of a camp fire—either an Indian hunting party or I have caught up with Starke.

Thursday August 23

A lovely day—really hot sunshine at last & the rolling hill country very beautiful in its autumn colours. The birches are all gold & the poplars starting to turn but mostly splendid of all are the scarlets of the blueberries, cranberries & small bushes. I caught up with Starke & Stevens as they were windlassing up a riffle. Not much gas left & the propeller badly dinged so Caribou Creek is the end of the trail for them this year & they were glad to hear it was so close. We had lunch together—they also had a fresh moose, shot when I got mine. They tell me that two planes were working up here this summer—not one only as I had supposed.

I went on & left them & passed Caribou Creek in another hour. Then on for 5 miles up the Flat, a little, winding river here with long points like those on the Nelson & many shallow riffles. There were many good camping places just above the Creek, & one strange hillside with hundreds of conical rocks standing out like goblins turned to stone. I was delayed for a while by a patch of blueberries & cranberries & finally camped at 6:30 of a sweet, calm evening. The river water is warming again, praise be. There are few steaks to equal the tenderloin of one's own moose when one is hungry.

Friday August 24

Lunch time of another perfect day—one of those days when, slipping along under the cut banks & the overhanging trees, one can smell the good earthy scents of the bush & the little plants & mosses. The colours become more lovely daily. The valley here is bounded by high rounded hills & the tops of many of them are scarlet against the postcard blue of the sky—either from a little low plant with crimson leaves or from masses & masses of cranberries & blueberries. There are moose & caribou tracks on every sand bar & fish jumping in every pool—grey mountain trout—so that it seems that in these fall months one need not starve in this Eden. One can hardly realise that winter is hard by—yet my snowshoes are in the canoe & now & then a fallen leaf drifts down the river. Far ahead, a line of jagged mountains, pale blue in the distance, cuts across the valley horizon—maybe the mountains of the canyon, beyond which the McLeods found their gold. I may be the only one to reach them this year—indeed, as far as I know, mine is the first canoe to come this way for many a long day.

Later   Made a long afternoon—nearly 5½ hours—& camped very tired in some big spruce on a shallow, still reach of river with a cliff opposite to me. There were cranberries there to eat & soft moss & boughs to sleep on—an old camping place of the Indians, evidently, & I see that Faille had been here last winter & had set a deadfall close by. There was a blaze on a tree with several names & the date July 30 '92—"Purcell & Ole" were all that I could make out—possibly Stanier's party. A gorgeous "ripple" sunset—red, green & gold—reflected on the calm water with the black points of the tall spruce standing into it—the Canada one sees in pictures.

Saturday August 25
Woke up still tired & not feeling fresh—its time I took a day off on dry land—one cant go helling on through cold mountain water for ever. Also I want a bath & a shave & clothes washed & the load needs drying in the sun. Moose meat turning mouldy so I cut off the mould & set an enormous potful on to boil. A morning that cannot be described—so perfect in its sunlight & clear blue colours. I set off a little wearily & in 1¼ hours came to Stanier's "creek with falls ½ mile up." So I am getting on, & his distances are madly overjudged. I tied the canoe & walked up the great moraine of stones to see if this were really the creek. It was. I found the falls booming over a ledge in a little canyon into a deep pool of the clearest, emerald green water I have ever seen. There was another deep pool 200 yards lower down the canyon & in a few minutes I had 3 fine trout. So I went back to the canoe & had the trout & a moose steak for lunch—either one seems to have

nothing or everything all at once in this wild country. I am sitting barefooted on the stones in the hot sun & feeling less weary. I'll make this my day on shore & not tomorrow & so now I'll move on & pick my camping place & unload the canoe.

On Thursday night I woke up & saw the Aurora flaming overhead for the first time this season. Long, curling streamers & ribbons in the northeast, & shafts of light to the centre of the sky.

Later   Evening now & I am shaved, bathed & cleaned & in my right mind. Everything is dry & I have attended to the moose meat problem & thrown away all that I couldnt possibly use before the blow flies turn it. There are always trout & I shall probably get another moose when I am out of meat. Another flaming sunset & now the stars are coming out in a cloudless sky with a pale green light along the northern horizon—the low, rounded mountains & the spruce black against it in silhouette. If only I could show these colours to people at home in England—there are none like it there.

And now, suddenly, even as I turned my head to stir the fire to flame, the Northern Lights are out—wreathing & twisting across the sky & putting out the stars. My bed of boughs is cut & laid & I shall lie there & fall asleep watching them & listening to the everlasting noise of water. And two months from now even that will be stilled & silent. Camp is between some big spruce & the river—facing N.W.—exactly what I needed to catch the afternoon sun. Under the trees here are masses of fat, ripe high-bush cranberries—the bushes over six feet tall. A pleasant land in its milder moods.

Sunday August 26
Started at 8:25 & travelled 4 hours—pulled up a rapid in a snye behind a spruce island last thing before lunch & am now having cold moose meat & tea at the mouth of a creek—an old camping place of the Indians, both here & on the far bank. A hot day with a gentle breeze—utterly cloudless, with a thin haze of heat softening the flaming colours of the woods & turning the red mountain tops to purple. The beauty of the country now beggars description—there are no words for it, & all mine. Probably not another soul from here to the Yukon. The fresh track of an enormous bear is on the sand here—there are ducks of a pale biscuit & dark brown colour swimming on the river—the squirrels are working hard in the bush—the whisky jacks are watching me—the red & black butterflies are about & the trout are lepping [*sic*: leaping] in the water, about their lawful occasions. The golden days of the year.

Evening   Went on 4½ hours & made camp on a little sand beach on a muskeg shore & opposite to a cliff. A little tarn lies behind in the trees, very still & with the hills reflected in it, & there are low bush cranberries which will cook well with rice & dried apples.

Monday Aug*ust* 27
Not so hot a day—the sun shines through a film of cloud with the ring round it & the mountain tops have a powdering of snow. A rotten bit of river this morning & many riffles, but one is rewarded now & then by the sudden opening up of a new view of the mountains to the westward—ever nearer. I have passed Stanier's "big, barked timber" & hope to reach Irvine Creek by night. The Flat here cuts its way through tremendous deposits of glacial boulder clay & I think that the wooded ridges that stand between the immediate valley & the hills behind are the old lateral moraines of the glacier that must once have filled this valley.

Evening   After 2½ hours of very hard going I came to Irvine Creek. I landed first on the south bank of the Flat opposite the creek mouth. The hot sun on shore was comforting after the hours wading in the cold water & I went back into the woods. There was an old Indian camping place in some good sized spruce & a little lake behind—& more high-bush cranberries than I have ever seen together in one place—ripe & warm & their leaves glowing red in the sunlight. Then I crossed to the far side to make certain that this was the creek & not the mouth of a snye. It was the creek sure enough & I found the carved tree—

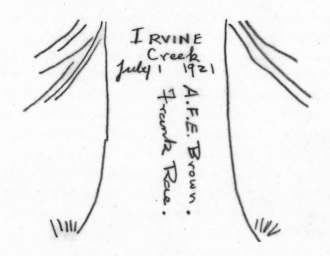

And on the other side, in pencil, was written:—

July 1. Rain

July 2. Rain

July 3. Rain

July 4 Rain.

So we are not the only ones who have suffered. Then I came upon masses of low bush cranberries—one trod upon them everywhere—& with them I dealt thoroughly. There was a long rapid ahead & the sun was getting down in the west. So I camped here & fished in the eddy & got me a nice trout for supper & two more for breakfast—& lost one the size of a whale, which I got to land but which wriggled off the hook & back into the water. I fetched him a clout across the back with my fishing rod—an alder pole—hoping to stop him, but the rod broke over him instead. A lovely evening & purple clouds in the west. Irvine Creek seems to run up a long valley between the high foothills & the actual mountains. A big creek.

Brown & Rae, I believe, came here across the mountains from the Yukon—staked here but never returned to their claims.

Tuesday August 28

Lunch time   At last—this far & no further. The river got worse after leaving Irvine Creek—simply one long, damned boulder rapid & for three hours I fought with it—soaked to the waist. One might as well try to take a canoe up a trout stream at home. Also I have the downstream run to think of—possibly in very cold weather & with the river even lower. So here I stop at the foot of a bad rapid, & make my camp & build a cache. And when I've climbed a hill & got the hang of the country I'll try to go on on foot. So the canoe is unloaded & beached & I am loafing in golden sunshine—& intend to go on loafing. This everlasting water travel upstream eventually plays one clean out—so tired through that a nights sleep no longer refreshes. Nothing will do good but a days rest on shore—warm & dry.

On the hill behind the camp are black & red currants—the finest I have ever seen growing wild, & equal to any from an English garden. Also a curious sweet tasting berry—a cross between a black currant & a gooseberry. I'll have a stew of them this evening—& a fresh bannock to go with them, & keep holy day & read my Jorrocks.

Wednesday August 29

Not everybody has eaten six different kinds of fruit at once—cold rice cooked with apples & cranberries, & over that poured cold stewed red currants, black currants, raspberries & gooseberries. A most pleasant eating.

Today I have been up onto the hills. I had my lunch 1700 *feet* above camp & from there I think I could see the canyon of the Flat—not so far away nor yet so long. Also I found an old Indian trail running in that direction so I may be able to reach Borden Creek on foot from here. Tomorrow I'll build a cache & then we'll see.

Thursday August 30

A clear, bright day of sun & wind, & now at dusk it looks as though rain might come in the night—a wind still blowing out of the N.W. & big, dark clouds rolling up out of the sunset. I have the cache built, my gear in order & myself shaved & cleaned & if the weather will let me I'll start away tomorrow—I only trust it wont be like my last adventure on foot, last September, from Fort Nelson into the Fish Lake hills. I'll be glad to be away from here—the noise of this rapid has come to be, in my ears, like the sound of the wind in the rigging of a ship in mid-Atlantic—a sound I'll rejoice to hear again. And there are voices & weird sounds in a rapid.

As I cleared round the cache I found black currants & many gooseberries—but there are no trout to be had here.

Friday August 31

A perfect day with a cooling breeze & never a cloud in sight. I broke up camp & put the stuff in the cache & then set out. Dont know how far I have come—its hard to say as one twists & winds through the bush, up hill & down dale, sometimes forcing a way through the trees & with a heavy pack & rifle to hamper one. I have made camp down by the river by a pool which gave me one small trout to add to my supper. I grilled him on a flat rock laid in the hot ashes before the fire & he tasted very good. The woods gave me cranberries & black currants so we keep on living. And now to bed.

Saturday September 1

Dead played out & back at the same camp. Yesterday I knew it but hated to admit it, & by midday today I had to give in & say that I could carry my load no further through the bush. It was beyond my strength, consisting of:—rifle, pistol (&

+

The Cascades of the Thirteen Drops, Flat River.

cartridges), shovel, pick & gold pan, food, tea pail, frying pan etc, axe, bedding, camera & the odd things that are necessary.

Last night it froze pretty hard &, after a cool morning the day became sultry with a hot sun & a thin blue haze of smoke over the mountains from some distant fire. Almost all the way lay through thickly tangled trees & deadfall & deep muskeg moss—often on a steep side hill. At times I had to climb—in one place 500 *feet* sheer from the river, notching footholds in the dry earth with my axe & every step & lift an effort with that damned weight on my back. My furthest point was a creek that flows into the Flat on the right bank in the canyon & there I considered things & gave up Borden Creek—or Gold Creek as some call it. So I shall go back to Irvine Creek &, if I can, try my luck & work there where I shall not be cut off from my canoe in the event of snow or a sudden freeze up. It's tough luck—but its too late in the year now to go venturing beyond the canyon with an unbroken trail-less country behind one.

The canyon of the Flat is bad—rapids that are almost falls & tremendous boulders. The country behind is a hard one to get into—no wonder it keeps its gold. Its difficult to see how to tackle it—if only I could have my four free Canadian years over again I'd try it.

Sunday September 2nd

A hot day of clear sunlight & wind. I made my way through the bush & reached camp about four o'clock—fairly well done in, but still energy enough to clean up on a few bushes of gooseberries, treat myself to a hot bath, bring the stuff down out of the cache, bake a bannock & make myself a good supper & bed.

On all this walk I never saw an animal—& yet there were tracks of moose, caribou, bear & wolves & the bush was honeycombed with moose paths. I saw three game birds—much like prairie chicken but very dark in colour—feeding amongst some small spruce. They flew before I could get a shot at them. The bush is very beautiful now—all colours of red & gold & floored with cranberries. But, of course, in those places where there is nothing but the small swamp spruce growing tightly together it looks—& is—just as damnable as ever. And main hard to travel.

Monday September 3rd

To get me:—The Border Book.

Also A Life of Cesare Borgia.

Another perfect day—over a fortnight now since it rained. I launched the canoe & loaded her & let her go for Irvine Creek & covered the four miles down in 28 minutes—a glorious ride—it made one feel alive again after these months of plodding toil, to be in control of a thing of speed & to be using the force of the river instead of fighting it. I ran all the rapids—my original cautious ideas of lowering the canoe down by wading soon fled. Its a splendid feeling—the sight ahead of a slope of dancing, white water—the sudden rush into the noisy waves— the sharp swing to avoid a rock & then the shooting out into the calm water of the pool below.

I fixed up my camp on the point at Irvine Creek & then held a much needed washing & mending day—fixed up some odd things in the outfit & cooked some grub. In the evening I fished & landed two good trout on my Indiana Spinner. One whale of a thing got off the hook just as I had him in the shallows, & then a thing the size of Leviathan himself broke the gut & went off with spinner & everything—blast him, as I now only have the Homesteader left & the trout dont seem to think much of him.

A starlit night & cold, with a very beautiful moonrise over the mountains— the moon reflected in the swirling river water along with the tall black spruce.

Tuesday Sept*ember* 4
Breakfast time   In the night it froze & there was an arch round the moon. Snow was in the air when I got up at five a.m. & some has just fallen on the far mountains & left them grey coloured. I'll let it make up its mind before I move.

Went up the creek a little way, to the top of a hill. Then the snow powdered over the mountain tops & a cold rain came down & I returned to camp. The creek is a big one & meanders through a wide, well wooded valley with many dry poplar & jack pine ridges, lots of spruce, a good deal of semi muskeg & some lakes. I should say a great trapping valley.

After lunch I dug down in the boulder as far as possible & panned a pan of dirt very carefully. Got nothing but a pinch of black hemalite sand & decided that I was doing no damned good up there at all & that I had better get back to *Gordon* & do some honest work & make some money. To prospect this upper country there should be two men with a good outfit & a year or two years to spend up here.

So I loaded up & for 3 ho*u*rs I raced down rapid after rapid on my way home. I bumped once but no harm was done. It was one of those cold, grey, still autumn afternoons which remind one of gardeners burning leaves, of "conquerors" & of jolly hot teas & books by the firelight. The world seems to have stopped for a moment—waiting for something to happen & you know that winter & its storms are not far behind.

I wanted meat badly & in the gathering dusk I came on a young cow moose, standing in the river watching me. Things always happen so. I came within ten yards of that moose & called to her & rattled my paddle before she *would* move. But a bad rapid—at the two islands—was just ahead. I was cold as a stone & wanted to make camp as a storm was chasing me down from the mountains & it was a place in which I couldnt land to skin the cow anyway. So I didnt shoot. I made camp & down came the rain, but no matter—I was comfortable.

Wednesday Sept*ember* 5

A morning like a glorious pearl, with the sun slowly clearing the silvery mists & now blazing down on a world in all its golden colours. In the night it froze. I have breakfasted, washed, shaved & broken camp & in a few minutes I shall be on my way—a warmer way, I hope, than yesterday's.

As I went on the day grew grayer & colder & at noon I was looking for a place to land & have lunch when I saw a young bull caribou ahead of me. He saw me—exactly at the moment when I was regretting the lost cow moose of yesterday evening & meditating fondly upon the virtues of a juicy steak—& swam the river across my course. I quickened speed & said "But for the devil's interference, there goes my supper." I fired as he landed on the bar at the run & dropped him on the stones with a smashed leg & a bullet through the heart— pleasing shooting at a running animal from a moving canoe. I had lunch there & skinned & cut up the caribou as snow fell on the hill tops & a cold rain fell on me. Then I went on down river & by six o'clock I sighted Starke & Stevens' camp in the big spruce, a few hundred yards up Caribou Creek. Their buildings were already up & almost finished—a shack, trim & well built, a cache & a smoke house for meat. And a sizeable wood pile to boot. I gave them a hind quarter of my caribou & they produced pickles, butter & jam & we made a devilish frying of meat & fell to—then sat & smoked & talked till a late hour. That night I slept in their shack, well sheltered from a cold drizzle that was falling outside. They are still in the tent & have not yet moved in—so I was the first to sleep in their cabin. But I had to have the door wide open & sleep upon the floor—having become used to the woods.

Thursday Sept*ember* 6

Up at six & put a fire in the stove & roused the others. The misty storm clouds hung in the valleys & fresh snow lay upon the hills—a cool damp morning. I didnt leave till after lunch. We made a feast day of it & had two excellent meals with unaccustomed dainties from the cache & choice pieces from the caribou. Overate ourselves, I suppose, but its the only form of conviviality that exists in this northland. And we gossiped & read & made plans to go out to Simpson & up the Mackenzie together next June—& to drink together in Edmonton. A pleasantly idle morning. I never knew before that you should parboil the liver of caribou before frying it.

We said goodbye & I ran on down the Flat for 3¼ hours of a splendid afternoon, with the sun out of a blue sky blazing down on a golden world. The river is very low now—in several places I had to jump out & wade my canoe down over shallows, & in others I was driven close to the dangerous water. As I slid along under a cut bank I came suddenly on a little black bear feeding quietly on the fruit of the wild roses. We were not 15 yards apart & saw each other simultaneously, but I had barely time to lay my hand on my rifle when he scampered back into the bush.

Now I am in camp amongst the big spruces by the Wish Pool—a lovely spot & a sweet camp with the smell of spruce boughs & cones under my lean-to & the light of the fire playing on the trunks of the trees. I camp here in honour of my granted wish—& also because I was hungry & ready to camp. So to my supper I ate delicious tender caribou & caribou tongue—luxuries that money couldnt buy at home. And now the frost is cracking down & I'm for bed—with Jorrocks to laugh me to sleep.

Friday September 7

Said farewell to the Flat River on a morning of frost & mist that cleared later to a pale autumn sunshine with a blue haze of smoke in the air that made the mountains look dreamlike & unreal. Travelled 5 hours & had a late lunch at the Gate—then 3 hours more & made camp by the old scow at the lower end of the Little Valley. The Nahanni has dropped tremendously—I had a difficult run in places, was thrown in close to the big waves in the riffles & came near to ripping the canoe both at the Portage & again just above the Gate. Saw no animals—lived well on caribou liver & cold jelly boiled from the bones—& very comfortable here before the fire.

(arrived home September 8th)

Friday September 14

Reached *Gordon*'s camp at Wheatsheaf Creek the next day at midday & found him working hard with a big clearing & the shack well under way to his credit. I suggested one or two alterations & we have put in a week's work on the building & things are looking more civilized. I made a work bench & a good, strong saw horse to make life easier for us.

Last Sunday *Gordon* took a holiday over to Prairie Creek & got a fat little black bear & in the evening we & the dogs packed home the meat, head & robe. Followed a prodigious rendering of lard & we got at least 20 lbs. of good white bear grease & set it up in tins—all of which will help to keep out the winter cold. On Tuesday we had a cold rain & snow fell on all the hills & still lies on the peaks even though the Chinook is roaring & blustering from the S.W. The geese & wildfowl are going south, honking overhead, & so the winter draws near.

Gordon cut his leg with an axe yesterday & is now mossing & chinking the shack. I am working on the gables & the roof & shall be more than glad to have them finished. Camp life goes slowly after the trail—yesterday one of the dogs ate my shaving brush by way of making variety in the daily round.

Saturday September 15

In camp, dog tired, up the Meilleur River, having crossed over the divide from Wheatsheaf Creek at a height of 2500 feet above the Nahanni—far higher than I need have gone as this camp is only 1500 feet. However, it took me across a beautiful moorland country with a splendid view of all Death Valley & the Nahanni up to the second canyon & down to the Cache Rapid. The jagged outposts of the Ram Mountains, snow powdered, have closed round me & shut off the open valley—for sound there is the roar of the mountain stream, the crackle of the fire & the rustling of a cold breeze from the snows. Sheep & moose tracks on the shore. A rotten camp—one cant move out of it in the dark without falling over tangled alder brush on loose rocks. Having already had several crashes in the dark I've now abandoned all idea of washing & am going to clean my rifle, sharpen my axe & go to bed.

Sunday September 16

Evening in camp on the Meilleur River, close to the timberline & 2500 feet above the Nahanni—I think the highest camp I have ever made. A wild & savage place with only a sprinkling of stunted spruce for trees, & the rest rockslides, blueberry bush & dwarf alder that catches & trips, the great cliffs & the snows. A thin rain is falling & I have my tarpaulin up & beneath it the sweetest smelling of beds cut from the little spruce. A grey, sunless day & this rain may turn to snow up here—the going is hard enough without it—all boulders, screes & the stunted alder brush. This morning I followed the wrong valley—a creek of yellow, iron tasting water that climbed sharply. At 3000 feet I could follow it no

+
A tarp rigged for a bivouac camp.

longer—the way lay over loose screes & up to the sheer cliffs—so I returned & took the main valley as being more probably Hunter's trail to his little lake. Saw one sheep in the far distance—many tracks & some bear tracks. Now reduced to rolled oats, bear's lard & tea—I trust I fall in with a sheep tomorrow. A cold wind getting up.

Monday Sept*ember* 17
Not much grub & I headed back home down the valley—a bright, sunny morning & a cold wind blowing in my face. I saw no game, crossed the divide lower down than before over a stretch of open moorland & then fought my way down through tangled alder & little spruce & so to camp. Pretty tired & my shoes cut to pieces on the rocks. Found *Gordon* putting fomentations on a swollen leg, had a good supper & then to bed. In the night it rained.

Tuesday September 18

Spent the day working on the shack floor & banking. Heard two shots in the afternoon from up river & presently there came into sight two canoes—each with two men. They landed & talked for a while but did not camp, being in a hurry to get to Simpson to catch the boat out on the 20th. They had been dropped by plane on August 4th above the Flat River canyon to prospect the country for gold—one name was Wrigley & another McLeod—I think the surviving brother of the dead McLeods who found the gold in 1904. I would give a deal to know what they found & how near I came to them—they had seen my tracks above the canyon. However, if a gold rush starts we are well on the way & can rush with the rest.

There are many ducks & geese going south down the river.

Wednesday September 19

Levelled off the shack floor, set up the stove & cut out the pipe hole. Mossed half the roof & threw a fair amount of clay on it. By way of amusement & recreation I had a haircut & a shampoo. A very workaday, ordinary sort of day—& a very calm, still day.

Thursday September 20

Lunch time I left *Gordon* at work on the shack & have come out a-hunting in quest of fresh meat. It froze hard in the night—our first severe frost—& there was ice in the bucket this morning. A perfect fall day now with sunshine & a west wind—a good hunting wind as I can head back against it towards Prairie Creek & may run into a bear or a moose. The running [*sic*: rutting] season of the moose is hard by now—I fancy I heard one calling this morning. I took the little canoe & dropped down below Prairie Creek & left her there on the shingle. Then I worked down through the bush & across the dry canyon moraine to a point opposite our old camp on the Meilleur River—& now back again & towards Prairie Creek. No luck so far—lots of moose, sheep & bear tracks on the bars & at least one wolverine & some wolf tracks.

The leaves are falling fast & the river is still dropping.

Later As I was scrambling along under an earth slide above Prairie Creek I came on three sheep feeding on the hips & haws of the wild roses. I shot them all—but it took me eight shots—rotten shooting. Two ewes & a young ram—the ewes fell dead into the creek but the ram lay up the slide with two bullets in him & I had to climb after him, knife him & throw him down. Twice my rifle jammed in a most annoying way—I must take down the bolt & see to it as things might have gone hard with me had I wounded a bull moose or a grizzly instead of a sheep. I set to work & cleaned them & left them on the stones with a fire burning by them to keep away the bears & wolves. I put the odd delicatessen in my pack & took half of the biggest sheep on my shoulders & packed him down to my canoe by the Nahanni, much as my forebears have packed English sheep back across the Border after a raid into Northumberland. And back to camp & to hot water & clean clothes & sheeps kidneys for supper.

Friday September 21
Up early on a perfect morning & we set out with the dogs to bring home the sheep. We found them untouched & safe & soon had them loaded up & packed on the dogs & on our shoulders & down to the river. I bathed while *Gordon* hung the meat & made a tremendous frying of mutton chops. Then we turned to the shack & finished the roof & the mossing of the chinks & banked the north side. A good days work.

Saturday September 22
I put in the windows, lit the stove to air & dry the shack, made the door & did various odd jobs. The shack is going to be very warm & light—an excellent refuge from the storms. The whisky jacks were busy on our meat & played fair hell with it before we noticed them. I shot one with the .22 & this seemed to warn them off the course. A grey day & looking like snow but the glass unusually high.

Sunday September 23
A grey morning, clearing later to a very still, beautiful day with a haze of smoke in the air. Early in the morning I heard a wolf howling over by Prairie Creek, but no other sound except from the squirrels & the whisky jacks—of which last I shot another. *Gordon* left in the little canoe for a two days hunt & a look at the McLeod Creek up towards the Second Canyon, so I am alone at home for the first time—& enjoying it. I hung & finished the shack door, started hewing out a table, did my washing, cooked, &, above all, discovered a new & most excellent way of making bannock—half frying the thing & half baking it in the oven—the result being a crisp, golden brown bannock, eminently eatable.

A year agone today I was caught on the Horse Track trail in the first snow— what a cold, hungry night that was!

+

Interior of Patterson and Matthews's Wheatsheaf Creek home.

Monday Sept*ember* 24

Frost in the night & a still, cloudless, golden day with the smoke haze thicker &
the mountains blue, dreamlike & unreal behind it. I hewed five heavy planks out
of spruce & made a table, like the Rock of Ages for solidity, in one corner of the
shack & made myself a chair out of a big log, with three rungs for a back to it,
& with the help of these two I have just had my first supper indoors—alone, as
Gordon has not come back. A great & momentous occasion—

> Menu
>
> Two large steaks from a hind quarter of wild sheep.
> Beans & barley cooked in mutton broth with much red pepper.
> Cold whole wheat porridge with milk, raisins & sugar.
> Bannock & tea.

And now I shall smoke & read an 18 months old Post. Almost all the afternoon I worked on my rifle & pistol—the pistol perfect but the rifle still partly
jamming. Maybe *Gordon* may have some ideas on the subject.

The winter wood pile grows apace—now & then I bring in a dry tree & cut
it up into stove lengths.

Tuesday Sept*ember* 25
Day just the same—still & smoky. I worked away at the shack—washstand, shelves, a cupboard & odd things. G*ordon* came back in the evening with no game but a string of beautiful trout so we made a good supper & I made my one & only savoury—a cheese one, discovered by me during a rainstorm in a lone camp at the mouth of the Second Canyon. G*ordon* had found strange rocks, good fishing, some weird old cabins of maybe 30 years ago, petrified trees, lots of partridges & signs of mink, lynx, marten & wolves.

Wednesday Sept*ember* 26
The same calm day again—but the smoke pall thicker. The hills are almost hidden now in the blue haze & the bitter smell of wood smoke is in the air. Wolves howling over by Prairie Creek at sunrise. I made a massive bed frame for myself in my corner of the shack—all it wants now are the poles & spruce tips for the mattress. Also I helped G*ordon* with his dog house, cut wood—& birch for a broom—& tinkered again with my rifle, which seems to be once more in order. At all events, I can do no more to it & must trust to my pistol if I get into a fix.

Thursday Sept*ember* 27
Dull & muggy all day & now raining hard—& nothing to write about except that I navvied unceasingly at uninteresting jobs, & am now going to spend my first night in the shack in a comfortable bed—the first bed for six months, even though it be but one of my own making. G*ordon* still in the tent as he hasnt fixed up his bed yet. A north wind at midday tried to remove our roof—which is somewhat of a sandy nature—but this rain will pack it down more firmly—especially if we get a frost afterwards.

Friday Sept*ember* 28
Rained all day—cut wood, cleaned rifles & looked over my kit. Large flights of ducks & geese heading southwards.

Saturday Sept*ember* 29
Woke up this morning to the first snow of winter—the usual damp, wet snow of the fall. Mist hung over the valley & the mountains, the sun never shone & there was a raw east wind biting on a grey wilderness. And all day it slopped & thawed & snowed again. I worked mainly at the window shutters—frankly, all

this carpentry is beginning to weary me, but it must be done. *Gordon* went after partridges & also fished, but had no luck. In the afternoon a curious wailing came on the wind to us from downstream, like the voice of a man in danger—probably the call of a lynx.

Sunday Sept*ember* 30
A grey morning & I left camp at 8:00 a.m. to try up Prairie Creek for bear or moose. Almost at once the snow came on the east wind & I saw no living thing except the ravens that rose from my old sheep kill, although I went on beyond the berry slope of the bears & through the Gap into the little, lonely valley, shut off from this one by the great rock walls. Probably there will not be much movement among the animals until this snow is over—though *Gordon* saw a big bull moose swim the river soon after I had left. Back to lunch & I worked all the afternoon cutting wood, finishing the window shutters & other odd jobs—we shall soon be settled now.

Monday Oct*ober* 1
Still the east wind & it has snowed all day—wet, miserable snow. All my work here is finished now—nothing more to fix up & only the everlasting wood to cut so, as soon as the change of weather comes, I hope to go a-hunting.

Tuesday Oct*ober* 2
Snowed all day—leaden & hopeless. I went about four miles this morning—maybe five—up the dry snye & beyond the old cabins after moose. I tracked a big old bull, who had passed by not more than ten minutes ahead of me, a good distance into the bush, but he was travelling straight & took to the hills. Also I saw one fresh wolf track. Home to lunch, the snow falling fast. Evening now & still snowing—we ate pancakes for supper—lots of pancakes until we could eat no more.

Wednesday Oct*ober* 3rd
More domestic jobs—*Gòrdon* away morning & afternoon, & returned with 7 trout from the little creek opposite to us, & having seen the fresh tracks of two foxes & a mink. It snowed until late in the afternoon & now seems to be clearing a little & colder. For six whole days now the mists have been low on the mountains & the sun has never shone.

Thursday Oct*ober* 4

Still grey & snowing—the seventh day now so I suppose, by the law of averages, the sun must surely soon return to us. I launched my canoe at 8:00 a.m.—cold east wind & snow—& came down to the mouth of the Meilleur River, hoping to run into a moose on the way. No luck, but in the calm water above the Cache riffles I came on wild duck & had a joyous burst of fire. I brought down six but could only pick up three—one diving & getting away & two being carried down the riffles where I couldnt follow them. I thoroughly enjoyed that shooting—got a good right & left & two of the best single shots I have ever made. It was cold in the canoe & the cliffs & the canyon mouth looked grim with the snow clinging to the ledges & the snow mists swirling in the clefts. I made my camp in the big spruce where the raspberrys grew this summer—Meilleur's old camp site—& after lunch went up the creek & back over the hills. Not a sign of life—except the tracks of one wolf—& the snow deep & wet in the bush. The beginning & end of winter are both alike—wet & wretched. But a good supper & a warm camp fire at night fall soon make one forget the grey, sunless day.

Friday Oct*ober* 5

Up early & went down in the canoe to the head of the Cache riffles & hunted around in the timber but could find no sign of the dog trail to the Hot Springs. Then I tried up the little creek & found an old trail which may be the one—at any rate McLeod & the prospecting party had camped & made a blaze nearby. But I could find no sign of the Upper Hot Springs that they mentioned. Then I went back to lunch & the sun blazed out for a little while & the west wind blew. Then the long track back home with two more ducks to my gun—making 5 in all—and a good pot of cranberries—not altogether a wasted trip. The night is bright starlight & the aurora in the north eastern sky.

Saturday Oct*ober* 6th

Hard frost last night & a bright dawn, but the mists & the east wind came again driving the snow over the valley harder than ever. This morning I went down in the canoe & landed below Prairie Creek—getting a duck on the way. I travelled all through the timbered flats & the snyes & saw nothing fresh but wolf tracks. Then I turned up the dry canyon—a silent place, without the sound of wind or water between its great, snow powdered precipices. Nothing there but old sheep tracks & towards noon I turned back to Prairie Creek & the bear garden.

There, by the Gap, the whirling snow shut down on the world &, as nothing was moving, I returned to the canoe & poled back home with the east wind driving me up river. I shot two more ducks on the way—single birds. Ice was forming on the Nahanni in the eddies & almost this seems like winter—ice on the pole & ice dripping from the paddles. Later *Gordon* went over to fish & got no fish but shot one coyote—our first fur.

Sunday Oct*ober* 7th

I landed *Gordon* on the opposite shore after breakfast & then paddled slowly down river in quest of food. It was a very calm, sunless morning & the cold green river flowed through a world of white, grey & silver—lifeless & silent. I got two ducks & then came home to work round camp—feeling rather stiff—the old trouble I suppose. In the afternoon I roved the Spanish Main once more but no ducks came of it. About four I picked up a tired & sodden *Gordon* & brought him across. He had followed three bull moose vainly into the hills, had found the home of another mink & also a dam full of beaver on the little creek—all hard at work felling trees for winter feed & hauling them into their pond. With him he had two ducks & a partridge, so our day has not been in vain. Afraid I am due for another bout of rheumatism. Damn—why cant these things be reserved for stay-at-home folk?

For supper—two roast duck & sauce of cranberries & wild roses.

Monday Oct*ober* 8

A grey, cold day & I was laid low & unable to move. Spent the day reading. *Gordon* got 5 ducks in the morning.

Tuesday Oct*ober* 9th

Still unable to do much but feeling much easier. Weather still cold but drier & brighter. *Gordon* went a-cruising all morning & came home with six duck. He has now departed for the night over to the little creek, to lie up by the beaver dam & try for a moose or beaver. Mademoiselle is busy having pups in the den that she had made under an old stump—the rest are chained up—peace reigns.

Wednesday Oct*ober* 10

Gordon returned early with two duck but no beaver—he then went a-roving in the canoe & banged six duck on the Nahanni, so the cold storage begins to look most impressive. I am still useless—a perfect log, & am alone again as Gordon has gone back to his camp by the beaver dam. It is colder & drier & the north wind has brought me the sound of one rifle shot.

Thursday October 11th
A cold dry day with a strong north wind & ice forming at the edges of the Nahanni. A lovely sunrise on the snow covered hills & a clear sunset in a cold, blue sky. Gordon back for breakfast, with one small duck. He had shot a young beaver, but with its last kick the animal had flopped into the water & lodged under the ice—indeed, our luck is clean out just now. Evening now & I'm still stiff in the hip, & Gordon has gone back to his camp to try once more for meat.

Friday October 12
A cracking frost at night & a clear, cold morning. There were strange, rustling noises from the river at night & sharp reports, & morning found the eddies & the edges frozen & mush ice in crowding, jostling cakes covering the river & floating downstream. Gordon came home empty handed—defeated by the frost, as the beaver dam was covered with thick ice & the beavers had spent the night banging & battering about under the ice in a vain effort to get out on the bank & get to work. Evidently this sudden frost has caught them unprepared & without enough trees felled for winter feed—& no houses built. On Thursday night, when the frost was not so severe, they had working parties out all night, breaking the ice as the water froze in their dam & keeping channels open. Gordon had a good chance at eight partridges on his way home but the bolt of the .22 was frozen solid.

From a rose & gold sunrise the day turned grey & there fell a thick, cold snow. In the evening the snow stopped, the clouds moved from the S.W. & there was the mutter of a Chinook on its way from the Pacific to comfort this cold east slope.

Saturday October 13
Chinook—sunshine—& the snow melting before that warm west wind, & the ice almost gone from the Nahanni. Maybe our luck is going to change—anyhow I have limbered up considerably & have actually got through some of the camp work & hope soon to be able to hunt. Gordon has gone up towards the mountain behind us & into the big, open basin that I found, in search of a moose, so I am here alone again.

Later   Gordon came home about six, very wet & weary but with a bag of three bull moose to his credit—all shot up in the basin, two together where they were feeding on the stunted alder brush, & the biggest of all by a salt lick. This one, an enormous old bull, was in his evil mood & charged Gordon who happily made good shooting. So now we have over half a ton of moose meat up in the hills & the problem is how to get it home before the wolves get at it.

Sunday October 14

After a good breakfast of wild duck, porridge & moose kidneys we took down the dog sled from the cache & while Gordon took off the canvas carry-all I did the chores, cut wood & shot a blue grouse & a couple of whisky jacks with the .22. It was a lovely Chinook morning, the sun blazing down through the white, bumbly clouds as they rolled across on the south west wind—but the mountains still snow covered & the Nahanni still running ice. We ran the dog team to the top of the first ridge, but there the Chinook had struck hard & the ground was warm & dry & clear of snow. So we left the toboggan & went on up to Gordon's camp on foot with the dogs & had lunch up there in the open moorland country. Then we worked on the two smaller moose, skinning & cutting up, & at four o'clock I set off homewards, leaving Gordon hard at it & taking with me a pack of meat. The moorland country looked very wild & lovely as the sun set behind the Ram Mountains & the blue shadows lengthened out over the snow & the purple & brown of the brush. And far below lay the Nahanni, the blue channels of Prairie Creek & the greens & drabs of the flats, backed everywhere by the mountains, cold against the sunset sky.

By the salt lick I turned round & looked back & saw a big bull moose walking down towards me out of the big basin. He disappeared into the lick & I could hear him snorting & pawing about near the dead bull. Being still very stiff, & also uncertain of my rifle, I climbed a spruce from the top of which I could see down into the lick. Swaying in the branches like an ape I got one long shot at the moose & think I wounded him, but couldnt be certain, as he disappeared into the trees. I waited a while & then headed for home which I reached in the twilight.

Monday October 15

A powdering of snow fell in the night but the day was clear & sunny. A day of odd jobs & camp work & in the evening I went down the river to the nearest moose pasture & waited for an hour or so on the chance of a shot. Gordon came home about sunset with all the dogs packed & himself with a heavy pack of meat. We had supper & decided to cut a dog trail through the bush to the hunting ground as packing meat on ones back that distance is an exhausting, bloody—in both senses of the word—& everlasting job.

Tuesday October 16

We set out early on a cold morning with the snow powder falling & went together, on a line that I suggested, to the top of the first ridge. The going was better than I had hoped so I left *Gordon* to go on with the dogs while I turned there to cut & blaze a trail down the hill & back home. I worked without stopping till 4:30 & then walked back here, with the last bit of trail over the flat to the Nahanni still to cut tomorrow. The cakes of soft mush ice are still running in the river & I think a day or two of the N. E. wind & two or three good frosts by night *would* freeze it over.

Wednesday October 17th

Hard frost at night & a warm sunny day. I set out early to cut the rest of the dog trail through the river flats to the Nahanni. Met three partridges on the way & made an unavailing din with my pistol—a row *which Gordon could* hear up in the moorland. He thought I had run into another moose. I finished the trail to the beach in about 3½ *hours* work & felt very stiff & weary—wish this ache *would* go away & leave me in peace again. So I came back home to lunch & later went out after partridges—saw none but got 2 squirrels worth about 20 cents apiece! *Gordon* turned up for supper with his rifle butt smashed by a fall, & calling on me to mend it for him. He had found the moose that I had shot on Sunday evening lying stone dead about 100 *yar*ds from his own big bull. My bullet had torn his inside to pieces—he had turned back into the lick, drank his fill of water & died. A very big bull, it seems, with one horn very like an elk horn & the other a perfect moose antler.

Thursday October 18th

Still pretty stiff but I went up the hill with *Gordon* & cut more trail until 1:00 p.m. when I turned for home. Lunched & worked on *Gordon's* rifle *which* is now firm & solid again & am now going out to cut the evenings wood. Soft sunshine, white clouds & a roaring Chinook today, *which* made it very warm & sloppy in the bush & is sweeping the country clear of snow & clearing the Nahanni of ice. The wild-fowl all seem to have gone south now—only the blue grouse & partridges are left to us.

Gordon returned with news of a black bear, only a few yards from our trail on a warm & dry spruce covered knoll, the den facing south as usual. Sammy's inquisitive nose found the den & Gordon came up in time to see a black paw reaching sleepily out of the darkness towards the dog.

Friday October 19th
A raw, roaring Chinook & a nasty, grey, damp day, verging on rain. Almost it might have been England—& very heartily we wished it had been—with two deep leather chairs drawn up to a smoking room fire. Worked in camp in the morning, making fur stretchers while Gordon tubbed & had a washing day, well earned after his work with the moose meat. After lunch we went out & cut more trail along the ridge, mainly through thick set young spruce. We took a stroll up to the bears den on our way home: the bear was abroad, maybe taking one last meal of grubs or berries before the winter sleep. The den was lined with moss, so evidently it must be the home of a female, made soft & comfortable for the cubs that are to be born there before spring. But maybe—& even probably—there is our next supply of lard, the recent debauch on pancakes having run our store very low.

Saturday October 20th
Nothing to report. Frost at night & a dry sunny day with a strong wind. I [am] still laid up with the remains of my stiffness—Gordon again packing meat down from the moorland.

Sunday October 21st
Trafalgar day, & a dull grey morning with a N. W. wind. I felt much better— almost human once more & able to get about & do things.

Monday October 22nd
A windy Chinook day, but drier & with more sunlight. I went up the hill with Gordon & cut more trail through the woods while he went on for a load of meat. We came back to lunch together & later took the canoe & went over to try for a beaver. I had a good look at their system of dams—two or three small, subsidiary dams lower down stream to raise the water & so take the pressure off the main dam which forms their home—a pool maybe 12' to 15' deep & about ½ mile long—the wings of the dam being curved back on what is now dry land in order to catch the spring flood water. Only one house was built, & that on the

bank—a dome shaped thing roofed with mud & sticks, with an entrance & an exit tunnel, both under water. On the banks, up into the woods where they were felling poplar for their winter feed, ran their trails, cut & cleared through the alder & willow & beaten smooth.

As we came near the main pool two warning smacks on the water from the flat tails of the sentries told us that we had been heard. We were a shade too late in the afternoon. I sat with my rifle on my knee for almost an hour on a fallen tree— the sunset, the black spruce & the snow mountains reflected in the calm water of the dam. Not a sound except the chattering of the squirrels & not a shot—only one beaver sighted, & he swam close beside us making no attempt to land.

Tuesday Oct*ober* 23rd
A fine sunny day & a little colder. *Gordon* brought down more meat & I cut more trail. We had lunch on the ridge & then worked together until the last of the trail was cut, & reached home about 3:30. A splendid sunset, turning the snow peaks all to rose, & now the moon & the stars in a frosty sky & the mountains & the river pale in the blue, cold light.

Wednesday Oct*ober* 24th
Grey & cold with the S. E. wind a-blowing, & now, at eight in the evening, snowing hard. I went away early over the Nahanni in the canoe. I had to break the ice in our eddy to launch her & all the way across the river the cakes of mush ice came hissing against her & shoving her down river. I went up Prairie Creek & through into the Hermitage where there were many high bush cranberries. From there along the ridges till I hit the head of Trowel Tail's (The Beaver's) creek & so down to the dam. I waited there for ¾ hour but the dam was frozen over & the Trowel Tail outfit were keeping to their own firesides & doing nothing further in the matter, like sensible animals. They may break the ice where it is thinner & come out & fell timber later on if the moon shows up. And so home to supper—wild duck & green peas. Trowel Tail's Creek doesnt freeze in its lower reaches—or not yet—& there are numbers of trout in it. Some warm spring, maybe, or perhaps the water seeps for a long distance underground & through the stones.

Thursday Oct*ober* 25th
A fairish deal of snow fell in the night & today has been grey & sunless with snow falling most of the time. I am writing by my fire, in camp by the salt lick in the

hills. I came up here slowly with my pack, rifle & axe this morning, while *Gordon* went on ahead with the dogs to bring home the sled load of meat that had lain on the trail so long, becalmed for lack of snow. As I came near to the salt lick I found the tracks of a wolf in the snow, & further on a piece of chewed moose hide. I was afraid for our meat but, though wolf tracks—monstrous tracks into which my fist fitted with room to spare—were all around, nothing had been touched but the offal. However, here I made my camp, close to the kill so that it may be safe from the wolves until we can get it home. I made a good camp & cut myself some steaks from *Gordon*'s bull for lunch & found the old boy to be amazingly sweet & tender for one of his years. Then I set off on the trail of the wolf towards the remains of our two moose that lay up on the open moorland. As I topped the last rise half a dozen great ravens rose screaming into the air & I saw a huge timber wolf start up from the kill—a great beast, looking much the colour of an Airedale through the falling snow. I dropped instantly to keep myself from view & was then unable to shoot for the maze of dwarf alder in my way, the twigs of w*hic*h would have split my bullet into pieces. So I started to wriggle through the snow but the breeze—or the breath of air that moved in the silence—blew from me to him, the damned corbies had given him the alarm, & at the first soft squawk of the snow he was away over the rise & out of sight in a long easy lope. I rose up, & as he breasted a slope about 300 y*ar*ds away I got in three shots, the spurts of flame stabbing sharply into the fading light of the October afternoon & the echoes from my monstrous cannon of a Männlicher rolling up the little basin & dying under the outpost spurs of the Ram Mountains. The first a wild miss—I never saw it at all: the second threw up the snow powder before his nose & made him tack sharply: the last fluffed the snow under his tail as he disappeared—two good shots although they missed. I'd have been lucky to get him, & he was lucky to get away—a matter of inches.

I came back to the spur between the big & little basins & waited there in a grove of birch until it grew too dark for me to see my sights, but no moose were travelling the trail. Bed time now & the moon shining down into my camp under the spruce through a veil of cloud, & a fine snow falling.

Friday Oct*ober* 26th

Another grey day with the tops of the Ram Mountains hidden in cold blue mist. *Gordon* came up with the dog team for a load of meat—I think it will take him another 5 loads at least to get it all home, w*hic*h means that I shall have to camp here tomorrow night as well, probably. Today I went up into the big basin—a great stretch of fairly open country, bigger than I had thought. There were no moose tracks, nor was any game moving, & I saw only the tracks of wolves & maybe of marten & fox. I crossed the spur down into the little basin but nothing was round our moose & the going was damnable on that side of the spur—a mass of alder & drifted snow. For rotten walking this valley beats any other part of Canada that I have yet seen. Later on I waited again, at sunset, by the moose trail, but in vain.

Saturday October 27th

I felt cold in the night & roused myself to see the clouds gone & the moon & the stars glittering in a dark blue sky with all the radiance of the frost. It was the first morning of winter—the sun came up with a roar of light into a frozen, shining world, the snow squalled underfoot, ones nose stung in the clear air & the moose steaks I had cut overnight were frozen like bricks. Also I had no more lard so I had to grill them on green willows over the embers. *Gordon* & the dogs came up soon after ten. He had with him a bannock & a couple of cold ducks—the white variety with the purple heads, the fattest & best of all that we have had so far. So I made tea & we had a good lunch & then loaded up more meat on the sled & he departed with it. I broke up my camp, leaving the Indian blanket hanging gaudily by the kill to scare away the wolves, & followed. A lovely day, sunny, cloudless & cold & the snow dry underfoot. I overtook *Gordon* on the steep hill where he had lost a trace & cracked a sled board, so I reached home before him & set about a much needed wash & shave.

A very cold, clear evening turning later in the night to a N.W. wind, cutting but actually less cold.

Sunday October 28th

Clear & sunny with a raw, hard wind & the river gradually freezing. I felt very stiff again & had to stay at home working at the innumerable things that crop up day by day, such as the mending of the sled. The wind has almost dropped now & a full moon is shining out of a cloudless sky on the half frozen Nahanni & the snow mountains.

Monday October 29th

A perfect winter's day—cloudless, cold & still. And I useless—a damned log, & at home.

Tuesday October 30th

Another glorious morning, the valley glittering like a jewel in the sunlight & the frost. I am less stiff, but still at home, & *Gordon* has taken the sled up onto the moorland for the last load of meat. This morning I saw a little white head looking at me from between the logs of the wood pile—an ermine, prime & in his winter coat. So I shot a squirrel & a whiskey jack & threw them down for him & he promptly hauled them inside. We should be able to catch him easily if we can keep the dogs away from him.

Wednesday October 31st

Still laid up—glorious day & the Nahanni jammed with ice.

Thursday November 1st

A clear sunny day with a strong N.W. wind. During the night the ice rose in the jam & pushed its way well up onto the beach, so this morning we carried up the little canoe & laid it by for the winter. *Gordon* went away with Quiz & Sammy & some traps to look over the tracks I found in the big basin & will camp up there tonight. So I am alone with the other two dogs & still pretty much of a cripple. South Africa, the South Seas or Australia for me the next time—I've wooed the frozen north & she has treated me very ill.

Friday November 2nd

A warmer day—I feel much easier now, but still too stiff to get about & so I have nothing to say for myself.

Saturday November 3rd

Coldish, sunny & still. In the night the weasel put his head in the trap & now one ermine is drying on the rafters. The two pups are now on their feet & come squeaking & tumbling out of their den to view the world—surely the fattest & healthiest pups in all Christendom. The Nahanni is playing odd tricks—it has opened a narrow channel for itself in the centre through which the open water flows fast & swirling, & black against the fields of tumbled ice on either side.

Sunday November 4th

A day of Chinook & at lunch time the river broke up again & piled its ice high on shore, & is now running much as in the spring break up. I am writing after supper—alone & with the west wind roaring outside & the warm breath of the Pacific Ocean in it. *Gordon* is again away up in the basin with Quiz, setting traps. This morning I went up the dry snye to the old cabins & set a couple of weasel traps. The snye is evidently a highway for the wolves & coyotes, the tracks of one big fellow being the size of saucers in the snow.

Monday November 5th

A perfect day, warm & sunny like a fall or spring day, with the river still running open. Opposite here it was like a lake, with most beautiful & unbroken reflections in its calm waters—evidently dammed back by some ice jam down below. I was out & doing once more though only a little—making canoe poles & felling trees. After supper we raised great bedevilment with Chinese crackers, rockets & the like—brought originally to impress the Indians, but now not needed, since the once dreaded Nahannis are down to a small & miserable remnant, gathered round the posts on the Liard.

Tuesday November 6th

A sweet morning—sunny & still & not more than a touch of frost. The sunlight shines in at the door & falls on the table here, glinting through the trees. *Gordon* has gone up to the old cabins to set wolf traps & I am hobbling around, cutting wood & boiling traps over the open fire.

Wednesday November 7th

Another pleasant day & I am better but still have to stay in camp & do the camp work—only wish I could be away on the trail once more. *Gordon* away down the shore to the driftwood bay to set traps & he returned with an old Munsey's Magazine that he had found in the prospector's camp—rather a godsend as, in this month of stiffness, I have read everything we have—including the advertisements—& most things twice.

The pups can almost run now & are getting to know me.

Thursday November 8th

A perfect fall day—the river now backed high up onto the beach & still not frozen across. Feel still better & am cutting wood & boiling the last of the traps. I managed to get a photo of the pups at midday, outside their den.

Gordon came home with one ermine—or, to call it by its more homely & less royal name, a weasel in his winter jacket. A big timber wolf had been caught in one of our No. 3 traps but had chewed through the toggle & gone away with the trap on his leg, so we may have him yet when the snow falls again & he leaves a trail. Dont like to think of the poor beast in misery & unable to hunt—too much like my own case these last weeks. And Faille lost ten wolves in the same way last winter.

Friday Nov*ember* 9th
A grey cold day with a threat of snow. Camp work & the chores take up my time.

Saturday November 10th
A still, sunny morning & the river almost frozen across. In a day spent in camp there's little to write about, & that little would only be monotonous in the telling.

Sunday Nov*ember* 11th
Cold, grey, & still—not a breath of air moving during the day, & now, in the evening, a fine snow falling. Armistice Day at home but there's no need of a Silence here—the Nahanni has frozen across & with that the last ripple of sound has gone from us. Frozen, that is, except at the mouth of Trowel Tail's creek which, I think, must have a warm spring feeding it. Unless it freezes it is going to be a nuisance to us all winter. I am almost limbered up again & have been out all day working on a big stretcher for wolves, coyotes & foxes.

Monday Nov*ember* 12
The snow has stopped—a fall of an inch or so—& it is sunny & still. *Gordon* away with traps in behind the old cabins & I am at work again on my fur stretchers. Also, in view of the fact that we were almost smoked out of house & home last night, I have cleaned the stove of ashes, & swept the chimney with an old sock on the end of a canoe pole.
Evening   *Gordon* home with one weasel—snow falling.

Tuesday Nov*ember* 13th
Calm with snow falling at intervals—about 1½ inches fell last night. Both of us were in camp today & I worked mainly on my stretcher boards.

Wednesday Nov*ember* 14th
A cloudless sky & a cold, whistling N.W. wind, driving the snow in a haze from the mountain tops & drifting it like sand down the frozen Nahanni & across the

bars—a bitter wind that freezes as it touches. I have been out all day, logging & working at my fur stretchers. *Gordon* went up to look over our traps in the basin & was back to lunch with a fully prime, medium No. 1 red fox—$35—for him we hope. Now Poilu & Quiz have disappeared—maybe the wolves have got them, or maybe they are freezing to death in traps that we have set. *Gordon* has gone up on his morning's trail to look over the traps for them, & its no night for a Christian to be out hunting for dogs. I hope we shall see them again but *Gordon* saw two timber wolves about the size of calves this morning, & these dogs are fools enough for any folly—spoilt by sparing the rod.

Later   The luck was with us, as *Gordon* met Poilu in the river flats, limping silently home with a No. 3 trap on his foot, while he found Quiz up at the salt lick, caught in a No. 3 & yelling his soul out for any wandering wolf to hear. Both dogs were thoroughly scared, had their feet badly nipped & partly frozen but no bones broken, & both have been well basted with a willow, so doubtless all is for the best in the best of best possible worlds.

And the wind is in the north now—rising to a scream & driving a burning blast of cold under a starlit sky.

Thursday November 15th

Cold & still. I was busy at home all morning, & after lunch I took my rifle & went up the snye to the old cabins to look at one or two traps. It was a perfect winter afternoon. The sun set early behind the Bald Mountain & left its aurora glowing in a sky of bronze that threatened snow—the ice in the snye was the colour of pale jade & the black spruce were reflected in it—all was still save for the faintest of cold airs that burned & stung on the cheeks & nose. And no game was moving.

In the evening we skinned the fox & set him on a stretcher that I had made—& later I dreamed wildly of an uproar in a pastry cook's at Red Deer & of an Atlantic crossing on which I insisted on wearing my dinner jacket at breakfast. In this cut-off existence one's dreams seem very real.

Friday November 16th

Snow fell in the night & with morning came a N.W. wind w*hich* by midday changed to a Chinook, roaring across the Bald Mountain & fanning out his beard—wetting the dry snow powder. This morning I crossed the river on the ice to the far side, but couldnt land as Trowel Tail's Creek was running, open as ever, & one small channel of the Nahanni remains free from ice. The sky was wonderful—the south westerly clouds a rich gold, rolling across a field of perfect blue. And for the moment the valley lay in shadow, while the snow slopes of the western mountains & of the Second Canyon Mountain lay golden in the sunlight.

The rest of my day, carpentry & camp work in the shadow of the trees, & now evening & the Chinook still blowing.

Saturday November 17th

Another damp day of west wind & we went down the shore together to look at the traps—down beyond the Little Butte as far as the Cache riffles. We found nothing, & except for the trails of one weasel & a coyote we saw no signs. The western walls of the valley were rose coloured in the dawn light &, at midday, gold in the half sunset light from a sun that only rises for a short while above the ridges to the southward. In a month's time, at midwinter, I expect we shall see little of the sun.

Sunday November 18th

Well before sunrise this morning we set off with the dogsled up to the ridge to dig our bear out of his winter den. But no luck—the bear had gone & the den was empty. The inside of the hole was dry & comfortably floored over with moss & twigs, so in all probability it was the den of a female—& I think that Sammy's visit & ourselves continually working & passing on the trail had scared her away to safer quarters. We dug & grubbed with pick & shovel, poked about with sticks, got head & shoulders into the den & lit matches inside, & at last convinced ourselves that there was nobody at home. So we went on up to the lick & the moorland to look over our traps & were home to lunch about two—having seen the fresh track of a fisher. A raw, half Chinook day of damp, slippery snow.

Monday November 19th

A day of snow & glorious sunshine & I spent it travelling about in the delta of Prairie Creek, on the far side of the Nahanni. I found the track of lynx, weasel & mink & set four traps for weasel—of wolves & foxes there was no sign, but Prairie Creek is open in many places & they are not fond of water. Also the Chinook, sweeping over the open stretches, soon wipes out the tracks of any animal by melting or drifting the snow. The short lived winter sun sank below Old Baldy before two o'clock, & by three there was a marvellously beautiful reflection in the calm reaches of open water—the tall spruce like sentinels, dark green against a blue green sunset sky, with rough, ragged, golden clouds driving across on a S.W. wind—the snow powdered cliffs of old Baldy as a background.

A burst of artillery in the distance, about nine this morning, heralded the deaths of four partridges at *Gordon's* pistol.

Tuesday Nov*ember* 20th
Weather much the same as yesterday's & my day was spent at home in camp work & chores. *Gordon* was away all day up to the McLeod creek & came back with a tale of sprung traps & of wolves & foxes & snowshoe rabbits in the muskeg beyond the old cabins, while mink & otter were moving on the creek. At dusk, as the dogs were feeding, we worked together on the bench, compounding various ghastly, decayed stenches as bait for the fur.

Wednesday Nov*ember* 21st
A grey day & from daylight to dark I was over by Prairie Creek setting traps for mink & weasel. Late in the afternoon I discovered that many of these Yankee made Victor traps were not springing properly, & consequently I returned home in no even temper. After supper I fiddled away at the traps with a file & an oil can & a superior smile from *Gordon*, & if some djinn would give me a bottle of old Burgundy, a good book & some cigarettes I'd thank him.

Thursday Nov*ember* 22nd
A roaring warm Chinook, toppling over trees, melting the snow & bringing overflow onto the ice. In the morning I was over to the Prairie Creek island, re-setting the stiff & frozen traps, & all afternoon I have worked on another fox stretcher which is now finished & ready for use—we need only the foxes, but in this warm, wet weather serious trapping is almost impossible.

Friday Nov*ember* 23rd
A cold, beautiful morning—one of the few winter mornings we have had. Together we went to the head of the dry snye & into the muskeg behind the third cabin where we made some fox sets by the little marsh lake. In there there were many tracks of wolves, foxes & rabbits—some weasels & the odd marten. A ring round the sun I think betokens the approach of another Chinook.

Saturday November 24th

I went away early over to Prairie Creek & lifted my frozen traps. Then I went on up to the banks & made a lynx set, & there, as I sat & ate my lunch in the low sunshine, the Chinook broke—a roaring warm wind—almost it might have been the hot breeze of June. In the afternoon I went through the Prairie Creek Gap on the ice—an awe inspiring place with its overhanging cliffs & its floor of jade green ice & rushing water. The Hermitage was silent & its snows without track of animal, & there I climbed the rock slides & took photos of the Gap from within. I went on up the deep valley—its cliffs red in the afternoon sunlight & a warm wind blowing—but I saw no signs of fur, & so turned back & homewards, crossing the great bar in the evening frost & with the western sky flaming behind the mountains. And now the Chinook has come again with the moonrise—warm as any summer evening's breeze.

Sunday November 25th

A Chinook day turning later to east wind & a threat of snow. No animal seems to move during this everlasting warm weather & I was at home all day—camp work & odd chores & I wrote a letter to George.

Monday November 26th

A grey, raw, silent day—& another day spent at home on odd, uninteresting jobs.

Tuesday November 27th

Over to Prairie Creek in the morning & round the traps, finding one weasel. A roaring wet west wind was blowing & in the afternoon I did camp work & later on wrote to Annette.

Wednesday November 28th

A sunny day & colder. We went away together as soon as it was light & spent the morning searching the ridges for bear dens but with no success. After lunch we went on & through the Prairie Creek Gap where I took two more photos with *Gordon* & Quiz in them. Then we separated & came home by different ways.

Thursday November 29th

This morning I went up to the lick. It was clear, frosty & still & not a thing was moving & as usual, nothing was in the traps. I reset four No. 3 traps from which the Chinook had swept the snow & leaves, & cut toggles for two new trail sets on my way home. *Gordon* spent the morning in the muskeg &, this afternoon, was over to Trowel Tail's Creek making a set for an otter. Feel decidedly blue today—I gave up so much for this trip & yet it seems that the luck & weather are always against us.

Friday Nov*ember* 30th
Colder with an east wind, & a fine snow falling during most of the day. I went away at daylight to explore the mouth of the McLeod River canyon & was not back until dark—no lunch with me so I came home with a monstrous appetite. The canyon was deep, wild, rocky & sunless, but very beautiful. I found it to be as I had expected & found a creek leading from it to what I think may be a high, open valley & possibly to the back of the Ram Mountains.

Saturday Dec*ember* 1st
A very cold, dirty morning with a bitter S.E. wind driving the grey snow powder up the frozen river. The water hole through the ice has to be cut open both morning & evening on these cold days—a sloppy, cheerless job in the dawn twilight. I went round my weasel traps by Prairie Creek & found one small weasel there, while *Gordon* came back at lunchtime from the muskeg with a marten, so the day has not been in vain.

The wind has dropped now & the night is starlit & still—the first cold night of winter. Outside, the trees of the bush & the river ice are cracking under the frost, & inside the shack the latch hole & door jamb are lined with hoar frost & rime.

Sunday Dec*ember* 2nd
About 2:00 a.m. the wind got up & swung into the N.W. & from that quarter it has blown a gale all day long—an icy wind that freezes as it touches, has driven the dogs to seek shelter in the doghouse or their burrows & made movement on our part pointless, as all animals will den until this blast of cold has passed. Never a cloud all day in the pale blue sky & the "sun of Austerlitz" shone unhindered but cheerless & futile. I devoted the day to mending moccasins & cutting wood, & now—at night—the gale still rages.

Monday Dec*ember* 3rd
Woke up with the wind still blowing out of a cloudless sky, &, as the alarm clock had frozen in the night, we overslept ourselves. I was away up over the ridges from ten until three, exploring a new part of our country—the wooded basin to the west of

the big basin. I was surprised to find that, at the height of a few hundred feet, one was above this wind & could look down from the silence of the frozen woods & hear the roar of the gale & see the tree tops bending in the valley below. On the way up I took an idiotic & wasteful shot at a blue grouse with my Männlicher. There was nothing left to bring home & the wretched grouse was scattered all over the map. I found rabbit tracks & signs of weasel up there but nothing else was moving, so I crossed the spur & came home by the lick & the old trail—nearly getting the skin blown off my face as I came up the shore. Later on I found that cutting open the water hole out on the river ice was a cold & perishing job but now the wind is dropping.

Tuesday December 4th

Woke up to a grey day & the snow falling, so, almost before it was light I set out up the mountain trail to make my trail sets. I made two & one weasel set but the snow stopped before my tracks were completely covered—my usual luck, these days. The sun shone but there was no warmth in it—only light & colour to the mountain slopes—& in the afternoon I made a long circle west of our own creek, along the hillside to the snye, in search of partridges—four of those that we were holding for Christmas having blown down from the cache & disappeared down some dog's throat.

Wednesday December 5th

Cold, clear, sunny & still. Day taken up with camp work, writing to Mrs Portman & looking over the weasel traps. Saw otter tracks by Prairie Creek.

Thursday December 6th

Away on foot for nine hours today in an effort to find a way into the high valley that I think lies behind the ridges at the McLeod Creek Gap. The snow was deep & much of the going tough but I think I have found the valley—a long, ridgy, wooded valley running southwards—& out of it we may get some fur. And over my trail today I found many rabbit & marten tracks. A cold day turning to a light snow & I did not get back till after dark.

Friday December 7th

A warm wet Chinook blowing & the snow melting in slop. I was at home all day doing various small jobs while *Gordon* went up to the mountain & returned with two weasel, one in my set & one in his. It has seemed a long, dull day.

Saturday December 8th

Colder—down to Prairie Creek in the morning & found the creek overflowing & nothing moving or in the traps. In the afternoon I went up the snye & out over the big bar setting weasel traps.

Sunday December 9th

We went together up to the mountain where, two days ago, another of the great timber wolves had gone off with one of our No. 3 traps on his foot. Beyond the lick we made two trail sets with heavy toggles of birch, & if they wont hold then we have done our best. The weasels are about again, & on our way home we made three weasel sets. A frosty day, but with a touch of west wind & not cold.

Monday December 10th

A still day with a hazy sun & coldish. I went up into the wooded basin & set some weasel tracks & picked some low bush cranberries against our Christmas day. On the way down I blazed & partly cut a trail as, later on, we may have trapping to do up there.

Tuesday December 11th

Cold & still. We went together round the marten & fox traps this morning but there was nothing doing—maybe we are to have the same luck as Faille had last year— nothing before the New Year. Cut wood, wrote & did the chores after lunch.

Wednesday December 12th

We went up together into the wooded basin as soon as it was light. *Gordon* went on up, finding many marten tracks amongst the spruce, & came home by the lick, while I cut out the rest of the trail & set two traps for a fisher whose tracks I had seen. A still, cold day with mists & grey streamers of cloud hanging on the mountain slopes.

Thursday December 13th

A cold, still & sunny day & we spent it in different parts of the wooded basin, setting marten traps. I covered a lot of ground & set seven traps—there were many tracks so some good should come of it. I had a wonderful view in that clear air down towards the canyon, & at sunset the mountain tops were all rose coloured in the evening light.

Friday December 14th

We went down the valley together, picking up my useless weasel traps by Prairie Creek & then going on to have a look at the Cache Rapid. We found it frozen & silent, although the Cache riffles were still partly open, & there was a good passage for a dog sled into the canyon. It was very cold in there—much colder than in the valley. A cold wind was blowing & we were glad to reach home again latish in the afternoon.

Saturday December 15th

A warmish day & a day of damp snow & I spent it around camp cutting wood & writing letters & cables. In the morning I got a brace of blue grouse up the creek with the .22.

Sunday December 16th

Up to the wooded basin & found a marten in one of *Gordon*'s traps. Then I went on alone over my own line & reached home late in the afternoon.

Monday December 17th

This was our Christmas eve, & in the morning *Gordon* went up the mountain trail while I did the camp work & shaved, bathed, tired my hair & attired myself in new & clean clothes—& felt exceedingly blessed. In the afternoon *Gordon* did likewise, while I cut wood & brought down good Christmas fare out of the cache. Then, in the evening, we made a batter & fell to eating hot cakes with butter, sugar & maple syrup on them. But when you have been a long time without rich, sweet food there's a distinct limit to the amount you can eat of it—I did my best but caved in at $4\frac{1}{2}$, while *Gordon*—unfairly skunking his sugar—managed to do in five. If only we could have our twenty one year old appetites back again. The day militated somewhat against a great eating—a warm Chinook day.

Tuesday December 18th

The day was passed largely in the eating of good things, in talking & in preparing for *Gordon*'s setting out. I finished & bound up my mail & handed it to him & cooked & cut wood & walked off a splendid midday meal of grouse & partridge— a brace apiece—with cranberries, & a lusty dessert, in an unavailing hunt for partridges. Quiz did better—I think the wolf in him is stronger than in the rest—

& he caught & ate one on his own. The more strength to any dog who can rustle his own feed. A colder day.

Wednesday December 19th
The day has passed by degrees from a pleasantly frosty morning into a tearing Chinook—a beastly wet, warm winter, & the worst I have yet seen in Canada. We had a good breakfast & then *Gordon* loaded up & left for Simpson—the pups in the carryall, very placid, & Poilu looking like a peasant evicted from his old cottage home by an unjust landlord. I went up to the marten sets & found a nice marten in one of my traps—but no means of telling what the marten are doing until a fresh snow fall comes. I spent the late afternoon clearing up our Christmas mess & preparing things to my own liking for a month or more of my own company.

Thursday December 20th
A grey morning, clearing to an evening of blue sky & ragged clouds—& the Chinook still blowing. I went up early to the marten sets but found nothing. Then I pushed on westwards, cutting & blazing a trail towards the last big basin—a larger distance than it seems from down below. The trail runs through what should be good marten country but until fresh snow falls one cant tell if anything is there or not. I was out about 6½ hrs & came home to a number of small chores—am now going to skin & stretch my marten.

Friday December 21st
More Chinook—cloudier, warmer & wetter. I went to the lake & muskeg traps but in this weather one might as well admit that one goes round for exercise & nothing else—there is nothing moving & this is the longest spell of Chinook that I have yet known.

Saturday December 22nd
The shortest day—thank God—& from now onwards the sun will be returning to us. It was very warm, & I spent the morning at home, working round camp, tackling my laundry & cleaning my armoury of two rifles, a shot gun & a pistol. After lunch I went up the mountain trail &, as I was setting a trap on the ridge, I heard the sound of a voice & the clatter of a dog sled on the river ice. I climbed a tree but *could* see nothing so I went on up, resetting traps, & came down home in the twilight—a warm, gusty Chinook melting the snow to slop. The light was

on in the shack & I found *Gordon* & the dogs at home again. He had been unable to get through the Lower Canyon owing to open water & had spent a couple of days trying to find a ledge of ice against the cliff to carry him & in crossing open places on a raft. Finally he had been forced to cache all his gear on the island & to turn back home to get the canoe. It seems that there is ice a couple of feet thick right up to the open water, & no rim of rotten ice—so it is possible that this latest peculiarity of the Nahanni is caused by warm springs. The day crowned itself by raining—at midwinter in the North West Territories—of all times & places. We went glumly to bed.

Sunday Dec*ember* 23rd

We were up early to a slightly colder day, & worked hard preparing for *Gordon*'s second attempt to get out. We cut nicely curved birch & hewed it into runners twelve feet long, & so made a strong & solid sled on which the canoe could be loaded & carried over glare ice down to the open water. We made everything ready & then had a second farewell supper & went to bed feeling that something had been achieved.

Monday Dec*ember* 24th

Christmas Eve—my fourth to be spent in a strange place away from home. It was colder & the wind had dropped to a dead stillness—luckily, as it would have been impossible to travel with the canoe on glare ice in a high wind such as sweeps through that canyon. We had a good breakfast & then lashed the little canoe onto its birch sled & put the dog sled into the canoe, & the pups, grunting their objections, into the dog sled. *Gordon* hitched up & I took two photographs of his outfit, & then away he went down river in the dawn light—I hope with better fortune. I made the round of the marten traps & found a large crop of squirrels in them. I brought home a tin full of cranberries & ate them with pancakes to my supper—& now have that torpor upon me that invariable comes of over eating.

I do now resolve—to buy myself a present when I get home, as a species of thank[s] offering. And it shall be a piece of old German glass, such as I have long coveted.

Tuesday Dec*ember* 25th

Christmas Day & a cold, still pleasant day for it. I felt stiff in the hip & spent the morning at home, mending moccasins for I suddenly found myself without footgear fit for the trail. Dinner at midday was off hot roast partridge with stewed cranberries & in the afternoon I went out in quest of more fowl for the larder & was rewarded with one partridge in the big spruce over by Trowel Tail's Creek. A wash, a good comfortable supper & now bed.

Wednesday December 26th
Afraid I overslept myself, but as we keep our clock far ahead of the sun it didnt matter so very much. I went up into the wooded basin & cut more trail, making six marten sets along it & reaching home in the twilight. The day was cold, clear & still & the night is turning colder with the clouds moving at last from the east.

Thursday December 27th
Woke up to a fine dry snow falling & after breakfast I went up the mountain trail to see that the trail sets were in order. The snow soon stopped & the day was still & coldish with the glass rising steadily.

Friday December 28th
Snow falling all day—not hard but steadily—& the mountains mostly hidden in cloud. I packed 8 traps up my hill trail, but left them hanging on a birch tree by the trail as I could see no sign of fur, & came home by a new way that led through a varied country & out into the snye.

Saturday December 29th
Snow & a cold east wind all day—grey & monotonous. Behind the old cabins I came on a big beaver meadow—deserted now & the dams broken.

Sunday December 30th
Cold & still & the clouds the colour of bronze as if the sun were trying to struggle through. I went up Prairie Creek to pick up two isolated traps & then turned west & hit for Trowel Tail's dam. From there I followed up one arm of the creek & found it to be merely a snye of the Nahanni winding through the woods. I went on up, exploring some big snyes, until I came opposite to the McLeod River, where I crossed the Nahanni & came home over the bars. In the night it snowed.

Monday December 31st
Mainly clear & sunny & I think the coldest day of winter so far. I went the round of the marten traps but nothing was moving except the odd wandering weasel. So

+
Cabin and dogs at Wheatsheaf Creek.

I came home & did the chores & made pancakes & roasted two blue grouse for supper—I thought the last meal of the year might as well be a decent one, & lets hope for better luck in 1929. Give '28 its due—it began wonderfully—too well to last. Dead still outside & the coldest night we have had. There is frost round the door, the hot air steams as it goes out of the shack & the smoke is rising thickly & heavily from the chimney.

Tuesday January 1st 1929
Very cold & still—& the night still colder. I went up the mountain trail & found tracks at last—wolf & fox, I fancy—& one of our traps had just missed getting the wolf.

Wednesday January 2nd
The north wind came with the sunrise & blew all day out of a clear sky—a strong, searing wind. I hunted unsuccessfully for partridges in the morning & cut wood all afternoon. Dead still now & slightly less cold.

Thursday January 3rd
Very cold[,] sunny & clear. I set out for the McLeod River again to try to find my way into the high, hidden valley, but when I came to the Gap, a cold blasting wind blew out of it, whirling the snow powder over the bars like sand. I couldnt face it

&, for the first time in my Canadian life, I made for a sheltered spot in the trees & lit a fire to warm myself—that wind went through every thing. I turned back & as I left the Gap behind I left the wind also. I went on up the Nahanni, exploring the narrow, winding snyes towards the second canyon, finding old beaver dams & fresh tracks of wolverine. There was a curious colouring high in the sky—pale green & orange—it might have been a sun dog or the play of the Aurora. The sun shone on me in the snyes for the first time for many days—it was pleasant to be out of the mountain shadow & once more in a glittering, golden world. Coming home over the bars I felt the cold.

Friday January 4th
Very cold & clear with an occasional breeze. I went up the mountain trail & found a wolverine in a trap—just caught & lashing & plunging on the chain. It took eight Luger 9 mm pistol bullets to kill that animal, so either the American cartridges are no good or else the wolverine is amazingly tough—both, probably. A powerfully built animal, something on the lines of a bear & with ferocious jaw & claws.

Saturday January 5th
Much warmer & a slight powdering of snow but no sign of a Chinook. A day of chores & spent at home—mainly in attending to the wolverine & in getting him stretched on a frame. A wearying day, as days spent in camp usually are.

Sunday January 6th
Cloudy & not too cold—just right in fact. I went up to the marten traps & found a well furred, lightish coloured marten in one of mine. Came down a new way & saw wolf & marten tracks on the way home. The wolverine is a brute to flesh as the hide cuts easily in cutting off the fat.

Monday January 7th
In the night snow fell—a heavy fall of three inches or so. A powdering of snow fell all day with a breath of east wind & I went up into the old beaver meadows & set traps there.

Tuesday January 8th
A grey day but not cold. I was away early—on snowshoes for the first time this season—up into the Nahanni snyes beyond the McLeod creek, & there I set two

No. 3 traps & a No. 1 for weasel. Got home latish—I believe there is already a lengthening out of the daylight hours—& feel a little stiff in the re-awakened snowshoe muscles. Found a small weasel in one of the traps at the old cabins.

Wednesday January 9th
This morning I sadly overslept & didnt waken until the dawn light roused me. I had intended to go up the mountain trail but it was so late by the time I had finished breakfast—& also it was snowing hard out of a hopeless sky—that I spent the day at home where there was much work to be done. Night now—still snowing with a strong south east wind.

Friday January 11th
Yesterday I took my pack & went up through the McLeod Creek Gap & camped there meaning to go on into the high valley. I had no luck—it seems that I cant get into that valley, somehow. This time it was overflow on the McLeod that stopped me—I went through into it yesterday afternoon & got feet & snowshoes soaked & this morning the water was creeping on down so that I had to pack up & leave—otherwise I should have been cut off beyond the Gap. I saw two moose tracks as I came over the bars—& then hills & everything vanished in a driving whirl of snow that is still coming from the east—the third big fall in six days.

Saturday January 12
A little snow fell in the night & I spent the day up the mountain trail lifting the traps. The going was heavy, wading in deep, powdery snow, & I was away over six hours.

Sunday January 13
A grey, snowy morning & the evening clear & cold. Found I had no footgear in sound condition so I devoted the long weary day to mending. Finished the last of the moose meat today.

Monday January 14
Still, clear, sunny & coldish & I went round the marten traps on snowshoes.

Tuesday January 15th
Clear & sunny & very cold. I went down the Nahanni on snowshoes & up the Meilleur River, looking for moose. I saw no signs of them—only wolf & weasel tracks.

+

The Nahanni country in winter.

Wednesday January 16th

Not so cold but grey & snowing. I looked over the nearer traps & chased around in quest of partridges—made a fresh mattress of spruce tips & did odd jobs at home.

Thursday January 17th

Clear, sunny & cold. I was up in the beaver snyes beyond the McLeod & towards the canyon. The sun is raising itself over Baldy & shone there all day—there was warmth in its rays for the first time, & it was very sweet to spend a day away out of the shadow.

Friday January 18th

Still, cloudless & sunny—a perfect winter's day. I wandered unsuccessfully up Trowel Tail's Creek & over the Prairie Creek bars looking for partridges & moose—lunched on a slice of bannock out on the bars & actually sat & felt warm in the glorious sunshine.

Saturday January 19th

Dull & warmer with N.W. wind. Went up the mountain trail.

Sunday January 20th

East wind & snow falling—turning later to clear, cold & still. Went over marten traps.

Monday January 21st

A clear sky & a moon last night & this morning it was very cold—the coldest day we have had so far. It must have been something towards 50° below zero & the open waters in the valley were steaming hard in the cold air & spreading a raw mist over the floor of the valley. I went up to the Second Canyon reach & came back over the bars, seeing nothing. Towards evening it clouded over & a very fine, cold snow started to fall.

These last few days I have been eating boiled wolverine & cooking with the soup—having no other meat. Its an acquired taste but one soon gets used to it.

Tuesday January 22nd

Clear & sunny but still colder—both last night & today. I dont know how cold, but certainly damned cold—of course this poor grub & lack of meat, sweets & fats doesnt help one to stand the cold any better. I spent the day wood cutting & in an unsuccessful quest for game. Even the squirrels are silent these days. About time Gordon was back from Simpson.

Wednesday January 23rd

Utterly still & very cold with a film of cloud in the sky. I cut wood this morning & got myself a partridge & after lunch I went up to the Prairie Creek Gap—still looking for the eternal moose.

Thursday January 24th

Just the same as yesterday & very cold. I thawed, cut up & boiled the rest of the wolverine & cut wood this morning & after lunch went round my traps in the snye. If Gordon doesnt show up soon theres going to be a shortage of grub in this outfit.

Friday January 25th

Last night still colder & today very cold, still & sunny. Had no luck with the partridges today but got a lot of odd jobs done & cut more wood.

Saturday January 26th

Cloudy & warmer with some north wind, but still I dont think above zero. Hunted very patiently today & got a nice plump, tender partridge for my supper, & then went up the mountain trail as far as my first trail set.

Sunday January 27th

Cloudy, a fine snow falling & not too cold. No sign of Gordon &, this morning, up in the cache, I made the pleasant discovery that we are almost out of grub. So in a day or two I shall hit the trail for South Nahanni to see just what the devil is happening.

Monday January 28th

Not cold & snowed all day. I spent the day cleaning up & preparing for my trip. A very, very long & wearying day it has seemed.

Tuesday January 29th

Dull & snowing heavily. I'm packing up to make my attempt on *South* Nahanni. Probably start tomorrow & if my leg doesnt turn bad & if I can get through the canyon I'll probably get there in four days or so—barring weather & accidents.

[Patterson's journey to Fort Simpson was challenging in the extreme. Because of frigid temperatures and high winds on the expansive plain of the frozen Liard River, he could not make daily journal entries, and had he brought his journals up to date at Fort Simpson, they would have lost much of their immediacy. At any rate, in The Dangerous River, *Patterson tells the story of his return to Fort Simpson and the subsequent return to Wheatsheaf Creek to trap for the remainder of the winter.]*

Annotations

R.M. PATTERSON'S NAHANNI JOURNALS, JUNE 7, 1927–OCTOBER 22, 1927

page 1, line 6:
...*shoved out into the river*: Patterson, *The Buffalo Head* (New York: William Sloane Associates, 1961), 74.

page 2, line 20:
...**one can sleep without a bar**: Patterson commonly uses the word "bar" to refer to a mosquito net.

page 2, line 24:
...**I have Jorrocks Jaunts & Jollities**: Patterson refers to *Jorrocks's Jaunts and Jollities* (1838) by Robert Smith Surtees.

page 2, line 25:
...**buy more than this**: The page following this one in the journal is the first of four pages depicting a map of the Liard River. The first two maps join together to show the Liard River from where it flows into the Mackenzie River at Fort Simpson up to a point a bit south of where the Nahanni enters it. The third map continues tracing the Liard upstream as far as the British Columbia border, and the fourth map follows up the Liard past the entrance of the Toad River and on to Hell's Gate. The place names on all the maps are obviously written in Patterson's hand and, presumably, the other parts of the maps are in his hand as well.

The placement of the maps at the beginning of the journal book but after the first two entries is curious. It suggests Patterson compiled them from information gathered somewhere after Fort Chipewyan (where he was when he composed the June 10, 1927, entry). David Finch, however, says the maps were copied in Edmonton from R.G. McConnell's 1887 map of the Liard, which geologists at the Imperial Oil Company Producing Department in Edmonton had allowed him to copy (*R.M. Patterson: A Life of Great Adventure* [Calgary: Rocky Mountain Books, 2000], 79). The "Table of distances" is not a table of distances travelled by Patterson (such as appears at the end of the journal), but a list of distances compiled, presumably, from the same source that supplied the information for the maps. Patterson has clearly already begun his journal, filling four pages thus far. Then the first of the four maps appears on a right hand page (or recto). On the back of that leaf is the "Table of distances" transcribed here, and this is followed on the next recto by the second map. Its verso is blank, but the following recto contains the third map. After leaving its verso blank, Patterson draws the fourth map on the next recto. He leaves its verso blank, then resumes the journal on the following recto with the entry for July 22, 1927. Perhaps he had left a few pages blank when he copied the map at Edmonton, and then later used those blank pages for the isolated entries for June 7 and June 10.

page 4, line 33:
...**green of the forest:** In the top margin of this page in the journal book, which begins with the words "in shades of blue according...," Patterson has written in darker pencil: "From here on set date one back." At some later time, he has obviously realized the dating error starting with the "Tuesday July 27th" entry that appears in the middle of this page of the journal. Although he does not mention it, the date should be set back by one day *only* up to the entry for "Saturday September 3rd."

page 5, line 1:
...**July 27th:** Here, Patterson's dates get out of sync with his days of the week. July 21, 1927, fell on Wednesday, not Tuesday. The days of the week remain one day off the correct date up to and including the "Friday September 3rd" entry. Given Patterson's comment in the top margin (see the previous annotation), it is the date—not the day of the week—that is incorrect.

page 5, line 2:
In Poole Field's: After working as a prospector, Poole Field opened a small trading post at the mouth of the South Nahanni, in competition with Jack LaFlair, whose post was similarly located.

page 5, line 7:
...**the end of a snye:** A snye is a distinctly Canadian word, derived from anglicizing the Québécois French word *chenail*, meaning "channel." It describes a side channel that departs from and then rejoins the main channel of a river, thereby creating an island. Snyes often provide river travellers with passage around turbulent stretches of the main channel (*http://www.billcasselman.com/ wording_room/snye.htm*, accessed February 20, 2007).

page 8, line 7:
...**thought of Bath:** The city of Bath, U.K., known for its mineral springs, is located about 150 km west of London. Patterson is at the Hot Springs of the Nahanni.

page 8, line 8:
...**Oxford & Lynmouth:** Lynmouth is a village in Devon, England, noted for its picturesque landscape.

page 8, line 8:
...**Hampton Court:** Patterson is probably referring to Hampton Court Palace, a former royal residence located on the Thames upstream from London. Every July, the Royal Horticultural Society still runs the Hampton Court Palace Flower Show.

page 8, line 23:
...**they saw Pan:** Patterson alludes to the chapter "The Piper at the Gates of Dawn" in Kenneth Grahame's *The Wind in the Willows* (1908).

page 8, line 24:
...**out of Eden:** From Genesis.

page 8, line 25:
...**all so far:** Lafferty's Riffle.

page 9, line 6:
...**drawing by Rackham:** Arthur Rackham (1867–1939) was a British illustrator especially known for his fine drawings in children's books and magazines.

page 9, line 9:
...**lard & Eusol:** Chlorinated lime and borax, used as a disinfecting solution and as a wet dressing.

page 9, line 19:
...**like the Cam:** The river on which Cambridge, England, is located.

page 10, line 2:
...**almost sheer:** In *The Dangerous River* (Sidney, B.C.: Gray's Publishing, 1966), Patterson offers a slightly modified version of the latter half of this paragraph. Although the words are not precisely the same, he says they are taken from a "battered old diary...a bit faded now but still legible" (51). None of the changes are substantial. Patterson and Faille "christened this chute the Cache Rapid" (52).

page 10, line 17:
...**in the rock:** This passage is closely paraphrased on pp. 53–54 of *The Dangerous River*, but the book only acknowledges the passage's relationships to the journal by enclosing it in quotation marks. Patterson is entering Deadmen's Valley here.

page 11, line 8:
...**from your pillow:** *The Dangerous River* (54) describes the morning "hunt" quite differently. It speaks of seeing a bull moose—not a cow and her calf—and shooting it from his sleeping bag. In the book, Patterson kills it with a single shot, gets up, dresses, lights the fire and has breakfast before going after the carcass.

page 11, line 12:
...**it blows:** A very loose paraphrase—disguised as a quote from the journal—appears on p. 55. The book adds "lunched off moose liver and bacon" before "and still it blows."

page 12, line 3:
...**Made good time:** A small "x" appears in the right margin.

page 15, line 7:
...**silently midget like:** Beginning with this sentence, the journal contains

several words and phrases written between the lines of the journal entry, suggesting Patterson was making notes toward revision—possibly for another accounting—directly on the journal manuscript. The relevant sentences, with the interlinear additions enclosed between pairs of ^, follows: "The whole thing was like a great gateway through which I ^the canoe could pass^ glided silently midget like. I have seen many beautiful places in my life ^time^ but never anything of this kind ^like this^. I took two photos & will take another on my way down if I have enough left. Followed a long battle in rough water in the high mountains—^in^ a rock strewn country of red screes—trees only where the rock slides cannot come." Patterson describes features now known as the Pulpit Rock and the Gate.

page 15, line 20:
...**life of Father Lacombe:** Albert Lacombe (1827–1916) was a French-Canadian Catholic missionary who worked extensively in the West. His evangelical work among the Cree and Blackfoot First Nations brought considerable stability to Western Canada during the nineteenth century.

page 15, line 27:
...**holt on myself:** One of the difficulties of transcribing Patterson (but also one of the pleasures of reading him) is that he occasionally plays with language. In this instance, he might be using Jorrocks's idiom, as he had done in the entry for August 8.

page 15, line 33:
...**Norwegian Logging Cake:** On the back pages of his journal, Patterson records the following recipe:
Logging Cake. Norwegian
1 tablespoon & a half (big)
of Barnyard [Yo-Lo?] eggs.
1½ heaping of milk.
a little salt & a handful of flour
2 tablespoons of lard
Start frying in cold lard

page 17, line 19:

...**Reeth is built on:** Reeth is a village in North Yorkshire, where Arkengarthdale joins Swaledale. It would not have been far from Patterson's boyhood home in Darlington.

page 18, line 7:

...**on Battle River:** Patterson often speaks of the Battle River in reference to his homestead in Peace River country. Patterson's Battle River is now known as the Notikewin River, a change perhaps implemented to avoid confusion with the Battle River in central Alberta.

page 18, line 7:

...**see Mr Fenwick:** The father of Patterson's boyhood friend, Edwin Fenwick.

page 19, line 4:

August 13: This date has been inserted later in what had originally been one long entry dated "Friday August 13th." The second date for August 13 has been inserted into the space created by the indentation for a new paragraph. Since the first entry for August 13 actually explains more fully what had happened the previous day (It begins "Yesterday morning...," i.e., the 12th), Patterson evidently realized the need to distinguish that his report of the activities of the 13th was actually beginning at this point—hence the double entry for August 13, 1927.

page 19, line 10:

...**I was up against:** Patterson describes Hell's Gate, although he also called the place where the two whirlpools meet "Rapid-that-Runs-Both-Ways." Faille named it "Figure-of-Eight Rapids," but "Hell's Gate" seems to prevail. Because of unusually high water over the past few years, a point of land has been washed away according to David Finch, and Hell's Gate is not the treacherous feature that it once was.

page 20, line 9:

...**into the bay:** Patterson made only three attempts, according to *The Dangerous River*, 64.

page 22, line 2:

...very few: By the time he wrote *The Dangerous River*, Patterson knew that a substantial number of travellers, both white and aboriginal, had seen the Falls. In fact, enough had portaged around them that a rough trail was evident when Patterson and Faille first saw them.

page 22, line 17:

...a beautiful picture: *The Dangerous River* tells a delightful anecdote about Patterson being caught between a cow moose and her calf (66–68) that has no parallel in the journal, other than this wasteful killing of the cow. In the book, Patterson made no attempt to shoot either the cow or her calf. It is interesting that his humorous and innocent recreation of events years later arises out of an event that disturbed him at the time it occurred.

page 23, line 4:

...five mile scramble: Patterson's information was very close. In fact, the Falls are at 61.6° N, 125.8° W, so they were even a bit nearer than he thought, as he would later discover.

page 23, line 22:

...rapid below them: This sentence and the preceding one are "quoted" in *The Dangerous River*. While the quotation is not exact, it is generally faithful to what appears in the journal. However, instead of saying he was "sickened by the sight of another cañon," the book merely says he "tracked on round the point, only to find yet another canyon" (68).

page 23, line 36:

...a Rocky Mountain ram: This is not a Rocky Mountain sheep, but a Dall (Dall's) sheep (*Ovis dalli dalli*).

page 24, line 21:

...the Kootenay Ram: Ernest Thompson Seton (1860–1946), author of such works as *Wild Animals I Have Known* (1898) and *The Arctic Prairies* (1911) and founder of the Woodcraft League, was born Ernest Evan Thompson in the north of England. A naturalist and an artist as well as an author, Seton tried on various monikers before he legally changed his name to Ernest Thompson Seton in 1901.

The story "Krag, the Kootenay Ram" originally appeared in Seton's *Lives of the Hunted* (1901).

page 26, line 33:
...the Tees at Dinsdale: The Tees is a river in Patterson's home County Durham. Dinsdale is situated on the Tees near Darlington.

page 27, line 12:
...solution of Condy's: Potassium permanganate was widely used as a disinfectant during WWI and hence familiar to Patterson.

page 27, line 36:
...isnt it Rowland Ward: Rowland Ward (1835–1912) was a Victorian taxidermist who worked for such eminent natural historians as John Gould, William Swainson, and John James Audobon. His Piccadilly shop—"The Jungle"—remained open until late in the twentieth century.

page 28, line 1:
...at Foresters Lodge: An 1880s-vintage country estate owned by the Fenwicks, the family of Patterson's close boyhood friend Edwin Fenwick. It is located near Wolsingham, northwest of Darlington.

page 28, line 3:
...also it: In the journal, Patterson accidentally repeats the word "it." The word appears as the final word on one page and the first word on the next.

page 28, line 14:
...South Nahanni Post: The small community situated where the South Nahanni River enters the Liard was known as "South Nahanni" up to the late 1930s, when its name was changed to "Nahanni Butte" to better distinguish it from a post called "North Nahanni" (Patrick Keough and Rosemarie Keough, *The Nahanni Portfolio* [Don Mills: Stoddard Publishing, 1988], 173).

page 30, line 4:
...girl I like best [now?]: Part of another letter precedes the word "now,"

possibly suggesting a different reading, although not an obvious one. Most likely, Patterson simply failed to strike out a false start before he wrote "now."

page 30, line 28:
...an aged gentleman: Much of this paragraph appears in *The Dangerous River* (78–79). Any mention of aiming his rifle at the bear, however, or of being out of sympathy with hunters, has been deleted and replaced by an ellipsis. Many of the remarks about wildlife observed at this period are "quoted" in the book, although most passages are silently revised, rather than accurately quoted.

page 31, line 25:
...give you Edenhall: Edenhall is an elegant estate on the Eden River, about 80 km west of Darlington. It was the ancestral home of Sir Thomas Musgrave, Knight. The manor Patterson would have known was constructed in 1821 in the Italian style.

page 32, line 15:
...scamps & neurotics (?): The question mark enclosed in parentheses is Patterson's. He evidently makes a joking reference to some conversation he previously had with his mother about his own tendency toward neurosis. See the entry for August 8.

page 32, line 16:
...western novelists say: Patterson's reference to "as the western novelists say" is somewhat confusing. E. Alexander Powell (1879–1958) wrote *Where the Strange Trails Go Down*, a travel book describing his adventures in Southeast Asia. A popular journalist and inveterate traveller, Powell was born in the United States, which might explain Patterson's perhaps faulty reference to "western novelists."

page 33, line 2:
...on the left: Caribou Creek.

page 36, line 2:
...Maurice Hewlett's "Rest Harrow": A 1910 book by English historical novelist Maurice Henry Hewlett (1861–1923).

page 36, line 3:
...epicure of Bourg: Patterson initially wrote "Bourge" but then struck out the "e."

page 36, line 3:
...en Bresse: Jean-Anthelme Brillat-Savarin (1755–1826) was a French lawyer and politician whose book *Physiologie du Goût* (1826) was one of the finest pieces of writing ever produced on the subject of gastronomy. Bourg-en-Bresse is a city in eastern France, near Lyon.

page 36, line 21:
...playing over them: About half a page of the journal remains blank after this entry, which is uncharacteristic. The next entry, for Sunday, August 29, does not begin until the top of the following page.

page 36, line 24:
...the Twisted Mountain: "Deadmen's Valley to the Twisted Mountain" is written in the upper margin of the page, most likely *after* the primary journal entry was made.

page 36, line 30:
...in Kensington Gardens: Kensington Gardens, formerly the private gardens of Kensington Palace, are located in London, immediately adjacent to the less formal Hyde Park.

page 37, line 12:
...Holy St James of Compostella: The pilgrimage to the shrine of St. James of Santiago de Compostela, the most popular of the Christian pilgrimage sites during the eleventh to thirteenth centuries, runs through southwestern France and over the Pyrenees to Spain. According to tradition, St. James was put to death in Judea, but his body was miraculously translated to Spain.

page 38, line 4:
...a humming bird: It is unlikely, but not impossible, that Patterson saw hummingbirds in the Nahanni valley. In *Birds of Nahanni National Park*, no species of hummingbird is listed, except to note that Patterson claimed to have sighted

them. In eight seasons at the park, biologist Doug Tate has not seen any, nor have his colleagues reported sighting them. Patterson might have mistaken large Clearwing Moths—which hover at flowers during the daytime—for humming-birds, a mistake that Canadian Wildlife Service staff in Yellowknife say is commonly made. On the other hand, it is certainly possible that Patterson saw hummingbirds.

page 38, line 28:
...was Le Fler's: Jack LaFlair operated a small trading post at Nahanni Butte, where the South Nahanni enters the Liard. In subsequent uses of the name in the journals, Patterson spells the surname "La Flair," although in *The Dangerous River,* it is spelled "la Flair" (223) and in *The Nahanni Portfolio,* Patrick and Rosemarie Keough use "LaFlair" (43).

page 40, line 1:
...Friday Sept*ember* 3rd: The original entry read "Friday Sept 2nd" but "2nd" was struck out and replaced by "3rd." Patterson's use of dates and days of the week is still confused, but is soon to be set straight with the next entry.

page 40, line 7:
...Saturday Sept*ember* 3rd: This is the first time since the journal entry for "Saturday July 23rd" that the date of the month and the day of the week correctly align. Possibly during his visits with the Georges or with Eppler and Mulholland, Patterson was able to ascertain the correct date, which he then maintained until the end of the 1927 journal.

page 41, line 21:
...end of volume: At the end of the book in which this journal is recorded, Patterson has made several lists. One list is headed "At Fort Liard" and includes the line "mits woolen mits, insoles, tie & pin." Some of the other items are "25 lbs flour," "moccasin rubbers," "Grub box *gun* rifle," and "canoe three paddles." On the verso of the same leaf is another list, headed "To get at Fort Liard." Both lists are written upside down; that is, when Patterson made these lists at the end of the journal book, he turned the book end for end before writing. Some seven or eight pages preceding these two lists have been cut out of the sewn volume.

page 41, line 31:

...to get them: The remainder of this recto or righthand page has been neatly cut out of the journal. The verso of this leaf, of course, is also missing, and across the top of what remains of that verso page, six lines appear that have been struck out so heavily that they cannot be deciphered except for the word "Beaver" in the second line. Nothing indicates when these pages were altered. The context of the journal would suggest that Patterson made some remarks in his entry about the contents of a letter or letters he had just received.

page 42, line 9:

...Wednesday Sept*ember* 7: Patterson has noted in the upper margin of the page: "First frost last night about 2 degrees."

page 42, line 22:

...on at Ascot: Ascot is a celebrated racecourse for horses in Berkshire, England, especially famous for the Royal Ascot , which is held every June.

page 43, line 3:

...it by anybody: Immediately below the end of this sentence, Patterson has used a straightedge to draw two horizontal lines across the page about 4 mm apart. One cm below these lines and beside the left margin, he has written the word "of." Three more horizontal lines have been drawn across the page and right through the word. The journal entry continues as normal below those lines. What is especially curious is that both sets of parallel lines are in ink, so they must have been added at a later time. Why Patterson would have left this blank space in his journal and why he would have left the word "of" hanging in useless isolation until that later time, however, is inexplicable.

page 43, line 6:

...at Alan Portman's: Alan Portman, an Anglican clergyman, was an older cousin or second cousin of Marigold Portman, Patterson's romantic interest at the time. Marigold was very fond of Alan and his wife, Violet, and visited them often at their house—Wheatsheaf—in Dorset, as did Patterson on at least one occasion.

page 43, line 10:

...much to see to: Perhaps Patterson is referring to information recorded on the pages that were cut out of the end of the volume (See the September 6, 1927, entry). Possibly the pages were removed because they revealed the location of potential gold deposits he intended to exploit.

page 43, line 11:
...by my birthday: Patterson's birthday was May 13th, so he was certainly thinking of an early push on the season.

Two more neat parallel lines in ink stretch across the page directly below this sentence. The ink indicates they were added later, probably at the same time as those earlier in the entry for September 7, 1927. The lines, especially in conjunction with the previous ones, evidently served some purpose, but not an obvious one.

page 43, line 34:
...down in July: Patterson originally wrote "June" here, then struck it out and wrote July beside it, possibly at a later time, to judge from the darker pencil.

page 46, line 7:
Teddy Trimble: Patterson might be referring to Ted Trindell, an accomplished Métis trapper and dog driver (Keough and Keough, *The Nahanni Portfolio,* 54).

page 46, line 26:
...flights of geese: Patterson originally wrote "cranes" here but at some point struck out "cranes" and wrote "geese ?" above it. This was likely done somewhat later, as the journal again refers to cranes in the entry for September 13. Doug Tate, Conservation Biologist at Nahanni National Park Reserve, says that Sandhill Cranes migrate through the park in spring and are likely to do so in autumn as well. Canada, White-fronted, and Snow Geese are also known migrants, so Patterson could well have seen either geese or cranes.

page 46, line 32:
...bellowing fechter: "A bonnie fechter" is "an intrepid fighter" (M. Robinson, ed., *The Concise Scots Dictionary*. [Aberdeen: Aberdeen University Press, 1985], 190). Remember that Patterson's father was a Scot.

page 47, line 2:
...**the Lake District:** A popular region in Cumbria, northwest England, noted for its lakes and mountains. The combination of its coastal situation and mountainous topography makes the Lake District one of the wettest parts of the country.

page 47, line 13:
..."**Magic Forest.**": Patterson probably refers to *The Magic Forest* (1902) by Stewart Edward White (1873–1946), an American adventurer, hunter, and author. Many of White's books were written for young audiences, and Patterson here seems to be speaking of a book that both he and his mother knew.

page 47, line 25:
...**if she likes me:** At the end of the sentence, Patterson draws a double line across the remainder of the page. Then, a few cm below that, he draws another double line from the left to the right margins. Like those in the September 7, 1927, entry, the lines were made with ink and, consequently, at a later time. As it was for some of the September 7 entry, Patterson's subject here is very personal.

page 47, line 34:
...**hear the cranes:** See the note regarding geese and cranes in the previous day's entry.

page 49, line 35:
...**British Columbia Police:** The British Columbia Provincial Police began in 1871 when the province entered Confederation, although their origins go back as far as 1858 when colonial forces were first established. The RCMP took over their duties in 1950, and the BCPP were dissolved.

page 50, line 4:
...**the Liard River:** What is likely nothing more than a false start on a word or letter appears here and is struck out.

page 50, line 5:
...**lived in Knightsbridge:** An area in central London, famous for expensive shops and prime residential properties.

page 50, line 8:
...**Charles Hawtrey's death:** Cyril Maude (1862–1951) and Charles Hawtrey (1858–1923) were celebrated stage actors and managers of the day.

page 50, line 34:
...**like Jezebel:** Jezebel, a queen of ancient Israel, is often involved as a Christian symbol of female seduction and abomination. In II Kings 9:30, when Jehu came to Jezreel, Jezebel "painted her eyes, and tired her head, and looked out the window." "Tired" here means "fixed" or "adorned."

page 51, line 24:
...**my happiest years:** While enrolled as a student at Oxford, Patterson spent time in Switzerland, obviously time he enjoyed.

page 52, line 9:
...**to meet Chehtaneta:** The spelling used in the caption to the photograph "At the Sikanni crossing" in *The Dangerous River* is "Chushnaneta." Patterson's spelling in the entry for October 7, 1927, is different again.

page 52, line 23:
...**since March 21[,] 1918:** The day Patterson was taken prisoner during the war.

page 53, line 2:
...**poor little dwellings:** In *The Dangerous River*, Patterson writes: "one of the little cabins was unlocked and I decided to camp there and dry out and warm up" (99).

page 53, line 16:
...**do it at Rossall:** The Lancashire boarding school Patterson attended as a youth.

page 54, line 7:
...**to Collier Law:** A small village on Wolsingham Park Moor, about 30 km west of Durham. It lies only 5 km farther west than Foresters' Lodge, the property belonging to the Fenwicks and mentioned by Patterson in his entry for August 19, 1927.

page 56, line 7:
...from the Chilterns: The Chilterns are a region of chalk hills in Buckinghamshire, a county in southeastern England.

page 56, line 9:
...school near Hereford: A city on the River Wye in the west of England, near the Welsh border.

page 56, line 26:
...came from Caux: A small village situated near Lake Geneva in the canton of Vaud, Switzerland.

page 57, line 3:
...by Joseph Conrad?: Polish-born English novelist and short-story writer, Joseph Conrad (1857–1924), wrote the title story of *Youth and Other Stories* (1902) based on his experiences aboard the ship *Palestine*.

page 57, line 5:
...between mouthfuls: Patterson first made the symbol he uses for "and," then crossed it out at the time of composition.

page 57, line 9:
...but anyhow youre: The next page begins with a note in the upper margin. It reads "N. B. I learn that Chief Belly Full 's real name is Belle Feuille." In English, the name means "Beautiful Leaf."

page 59, line 12:
...a little sour: Patterson apparently meant to say that the stew had caused their discomfort, but does not quite communicate that.

page 59, line 35:
...my beloved Urchin: Urchin was Patterson's horse at his Battle River homestead.

page 60, line 28:
...& Chuhnaneta: See the note on variant spellings for the September 21, 1927, entry.

page 61, line 7:
...Earl Haig: Douglas Haig (1861–1928) was a senior military commander of British forces during WWI. He led the British Expeditionary Force during the Battle of the Somme and was created Earl Haig after the war, although his leadership was not without controversy.

page 61, line 9:
...lower Liard Indians: Archie Gardiner might simply be passing on rumours he has heard, as there is no other recorded basis for his explanation of the meaning of "Nahanni." On the other hand, it is an amusing possibility that he was pulling the leg of his somewhat green travelling companion.

page 65, line 30:
...in the cooks: A mark something like a double dagger (‡) appears on the line immediately after "cooks." Yet because it is not linked to any similar marginal mark or to another page, it is probably only the result of Patterson having started the vertical line of a letter, then struck it out with two short horizontal marks.

page 66, line 13:
...him & Woods: Woods Streeper, according to *The Dangerous River*, 107.

page 67, line 29:
...extending the P.G.E: Patterson might be referring to the Pacific Great Eastern line.

page 71, line 27:
...Alberta Provincial Police: Alberta had its own provincial police force from 1917 until 1932.

page 72, line 12:
...for the Battle: Patterson leaves an unusually wide space between this sentence and the paragraph that follows, indicating a form of closure to the 1927 journal.

page 72, line 18:
...as may be: Patterson fails to complete the sentence with "estimated" or "calculated" or some such word.

page 76, line 12:
...at **Kenei Creek:** Spelled Kenai Creek on modern maps.

page 81, line 2:
...**O'Brien's Mountain:** In the early 1920s, a trapper named John O'Brien died atop what Patterson and Faille called the Twisted Mountain, giving this variant name to the mountain (Keough and Keough, *The Nahanni Portfolio*, 49). See also Patterson's entry for June 6, 1928.

page 84, line 10:
...**masses of thunderstorms:** A small "x" appears in the left margin, immediately beside the word "thunderstorms," as if to mark this passage or sentence for editorial reference.

page 85, line 9:
...**of calves liver:** Another small "x" appears in the left margin.

page 86, line 26:
...**Wednesday June 13:** Patterson initially wrote "June 14" but the "4" has been struck out and replaced immediately above with "3."

page 87, line 1:
...**Thursday June 14th:** Patterson initially wrote "June 15" but the "5" has been struck out and replaced immediately above with "4."

page 87, line 19:
...**a mosquito hawk:** Locals in the Fort Nelson area frequently use "mosquito hawk" in reference to the common nighthawk. The "thrum" is the noise the hawk's wings make as it dives.

page 87, line 22:
...**to Anceindaz:** Anzeindaz—not Anceindaz as Patterson spells it—is a popular ski area in the canton of Vaud, Switzerland.

page 87, line 22:
...**& the Cerdagne:** The French Cerdagne is a high mountain region along the border with Spain in the Pyrenees Mountains.

page 87, line 24:
...**Randa & Zermatt:** Sion, Randa, and Zermatt are villages in the southern Valaisan Alps of Switzerland.

page 88, line 6:
...**by young liards:** Balsam poplar.

page 91, line 3:
...**a driftpile, while:** Initially, Patterson wrote "which" here, but at the time of composing the entry, struck out the "ch" and replaced those letters immediately above the line with "le."

page 91, line 5:
...**Alexander & the B—t:** Patterson's cryptic abbreviation remains a mystery.

page 93, line 32:
...**of the Greeks:** Trinacria is the name by which the Greeks knew Sicily. Why Patterson referred to an island in the Nahanni by that name is unknown, although it likely had a triangular shape.

page 94, line 29:
...**anybody's pet dogs:** At this point in the journal manuscript, Patterson has left a blank space of about 3 cm in the line. Although he does not drop down to the next line, this is a way of indicating a new paragraph, while conserving paper. He did not follow such a practice in the 1927 journal, and it is only an occasional manner of indicating a paragraph break in the 1928–1929 journal. This is the first occurrence of the practice. Subsequent spaces between sentences are not marked in this edition; rather, a new paragraph is indicated in the conventional manner.

page 95, line 21:
...**day—by the:** Patterson initially wrote "camp" here, then crossed it out and continued his sentence as it appears.

page 95, line 33:
...**make up for it:** Originally, the word "all" appeared immediately after "make up for it," but has been struck out by three neat horizontal lines through the word. When this style correction was made is impossible to determine.

page 99, line 13:
...**in Piccadilly:** Hatchards, booksellers since 1797, is still in business at 187 Piccadilly, London.

page 99, line 14:
...**from the Leads:** Giacomo Casanova (1725-1798) was imprisoned in the Venetian Ducal Palace, a prison commonly referred to as "the Leads" because of its lead roofs. He orchestrated a spectacular escape in 1756, which was first published in Leipzig in 1787 as *The Story of My Escape*.

page 99, line 15:
...**on the Yukon:** London-born Frederick Courteney Selous (1851-1917) was a hunter and adventurer best known for his travels in Africa. At least two books by Selous contain sections having to do with the Yukon: *Sport and Travel, East and West* (1900), and *Recent Hunting Trips in British North America* (1909), the latter book devoting more than half its pages to Selous's 1904 and 1906 hunting expeditions to the Yukon.

page 99, line 16:
...**Lands Forlorn:** Patterson is confused here. George Mellis Douglas (1875-1963) published *Lands Forlorn: a Story of an Expedition to Hearne's Coppermine River* (1914), relating his experiences on the east end of Great Bear Lake and the Coppermine River in 1911-1912. David Hanbury (1864-1910) travelled the Thelon River on the Barrenlands, which he wrote about in *A Journey from Chesterfield Inlet to Great Slave Lake, 1898-9* (1900) and *Sport and Travel in the Northland of Canada* (1904).

page 99, line 17:
...**very well bound:** Patterson could be referring to *The Memoirs of Jacques Casanova de Seingalt*, advertised as a "rare unabridged London edition of 1894 translated by Arthur Machen to which has been added the chapters discovered by Arthur Symons."

page 100, line 19:

...the 'Inchcape Rock': A verse ballad by Robert Southey (1774–1843), an influential poet and friend of William Wordsworth, P.B. and Mary Shelley, and Samuel Taylor Coleridge.

page 100, line 19:

...'Death of Nelson': "The Death of Nelson" is best known as an 1806 painting by Benjamin West, although the *Fourth Canadian Reader* might have included the chapter "The Death of Nelson" from M.B. Synge's *The Struggle for Sea Power*, a classic lesson in Empire often retold in Canada around the turn of the century.

page 100, line 19:

...from Pickwick Papers: *The Pickwick Papers: The Posthumous Papers of the Pickwick Club* by Charles Dickens (1812–1870) was the author's first novel and much lighter in tone than the many that followed. Patterson had carried his own copy of the novel during his ascent of the Nahanni the previous summer.

page 102, line 17:

The sun: Another small "x" appears in the left margin beside the word "sun."

page 102, line 33:

...the creek valley: According to the entry for August 10, 1928, Fenley Hunter later named this creek after Patterson.

page 103, line 6:

...boulders & there: Patterson originally wrote "the" and at some time afterwards, added a caret and a raised "re" to the word.

page 103, line 28:

...of a cri-cri: From the French for "cricket."

page 103, line 28:

...but the very: The word "very" is added above the line, with a caret inserted between "the" and "perfectest."

page 104, line 7:
..."**The Dream Ship.**": Ralph Stock (1882–1962) was a frequent contributor to *Boy's Own Paper*. The full title of the work to which Patterson refers is *The Cruise of the Dream Ship* (1921).

Patterson has made a vertical line about 5 cm long in the left margin beside this sentence, as though to mark it, similar to what he has done with a small "x" in other places.

page 104, line 31:
...**country of Sussex:** The South Downs stretch about 80 km across the southeastern English county of Sussex. The Downs are famous for their Southdown breed of sheep.

page 107, line 11:
...**by the eddy:** A small check mark in ink appears above the word "eddy," perhaps further evidence—like the small "x" and the vertical line mentioned in previous notes—that Patterson was using his journals as he composed other accounts of the Nahanni trip.

page 108, line 7:
...**or Death Valley:** Patterson likely meant to say "Deadmen's Valley."

page 109, line 16:
...**sheep which had:** Another small "x" appears in the left margin beside this sentence.

page 112, line 29:
...**on the Nahanni:** In the entry for June 6, 1928, Patterson mentions seeing the blooms of saskatoons, but not the berries.

page 113, line 18:
...**on this country:** See the entry for August 15, 1927, "Later." Seton was never in the Nahanni country proper.

Two parallel vertical lines appear in the left margin beside this sentence. The marks are quite broad, as if made with a pencil in need of sharpening. The text in this journal entry is also written with an unusually dull pencil, suggesting that

Patterson made the marks in the margin at the same time he composed the entry. The marks, then, might have been made so that Patterson could easily find his note to himself, rather than having been made at some later editorial stage.

page 114, line 22:
...**Hunter F.R.G.S**: Fellow of the Royal Geographical Society, London, England.

page 114, line 23:
...**man George _____**: The surname is "Ball," according to Patterson's entry for August 10, 1928.

page 114, line 23:
...**of Dease Lake**: There are two short parallel vertical lines in the margin here, perhaps to mark this particular passage for future reference. There is no evidence as to when these marks were added.

page 115, line 11:
...**our valley behind**: Two short diagonal marks appear here, obviously intended by Patterson to be some sort of marker, although nothing indicates why or when they were made.

page 115, line 25:
...**his party—though**: The word "though" was added above the line.

page 117, line 25:
...**"Brownie Books."**: Palmer Cox (1830–1924) was a Canadian-born illustrator of children's books who grew immensely popular for his stories and accompanying illustrations of Brownies, mischievous but friendly elf-like creatures.

page 117, line 27:
...**of the Clouds."**: B.O.P. stands for *Boys' Own Paper*. *The Clipper of the Clouds* was the subtitle of Jules Verne's book *Robur the Conqueror* (1887). "The Star of the Settlement" might also be a Verne story appearing in *Boy's Own Paper*.

Two parallel 5 cm vertical lines in the left margin mark this particular passage about the books and reading material, perhaps for easy reference at a later time. Nothing indicates when these marks were made, however.

page 118, line 2:
...**the Little Valley:** In the left margin are two marks. The first is a small "x," similar to what has been noted elsewhere, and the second is the numeral "1" with a circle around it. Nothing indicates why or when these marks were made.

page 122, line 8:
...**sorry to think:** As in previous situations, Patterson initially wrote "thing" here instead of "think." But in this instance, the "g" has been struck out and "k" written above it. Nothing indicates when this change was made.

page 122, line 22:
...**smoking & drying:** Patterson first made his shorthand sign for "and" (indicated by "&" in this transcription), but then struck it out with two parallel diagonal lines before continuing the sentence as it appears here.

page 123, line 15:
...**A lovely day:** A small numeral 2 appears in the left margin between the date and the first line of the day's entry, likely made at some later editorial stage.

page 123, line 30:
...**one is hungry:** A small number 3 appears in the left margin beside this sentence. As with the number 2 above, nothing indicates when it was added.

page 124, line 21:
...**sees in pictures:** A small number 4 appears in the left margin, obviously serving a purpose similar to the other numbers in the margin.

page 125, line 15:
...**suddenly, even:** Patterson originally wrote "evening," then struck out the "ing."

page 125, line 22:
Sunday: A small "4½" is written in the left margin, separate from but just above the word "Sunday."

page 125, line 29:
...**& all mine:** Two nearly vertical parallel lines appear in the left margin beside this sentence.

page 126, line 4:
...**& dried apples:** The number "5½" appears in the left margin next to this sentence.

page 127, line 17:
...**to their claims:** A small "6¼" appears in the left margin.

page 127, line 34:
...**read my Jorrocks:** In the left margin, Patterson has written "6½ days travelling time from mouth of *Flat*."

page 130, line 18:
...**three game birds:** "Blue grouse" is written in the left margin.

page 130, line 25:
...**of Cesare Borgia:** Patterson is probably thinking of *The Life of Cesare Borgia* (1912) by Rafael Sabatini (1875—1950), but the reference to *The Border Book* is unclear. In the journal, Patterson has framed this shopping list of reading material with vertical parallel lines on either side.

page 134, line 18:
...**the Ram Mountains:** Patterson's Ram Mountains are properly the Tlogotsho Mountains, which means "Big Prairie Mountains" (*The Dangerous River*, 158).

page 134, line 22:
...**in the dark:** The phrase "in the dark" has been inserted above the line.

page 137, line 6:
...**the Nahanni, much:** The word "much" appears above the line.

page 137, line 32:
A year agone: Patterson chooses an archaic, poetic expression for "ago."

page 138, line 13:
...**months old Post:** *The Saturday Evening Post*, a popular weekly magazine in North America for many decades.

page 139, line 23:

...but this rain: Patterson initially wrote "wind" here, but the word has been crossed out and replaced above the line by "rain."

page 146, line 22:

Trafalgar day: Trafalgar Day celebrates Britain's defeat of the Spanish and French fleets on October 21, 1805.

page 148, line 18: .

...the damned corbies: "Corbie" is Scots for raven or crow, so Patterson is clearly referring to the ravens he had seen rise from the kill. "Gorbie" is an older name for the Canada Jay or Whisky Jack.

page 150, line 24:

...on the rafters: As Patterson explains in the November 8, 1928, entry, an ermine is merely a weasel in its winter coat.

page 151, line 23:

...old Munsey's Magazine: A highly successful popular magazine started initially as a weekly in 1889 but changing to monthly publication within a few years. Declining circulation caused it to merge with another serial in 1929. It included fiction, numerous illustrations, and reproductions of works of art.

page 151, line 29:

...of the traps: A small "x" appears in the left margin.

page 152, line 12:

...Armistice Day: The day marking the official end of WWI on the Western Front, although hostilities continued elsewhere. Since WWII, this day of commemoration has been known as Veterans' Day or Remembrance Day. Two minutes of silence traditionally recognize lives lost in war.

page 153, line 22:

...a sky of bronze: Patterson made an asterisk-like mark here, which is repeated at the bottom of the left margin on this journal page beside the following words: "This, in the S.W., is a sign of a Chinook. R.M.P. November 2nd 1952."

page 154, line 4:
...of the Second: The word "Second" was added above the line, but when the addition was made cannot be determined.

page 155, line 1:
...& by three: The words "& by three" have been inserted above the line.

page 155, line 19:
...if some djinn: A genie, from the Arabic "jinn" or "djinn."

page 156, line 16:
...letter to George: Patterson's childhood friend Edwin "George" Fenwick.

page 157, line 11:
Saturday Dec*ember* 1st: Patterson initially wrote "Dec. 3" here, but changed the "3" to "1st."

page 157, line 26:
..."sun of Austerlitz": A reference to Napoleon's decisive victory over Russian and Austrian troops at the Battle of Austerlitz, in the modern Czech Republic. A French division advanced under a dense fog, which lifted suddenly—the fabled "Sun of Austerlitz"—giving Napoleon's army the advantage of surprise.

page 158, line 3:
...up I took: Originally, Patterson had written "I to an idiotic & wasteful shot..." At some later time, he noted the error and added a small "ok" above the line, thus converting "to" into "took."

page 160, line 10:
...I got a brace: i.e., two.

page 161, line 4:
The day: The word "day" was inadvertently omitted in composing the sentence, and it has been added above the line. When this was done is uncertain.

page 164, line 7:

Tuesday Jan*uary* 1st 1929: On this first entry of the new year, Patterson first wrote the year as "1928" but then changed the final digit to "9" by overwriting the original numeral.

Appendix II

WHILE THE PUBLISHING HISTORY of *The Dangerous River* is far from the centre of *Nahanni Journals* and is even more remote from Patterson's adventure on the river, it is indeed a peculiar bibliographic matter. Nor is it without relevance to how readers have come to understand the events of the 1920s. Some will never have encountered Patterson's life-threatening return home to the Peace River district in 1927. Others—especially those who have ever tried to write about Patterson's book—will wonder whether the correct title is *The Dangerous River* or simply *Dangerous River*. While the section entitled "The Evolution of *The Dangerous River*" in the Introduction addresses facets of the book's history that are specifically relevant to the journals and how we read them, this Appendix provides far more comprehensive bibliographic information for those bibliophiles wishing to wander up this tributary.

Some readers will obviously want to compare Patterson's journal account to what is related in the book. In the same way, a smaller group of readers who are especially interested in travel writing —and not simply in travel itself—will want to examine the considerably different editions of Patterson's book that have been made public over the past 50 years. Especially when read in conjunction with *The Dangerous River*, the journals caution us that written accounts of historical or autobiographical experience are not to be confused with the experience itself. And just as the journals differ from the book, the various editions of the book also tell different stories. This Appendix attempts to understand how all those stories evolved.

As we have seen, Patterson's book was published simultaneously on both sides of the Atlantic in 1954. Extant correspondence between the London publisher Allen & Unwin and the New York firm of William Sloane Associates shows that publication was first secured with the London house, which in turn granted rights to William Sloane Associates to publish an American edition at a negotiated price. Allen & Unwin offered "to place [the book] successfully for [Patterson] in the United States,"[1] and six weeks later, Helen King wrote that the president of Sloane Associates had offered the London publishing house "a general option of $250 on the United States book rights to this work."[2] It looks as though the publishing industry itself hammered out its negotiation of rights and costs on the industry's own terms, with the American firm compensating the U.K. publisher for the editorial effort that house had already invested.

The publishers' correspondence refers to communications going back at least to February 25, 1953,[3] although no correspondence from quite that far back has survived. As well, in a letter of January 27, 1954 from William Sloane Associates to Allen & Unwin, the correspondent expresses his delight that "this rather prolonged discussion of contract terms and forms has been concluded with such good temper on both sides," and hopes that "this is but the first of many books that we shall work on together."[4] The release dates for Patterson's book were June 3, 1954 and October 27, 1954, respectively, for the British and American editions,[5] so ample time certainly passed for Patterson to have received advice from editors on *both* sides of the Atlantic, thereby doubling his tutelage.

This correspondence also makes clear that the American edition constituted a "different" text over which Allen & Unwin would have "no control."[6] Notwithstanding its status as a "different" text, an artist for the British publisher prepared six line drawings to illustrate the book, and the American firm negotiated a price with Allen & Unwin that allowed them to reproduce exactly the same drawings in their edition. Similarly, the U.S. publisher purchased from Allen & Unwin the Vinylite moulds of the photographs reproduced in the British edition and then printed almost exactly the same photographs, even though Patterson had offered a wide selection that could have supplied alternate visual images.[7] Of the 22 black and white photographs appearing in the U.K. edition, 19 of them reappear in the U.S. publication. Both texts even use the same full-page image, "The Pulpit Rock, looking upstream," as the frontispiece facing their title pages. The only reason the few photographs were changed is that the three in question illustrate Patterson's autumn 1927 journey homeward from the Nahanni's mouth, a section of the adventure that was entirely cut from the U.S. edition of *Dangerous River* as a result of deleting "The Trail South" chapter. The three photographs cut as Patterson's book crossed the Atlantic are "At the Sikanni crossing"; "Roche qui trempe à l'eau. Fort Nelson River"; and "Hudson's Bay Co.'s cache at the Forks of the Nelson." In their place, the American edition supplied three new photographs, all relevant to the Nahanni watershed only: "The open places in the Lower Canyon had frozen over"; "The Cascades of the Thirteen Drops, Flat River"; and "The following afternoon we came to the foot of the Falls." While the Allen & Unwin edition had interspersed individual pages of photographs throughout the book, William Sloane Associates tipped all the photographs together in a single cluster, except for the frontispiece.

The maps printed on the front and back endpapers of both editions are identical, having been supplied by the author. Correspondence reveals that Patterson had sent the maps to the British publisher, who then sent them to William Sloane Associates, with a request that they be returned directly to Patterson when no longer required.[8]

The publishers' correspondence also explains another bibliographic oddity about the book. Occasionally, one sees the 1954 U.S. edition of *Dangerous River* ascribed to William Morrow, not William Sloane Associates. Confusingly, in a letter—certainly not the first in the numerous trans-Atlantic exchanges—from C.A. Furth of Allen & Unwin to John C. Willey, the recipient's address is given as "John C. Willey, Esq.,/ Messrs. William Morrow & Co. Inc./ 425 Fourth Avenue,/ New York." But in Willey's reply, written on "William Sloane Associates Inc." letterhead bearing the same street address of 425 Fourth Avenue, New York, to which Furth had addressed his outgoing letter, Willey makes reference to needing to change the two firms' contract to work collaboratively on Patterson's book: "namely, that the option was granted not to Morrow, but to William Sloane Associates."[9] Obviously, the two New York firms were closely allied, but even their British counterpart was somewhat confused about just how they were connected. On different occasions, Editor Helen King corresponded with Patterson in February 1953, using *both* William Sloane Associates and William Morrow & Company letterhead,[10] and in the latter correspondence, she explained: "William Morrow and William Sloane are, both business-wise and corporate-wise, two separate and distinct publishing houses. Sloane has its own editorial department and its advertising and imprint are separate and distinct. William Morrow acts as sales agent for Sloane." That same letter, by the way, remarks that Roderick Haig-Brown "is one of the brightest stars in the crown of Morrow." However, to plumb further the relationship between Sloane and Morrow is unnecessary, even here in this Appendix. Like the London banker-gone-bush, who was entirely capable of holding his own in such complicated corporate positionings but opted instead for the simple appeal of the Nahanni, readers will be most interested in Patterson's travels, not in the legal and commercial intricacies of the firms that published his accounts of them. Nonetheless, it is through the words that we engage as readers; the commercial events of production that shape what we read should not be taken for granted.

Clearly, the 1954 publication of Patterson's narrative—both in London and New York—initiated a lengthy and curious publishing history. The book has been translated into Dutch and Spanish, and has not been out of print in English for over a half-century.[11] The American edition was the Sportsman's Book Club selection in 1955, which also provided about 100 Canadian club members with access to *Dangerous River*.[12] Allen & Unwin's 1954 edition was reprinted in 1955 and again in 1957, at which time a reprint identified on the title page as "London: George Allen & Unwin Ltd.; Toronto: Thomas Nelson & Sons (Canada) Ltd." appeared, with pagination identical to the 1954 original and with only minor changes to the title and preliminary pages.[13]

Also in 1957, Panther Books, London, published a paperback edition in a pocketbook format. The text is more or less the same as the 1954 Allen & Unwin original and includes "The Trail South" chapter, but the type has been totally reset. There is no Table of Contents, and the front and back endpaper maps have been relocated within the text itself—one immediately after the Foreword, the other between the Afterword and the Appendix. Only five of the original six drawings are retained, "A Lean-to Camp" being dropped. And of the 22 photographs that appeared in the original British edition, 17 reappear in the Panther edition, all tipped in together, except for photos of Patterson and Matthews on the outside of the back cover. In spite of the common date of 1957, the George Allen & Unwin/Thomas Nelson edition mentioned above and the Panther edition have little in common.

In 1966, the first genuinely Canadian edition was published by Gray's Publishing Ltd. of Sidney, British Columbia. The British Allen & Unwin edition seems to have been a closer "parent" than was the American William Sloane Associates edition, since this first Canadian edition includes "The Trail South" chapter and retains the definite article in the title, *The Dangerous River*. Gray's edition also uses the same photographs as the original Allen & Unwin volume, but it reproduces only one ("Diagram of Operations at the Cache Rapid") of the six line drawings that were prepared by the London firm's artist for the 1954 edition and that also appeared in the New York edition. Two other illustrations

("Single Man Tracking" and "Hell's Gate Rapid") that appeared originally, however, have been redrawn by another artist before being reprinted in Gray's edition. The other three illustrations have been dropped entirely. Gray's volume adds a "Foreword to Canadian Edition," written by Patterson and dated Victoria, February 1966, but it also retains the original Foreword. The map endpapers are obviously based on the same maps Patterson had previously loaned out in 1954, but they show very slight modifications, especially to the lettering of the placenames. Despite these similarities, the layout and pagination of the Canadian edition bear no resemblance either to the British or to the American 1954 editions. A second printing of the 1966 Gray's edition was made in 1969 and a third in 1972. The 1972 printing was in the same size format as the 1966 original and, presumably, so was the 1969 printing, although that has not been visually confirmed. In 1973, Gray's issued what the copyright page refers to as an "edition" (rather than a "printing," "reprint," or "impression") but this seems only to be the 1966 edition reprinted in a smaller, less expensive "pocketbook" format (with paper covers and glued pages). Its pagination, maps, and all illustrations are identical to the first Canadian edition, and it differs from the other reprintings of that edition only in its substantially reduced size. In 1980, Gray's made another impression of the original 1966 edition, in the same larger format of the 1969 and 1972 reprintings. That 1980 reprint was especially important because it was the last edition printed anywhere that included "The Trail South" chapter. All subsequent editions and reprintings of Patterson's book follow the William Sloane Associates' model of dropping the chapter and the definite article in the title.

In 1989, Stoddart, of Toronto, published an edition that again reproduced all six line drawings from the 1954 editions, *some* of the original photographs, and *some* new photographs that had not appeared in any prior editions. Oddly, even though the Stoddart edition drops "The Trail South" chapter, it reproduces a photograph that bears no relevance to Patterson's journey up the Nahanni, but only to his homeward—and substantially overland—return from the mouth of the Nahanni in the autumn of 1927. The photograph in question is labelled "Old Timers at Sikanni Crossing" in the Stoddart volume, but when it appeared originally in the Allen & Unwin edition (and was subsequently reproduced in all the Gray's editions), it bore the label: "At the Sikanni Crossing: (l. to r.) Chushnaneta, the Sikanni Chief, Barber, Archie Gardiner, Bellyful." These individuals play significant roles in the section of Patterson's journey related in "The Trail South" chapter, but are not mentioned elsewhere in the book. Accordingly, the caption to this interesting photograph has made colourful "old timers" out of these principal actors in Patterson's full travels.

Much of the original end matter (Appendix, Glossary, etc.) is retained in the Stoddart edition, but it drops the brief biographies of Patterson and Matthews that had appeared in all prior editions. There are some other very minor changes, such as the chapter title "Deadmen's Valley" (as it had appeared in both 1954 editions) has been changed to "Deadmen Valley." In spite of having been published in Canada, it does not reprint Patterson's "Foreword to Canadian Edition." No map of any kind appears in the book.

The following year, 1990, Chelsea Green Publishing Company of Post Mills, Vermont, produced a paperback edition of *Dangerous River*. It was "[p]ublished by arrangement with Stoddart Publishing Co. Limited," and with the exception of the title page, appears to be a mirror image of the Stoddart edition produced in Toronto the previous year. It uses the same front and end matter, pagination, and illustrations, and lacks any sort of map. Both the definite article in the title and "The Trail South" chapter are missing.

In 1999, Boston Mills Press of Erin, Ontario, published a paperback impression of the 1989 Stoddart edition. It, too, shares the same pagination, illustrations (i.e., both line drawings and photographs), and modified end matter with the Stoddart publication, but positions a most welcomed map of the Nahanni/Liard watersheds on the page facing the Contents page. The map, nevertheless, is vastly inferior to the map endpapers that had appeared in the two original 1954 editions and Gray's first Canadian edition. The Boston Mills' edition also adds a subtitle to the title for the first time, so that the full title reads *Dangerous River: Adventure on the Nahanni*. Significantly, while the subtitle has been added, no definite article appears in front of *Dangerous River*. Otherwise, only a modified title page and different information on the reverse of the title page distinguish it from the Stoddart or Chelsea Green editions. Boston Mills Press, according to the verso of the title page, is "[a]n affiliate of Stoddart Publishing Co. Limited." Although Boston Mills reprinted the book in 1999, the copyright date of "1989 by the estate of R.M. Patterson" appears on the copyright page, further indicating the book's connection to the 1989 Stoddart edition.

Notes to Appendix

1. Furth to Patterson, January 6, 1953. Correspondence between R.M. Patterson and various publishers, 1947–1979. British Columbia Archives and Records Service, Victoria, B.C. MSS 2762, box 6, file 5.

2. King to Patterson, February 26, 1953. British Columbia Archives and Records Service, Victoria, B.C. MSS 2762, box 6, file 5.

3. Furth to Willey, February 2, 1954. Correspondence between George Allen & Unwin Ltd. and William Sloane Associates. MS 3282, University of Reading Library, Reading, U.K. Records of George Allen & Unwin Ltd., AUC 655/10. This is a folder containing 24 items related to the publication of *The Dangerous River*.

4. Willey to Furth, January 27, 1954. MS 3282, University of Reading Library, Reading, U.K. Records of George Allen & Unwin Ltd., AUC 655/10.

5. Harrow to Furth, August 13, 1954; Furth to Harrow, August 17, 1954. MS 3282, University of Reading Library, Reading, U.K. Records of George Allen & Unwin Ltd., AUC 655/10.

6. [Furth] to Willey, January 18, 1954. MS 3282, University of Reading Library, Reading, U.K. Records of George Allen & Unwin Ltd., AUC 655/10.

7. [Furth] to Helen King, April 6, 1954; Stevenson to Furth, May 21, 1954. MS 3282, University of Reading Library, Reading, U.K. Records of George Allen & Unwin Ltd., AUC 655/10.

8. [Furth] to King, April 6, 1954. MS 3282, University of Reading Library, Reading, U.K. Records of George Allen & Unwin Ltd., AUC 655/10.

9. Willey to Furth, January 27, 1954. MS 3282, University of Reading Library, Reading, U.K. Records of George Allen & Unwin Ltd., AUC 655/10.

10. February 6, 1953; February 26, 1953. British Columbia Archives and Records Service, Victoria, B.C. MSS 2762, box 6, file 5.

11. Finch, *Life of Great Adventure*, 241.

12. Willey to Furth, November 30, 1954. MS 3282, University of Reading Library, Reading, U.K. Records of George Allen & Unwin Ltd., AUC 655/10.

13. The 1966 Gray's Publishing edition of *The Dangerous River* gives slightly different dates for the various Allen & Unwin reprints: "Second Impression 1955 Third Impression 1956 Published by Panther Books 1957" is shown on the copyright page. I haven't encountered any other reference to a 1956 third impression of the book, except in other editions of Gray's publications.

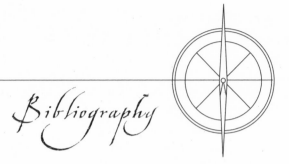

Bibliography

Addison, W. D. & Associates. *Nahanni National Park Historical Resources Inventory.* Vols. I & II. Manuscript Report Number 196. Parks Canada, Department of Indian and Northern Affairs, 1975–76.

Allen, George. Correspondence between George Allen & Unwin Ltd. and William Sloane Associates. MS 3282 "Records of George Allen & Unwin Ltd.," AUC 655/10. Folder containing 24 items related to the publication of *The Dangerous River.* University of Reading Library, Reading, U.K.

Berton, Pierre. *The Mysterious North.* New York: Alfred A. Knopf, 1956.

Black, Samuel. *A Journal of A Voyage From Rocky Mountain Portage in Peace River To the Sources of Finlays Branch And North West Ward In Summer 1824.* Hudson's Bay Record Society, 1955.

Chadwick, Douglas H. "Nahanni: Canada's Wilderness Park." *National Geographic* 160, no. 3 (September 1981): 396–420.

Correspondence between R. M. Patterson and various publishers, 1947–1979. British Columbia Archives and Records Service, Victoria, B.C. MSS. 2762, box 6, file 5.

Davis, Richard C. Review of *R. M. Patterson: A Life of Great Adventure. Arctic* 54, no. 3 (September 2001): 342–43.

———. Correspondence from M.T. Myres to Richard Davis, November 21, 2001.

———. *Voyages of Discovery: 20th Century Evolution of the Narratives of Wilderness Travel in the Canadian North.* PhD dissertation. University of New Brunswick, 1979.

Fiennes, Ranulph. *The Headless Valley.* London: Hodder and Stoughton, 1973.

Finch, David. *R. M. Patterson: A Life of Great Adventure.* Calgary: Rocky Mountain Books, 2000.

Grahame, Kenneth. *The Wind in the Willows*. New York: Charles Scribner's Sons, 1908.

Hartling, R. Neil. *Nahanni: River of Gold...River of Dreams*. Canadian Recreational Canoeing Association, 1998.

Jowett, Peter, and Neil Hartling. *Nahanni River Guide*. 3rd ed. Calgary: Rocky Mountain Books, 2003.

Keough, Patrick, and Rosemarie Keough. *The Nahanni Portfolio*. Don Mills, Ontario: Stoddart Publishing, 1988.

Lewis, A.C. *Nahanni Remembered*. Edmonton: NeWest Press, 1997.

Mason, Bill. *Path of the Paddle: An Illustrated Guide to the Art of Canoeing*. Toronto: Van Nostrand Reinhold, 1980.

Mason, Michael. *The Arctic Forests*. London: Hodder and Stoughton, 1924.

Milne, A.A. *Winnie-the-Pooh*. 1926. Reprint, Toronto: McClelland & Stewart, 1994.

Moore, Joanne Ronan. *Nahanni Trailhead: A Year in the Northern Wilderness*. Ottawa: Deneau & Greenberg, 1980.

National Film Board of Canada. *Nahanni*. Montreal, 1962.

Patterson, Raymond Murray. *The Buffalo Head*. New York: William Sloane Associates, 1961.

———. *The Dangerous River*. London: George Allen & Unwin, 1954.

———. *Dangerous River*. New York: William Sloane Associates, 1954.

———. *The Dangerous River*. 3rd impression. London: George Allen & Unwin and Toronto: Thomas Nelson & Sons (Canada) Ltd., 1957.

———. *The Dangerous River*. London: Panther Books, 1957.

———. *The Dangerous River*. First Canadian edition. Sidney, B.C.: Gray's Publishing, 1966.

———. *Dangerous River*. Toronto: Stoddart Publishing, 1989.

———. *Dangerous River*. Post Mills, Vermont: Chelsea Green Publishing, 1990.

———. *Dangerous River: Adventure on the Nahanni*. Erin, Ontario: Boston Mills Press, 1999.

———. *The Dangerous River: Adventure on the Nahanni*. Surrey, B.C.: TouchWood Editions, 2009.

———. *Dear Mother: A Collection of Letters Written from Rossall between May 1911 and March 1917*. Self-published, 1951.

———. *Far Pastures*. Sidney, B.C.: Gray's Publishing, 1963.

———. *Finlay's River*. Sidney, B.C.: Gray's Publishing, 1968.

———. "Fort Simpson, McKenzie's River." *Blackwood's Magazine* (March 1955): 239–52.

———. "Interlude on the Sikanni Chief." *Blackwood's Magazine* (July 1952): 1–14.

———. Journals, 7 June 1927–22 October 1927, British Columbia Archives and Records Service, Victoria, B.C. MSS. 2762, box 4, file 1.

———. Journals, 17 March 1928–29 January 1929, British Columbia Archives and Records Service, Victoria, B.C. MSS. 2762, box 4, file 3.

———. "Liard River Voyage." *The Beaver* (Spring 1955): 20–26.

———. "Nahanni Revisited." *The Beaver* (June 1952): 12–19.

———. "Nahany Lands." *The Beaver* (Summer 1961): 40–47.

———. "Peace River Passage." *The Beaver* (Winter 1956): 14–19.

———. "River of Deadmen's Valley." *The Beaver* (June 1947): 8–13.

———. "A Thousand Miles by Canoe." *Country Life* (July 28, 1950): 284–87.

———. *Trail to the Interior*. Toronto: Macmillan of Canada, 1966.

———. "Trails of the Canadian West." *Country Life* (June 25, 1928): 1272–74.

Robinson, M., ed. *The Concise Scots Dictionary*. Aberdeen: Aberdeen University Press, 1985.

Scotter, George et al. *The Birds of Nahanni National Park*. Special Publication No. 15. Regina: Saskatchewan Natural History Society, 1985.

Turner, Dick. *Nahanni*. Saanichton, B.C.: Hancock House, 1975.

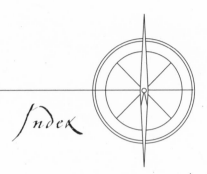

Index

RMP=Raymond M. Patterson
bold page numbers indicate
   illustrations

ailments. *See* injuries/ailments
airplanes, xxiv, 114, 120, 123, 136
Alberta Provincial Police, 71, 187
Alexander & the B—t, 91, 189
Allen & Unwin Ltd., xxxix, li, lii,
   liii–liv, lv, 199–202, 205–13
Amy (RMP correspondent), 58
Annette (RMP correspondent), 156
The Arctic Forests (Mason), xxiv
Ardill of Halfway River, 68
Astley (prospector), 90
Athabasca River, 1
aurora borealis. *See* northern lights
axes, 82, 90, 100

Bald Mountain, 153, 154–55, 167
Ball, George, 114, 115, 116
Balsam Creek, 60
Barber, Corporal
   quoted, 94
   as RMPs host, 49, 50, 55, 56, 57,
     58

   as RMPs travelling companion,
     59, 60–**61**, 62–66
Barber, Mrs, 49, 50, 55, 56, 58–59
Battle River, 48, 87, 176
bear
   hunting, lx, 30, 71, 110, 134, 154
   sighting, 6, 13, 38, 89, 133, 146
   tracks, 38, 60, 108, 125, 130, 135,
     136
Bear River, 71
bearberries, 83
Beatton, Angus, 62, 65
beaver
   hunting, 91, 123, 143, 146–47
   sighting, 6, 36, 142
   signs of, 8, 31, 76, 163, 165
The Beaver, xxxviii, xli, li, lxiii, lxxv,
   lxxvi, lxxvii
Beaver River, 44
bees, 12, 16
Belly Full (Belle Feuille), 57, **61**, 186
Bennett, Jim, xxxix, l
Berton, Pierre, lxxvii
big horn sheep, 23–24. *See also* mountain sheep
Big Willows, 75

Bigfoot, Chief, 61
Bird, Joe, lxxii
birds
    on Flat River, 30, 130
    on Lake Athabasca, 1, 2
    on Liard River, 42
    on lower Nahanni, 12, 17
    migrating, 134, 136, 139, 145. *See also* specific birds
black currants, 8, 108, 127, 128
Blackwood's Magazine, xxxviii, li, lxxvi
Blanchet, Janet (RMPs daughter), xliii, lxii
blue grouse, 144, 145, 158, 160, 195
blueberries, 35, 120, 123, 134
Blueberry River, 64, 76
Bluefish River, 76
Borden Creek, 128, 130
Boston Mills Press, liii, 204
Boucher (RMPs friend), 43, 49
Box Canyon portage, 120, 121
Brant, Charlie, 56, 63
Brillat-Savarin, J-A., 36, 180
British Columbia Police, 49, 184
Brodrick, Mr., 48
Brown, A. F. E., 126, 127
Brown, Dick, 30, 67
Bryan (journalist), 71
The Buffalo Head (Patterson), xl, lxiv
Buffalo Head ranch, xxxvii–xxxviii, xxxix, l
bush planes, xxiv, 114, 120, 123, 136
Buttercup (cow), 70, 71
butterflies
    on 1927 journey, 9, 11, 12, 30
    on 1928 journey, 83, 87, 89, 90, 100, 104, 114, 120, 125

cabin at Wheatsheaf Creek. *See* Wheatsheaf Creek cabin
Cache Creek, 67, 70, 109
Cache Rapid, 106–07, 112, 115–16, 141, 154, 160, 174
caches, food
    building, 79, 88, 93–94, 111–12, 116, 127, 128
    discovering, 86, 117
    near Hot Springs, 37, 97, 100
    near Virginia Falls, 25, 26
    at the Splits, 77, 78, 80, 99
    on Trail South, 53
Campbell, Gray, xli
Canada, Government of, lxxiii–lxxv, lxxix, lxxx, lxxxii
Canadian Nature Federation, lxxix
Canadian Wildlife Service, lxxiv, lxxix
Canadian Zinc Corporation, lxxx
Canadusa, xxxv, 3
canoes/canoeing
    distance travelled in, xxvi
    poling, xxxv–xxxvi, 4, 78, 87, 93, 94, 102, 108
    repairing in 1927, 11, 12–13, 25, 34, 38
    repairing in 1928, 77, 78, 107, 108
    RMPs early experience with, xxiv, xxxiii. *See also* rapids
Cantung Mine, lxxx
caribou
    eating, 28, 29, 132–33, 133
    habits of, 85
    hunting, lx, 27, 92, 132
    sighting, 32
    tracks, 124, 130
Caribou Creek, 123, 132

RMPs' feelings about, lxxxiii
of rocks, 3, 12, 13, 14, 15, 96, 119
and safety of photos, 58
of sled, 162
of travelling companions, 60, 61,
156
of Virginia Falls, xl, lviii, lxxvi, 35
of Wheatsheaf Creek cabin, xxvii,
138, 164
The Pickwick Papers (Dickens), xlv, 100,
191
Pocaterra, George, xxxvi–xxxvii
Poilu (dog), 94, 97, 111, 153, 161
portaging
on 1927 journey, 15, 20, 21, 26
on 1928 journey, 105, 106, 119,
120, 121
journals v *The Dangerous River*
version, lix
Portman, Alan, 43, 182
Portman, Mrs. (RMPs mother-in-law),
117, 158
powder horn, 44
Powell, E. Alexander, 179
Powers, Phil, lxv
prairie chickens, 65
Prairie Creek
camping on, 109
hunting on, 136, 141–42, 144,
147, 167, 168
trapping on, 111, 154–55, 157,
158, 159, 160, 163
Prairie Creek island, 155
preservation of Nahanni, lxxviii–lxxxii
Pulpit Rock, 14, 15, 119, 175
Purcell & Ole blaze, 124

quartz, 103
Quiz (dog), 78, 94, 109, 150, 151, 153,
156, 160-61

rabbits, 155, 158
Rackham, Arthur, 9, 173
Radcliffe (policeman), 71
Rae, Frank, 126, 127
Rafaelle (RMP correspondent), 42
railroad, 67–68, 69
Ram Mountains, 134, 144, 148, 157,
195
rapids
on approach to Virginia Falls, 23,
35
at Cache Rapid, 106–08, 109–10,
111, 112, 115–16, 160
on Flat River, 31, 33, 121–22, 123,
126, 127, 128, 133
on Irvine Creek, 130, 131
on Liard River, 41, 44
in lower canyon, 8–9, 101–02,
104, 105, 118, 120, 121
on lower Nahanni, 8–9, 10, 13, 15,
18, 19–20, 21, 26, 150
near Hot Springs, 37, 82, 97
on Nelson River, 49
on Peace River, 69, 71
on a scow, 84–86, 87–88, 112–13,
123
in the Splits, 36, 77, 78, 81, 82, 89,
90, 93, 94–95
raspberries, 4, 8, 13, 23, 35, 84, 108,
112, 118
ravens, 140, 148, 196
red currants, 4, 8, 13, 103, 108, 127

sighted, 163
signs of, 158
tracks, 154, 166
traps, 150, 155, 158, 159, 160, 166
Weaver, Harry, 65, 66–71
Wheatsheaf Creek, xxvii, 116, 134
Wheatsheaf Creek cabin
  building, xxvii–xxviii, 133, 134,
    136, 137, 138, 139–40
  cache, 111–12, 116
  choosing site for, 111
  pictures, **xxvii, 138, 164**
whisky jacks, 32, 35, 125, 137, 144,
  150, 196
White, Stewart Edward, 184
wildlife. *See* specific birds and animals
Willey, John C., 201
William Morrow, 201
William Sloane Associates, xl, lii,
  liii–liv, lv, 199–201, 202

The Wind in the Willows (Grahame), xlv,
  lxvii, lxix–lxx, 173
Winnie-the-Pooh, lxviii
Winnipeg Electric, 30
winter cabin. *See* Wheatsheaf Creek
  cabin
Wish Pool on Flat River, 122, 133
wolverines, 6, 92, 136, 165, 168
wolves
  hunted, 148
  sighted, 54, 111, 153
  signs of, 6, 34, 64, 92, 137, 139
  tracks, 34, 130, 136, 140, 141, 149,
    151, 164, 165, 166
  traps for, 151–52, 164
Woods (Streeper), 66, 70
Wrigley (prospector), 136